HATE CRIMES

Studies in Crime and Public Policy
Michael Tonry and Norval Morris, *General Editors*

Hate Crimes

Criminal Law & Identity Politics

JAMES B. JACOBS
KIMBERLY POTTER

New York • Oxford
Oxford University Press
1998

Oxford University Press

Oxford   New York
Athens   Auckland   Bangkok   Bogota   Bombay
Buenos Aires   Calcutta   Cape Town   Dar es Salaam
Delhi   Florence   Hong Kong   Istanbul   Karachi
Kuala Lumpur   Madras   Madrid   Melbourne
Mexico City   Nairobi   Paris   Singapore
Taipei   Tokyo   Toronto   Warsaw

and associated companies in
Berlin   Ibadan

Published by Oxford University Press, Inc.
198 Madison Avenue, New York, NY 10016

Library of Congress Cataloging-in-Publication Data
Jacobs, James B.
Hate crimes : criminal law & identity politics / James B. Jacobs
and Kimberly Potter.
p.   cm — (Studies in crime and public policy)
Includes bibliographical references and index.
ISBN 0-19-511448-5
1. Hate crimes—United States.   I. Potter, Kimberly, 1965–
II. Title.   III. Series.
KF9345.J33   1998
345.73'025—dc21   97-37802

9 8 7 6 5 4 3 2

Printed in the United States of America
on acid-free paper

From JBJ to Franklin E. Zimring, teacher and mentor, colleague and friend; and to Yoram Dinstein, who started me off on the study of hate crimes

From KP to my family, especially Sammy

Acknowledgments

We wish to express our appreciation to the New York University School of Law, Dean John Sexton, and the Center for Research in Crime and Justice for the support that made this book possible. There could not be a more stimulating and supportive environment in which to carry out research.

We received more than our just deserts in the form of generous assistance from friends and colleagues. We especially thank Jacob Buchdahl, Deborah Denno, Mitchell Duneier, David Garland, Susan Gellman, Milton Heumann, Graham Hughes, Stephen Morse, Jerome Skolnick, and Franklin Zimring. The Center's secretary, Judy Geissler, has provided all kinds of assistance with professionalism and good humor. Thanks to Emily Zocchi and Nick Quinn Rosenkranz for copy editing our various drafts, and to Terry Maroney who provided effective research assistance on several chapters.

While this book has been written "from scratch," some of the research and ideas were developed in previous publications. We have benefited from the comments and suggestions of those colleagues, anonymous reviewers, and journal editors who commented on the following Jacobs' articles: *Israel Yearbook on Human Rights*, "The Emergence and Implications of American Hate Crime Jurisprudence," 22: 113–139 (1993); *Criminal Justice Ethics*, "The War Against Hate Crimes: A New York City Perspective," 11: 55–61 (Summer/Fall 1992); *Criminal Law Bulletin*, "The Hate Crime Statistics Act of 1990: A Critique," 29: 99–123 (February 1993) (coauthor Barry Eisler); *The Public Interest*, "Should Hate Be a Crime?", 113: 1–12 (Fall 1993); *Annual Survey of American Law*, "Implementing Hate Crime Legislation: Symbolism and Crime Control," 1992/93: 541–553 (1993); *Journal of Criminal Law*

& Criminology, "The Social Construction of a Hate Crime Epidemic," 86: 366–391 (Winter 1996) (coauthor Jessica Henry); *Crime & Justice: An Annual Review of Research*, "Hate Crime; A Critical Perspective," vol. 21, Michael Tonry, ed., University of Chicago Press (1997) (coauthor Kimberly Potter). We especially thank Barry Eisler and Jessica Henry, two former New York University law students, who each coauthored an article that served as a stepping-stone to this book.

Contents

HATE CRIMES

1

Introduction

> If a person . . . intentionally selects the person
> against whom the crime . . . is committed or
> selects the property which is damaged or
> otherwise affected by the crime . . . because
> of the race, religion, color, disability, sexual
> orientation, national origin or ancestry of that
> person or the owner or occupant of that
> property, the penalties for the underlying
> crime are increased . . . [by as much as triple]
> Wisconsin hate crime statute, upheld by
> the United States Supreme Court in
> *Wisconsin v. Mitchell.*

ALTHOUGH THE UNITED STATES is one of the most successful multiethnic, multireligious (if not multiracial) societies, its history is also blighted by many deplorable incidents—sometimes campaigns— of anti-Semitic, anti-black, xenophobic, homophobic, and anti-Catholic violence, and all kinds of criminal conduct motivated by other prejudices. Only recently, however, have such incidents been defined as "hate crime."

Before the mid-1980s, the term "hate crime" did not exist. "Hate crime" as a term and as a legal category of crime is a product of increased race, gender, and sexual orientation consciousness in contemporary American society. Today, hate crime or, as it is sometimes called, bias crime is quickly becoming a routine category in popular and scholarly discourse about crime. These terms add a new component to our criminal law lexicon and to our way of thinking about the crime problem. Consequently, we now (or will soon) find it natural to think of the hate crime problem and the hate crime rate as distinct from the "ordinary" crime problem and the "ordinary" crime rate. This reconceptualization of crime is both reflected by and furthered by hate crime data collection initiatives, especially the federal Hate Crime Statistics Act of 1990 (HCSA),[1] which gave national recognition to hate crimes as a bona fide category of crime. Before hate crime as a political and legal category becomes entrenched, we think the term and the assumptions that launched it ought to be thoroughly examined. Toward that end, we offer this book.

Origins of the Term "Hate Crime"

Credit for coining the term "hate crime" belongs collectively to Representatives John Conyers (D-Mich.), Barbara Kennelly (D-Conn.), and Mario Biaggi (D-N.Y.). In 1985, they cosponsored a bill in the House of Representatives entitled, "Hate Crime Statistics Act." The bill sought to require the Department of Justice to collect and publish statistics on the nature and number of crimes motivated by racial, religious, and ethnic prejudice. From 1985 onward, the use of the term increased dramatically as evidenced by its appearance in newspapers. In 1985, 11 hate crime articles appeared in newspapers nationwide. In 1990, there were 511 stories about hate crimes, and three years later, more than 1,000. Most of these articles either asserted that the United States was experiencing a hate crime *epidemic*, or reported that politicians, advocacy groups, or academics had declared such an epidemic to be at hand.

The term "hate crime" first appeared in a popular magazine in the October 9, 1989 issue of *U.S. News and World Report*, in an article entitled, "The Politics of Hate." The author, John Leo, questioned the wisdom of a proposed District of Columbia law that enhanced the sentence for criminal conduct motivated by prejudice.

> Most of the time it comes down to any . . . epithets hurled during the crime. This gets courts into a maelstrom. . . . If a white mugs a black and delivers a slur in the process, is it a "hate crime" or an ordinary mugging with a gratuitous slur attached? Why should courts be in the business of judging these misty matters? If the skulls of all Americans are equally valuable (i.e., if this is a democracy), why not give everyone [the same sentence] for cracking any cranium at all.[2]

Legal scholars began using the terms "hate crime" and "bias crime" in the early 1990s. In 1991, the *Guide to Legal Periodicals* listed nine articles under a newly created "bias crime" subject heading. The first of these articles, "Hate Violence: Symptom of Prejudice," published in the spring 1991 issue of the *William Mitchell Law Review*, focused on violence against gays and lesbians.[3] The author, Lester Olmstead-Rose, a gay rights advocate, argued that a national atmosphere of intolerance had caused an increase in hate crimes directed at homosexuals, resulting in "the universal victimization of lesbian, gay and bisexual people."[4] The *Guide to Legal Periodicals* lists 86 law review articles (published between 1993 and 1995) dealing with hate crimes.

The passage of hate crime laws by the federal government and a majority of states since the mid-1980s did not occur because of a lacuna in the criminal law, or because some horrendous criminals could not be adequately prosecuted and punished under existing laws. Insufficient or unduly lenient criminal law is not a problem that afflicts the United States. Law enforcement officials certainly have adequate tools to prosecute criminals who commit murders, rapes, assaults, or other crimes, whether they are motivated by prejudice or not.

To understand why American society passed hate crime laws in the 1980s requires examining the history of the post-World War II period, especially the civil rights movement and the subsequent triumph of identity politics. Since the middle of the twentieth century, bigotry based on race, ethnicity, gender, and—more controversially—sexual orientation has been increasingly condemned by American society, especially its political leaders. One area of law after another prohibits discrimination and many institutions and organizations have created affirmative action programs to promote educational and employment opportunity for members of historically disadvantaged groups. Hate crime statutes extend the drive against prejudice to matters of crime and punishment. The hate crime laws do not seek to benefit minority groups by punishing their members less severely. Rather, they seek to punish bigoted offenders more severely. In addition, the hate crime laws seek to send a symbolic message of support to members of certain groups.

The term "identity politics" refers to a politics whereby individuals relate to one another as members of competing groups based upon characteristics like race, gender, religion, and sexual orientation. According to the logic of identity politics, it is strategically advantageous to be recognized as disadvantaged and victimized. The greater a group's victimization, the stronger its moral claim on the larger society.[5] The ironic consequence is that minority groups no longer boast about successes for fear that success will make them unworthy of political attention. For example, some Asian-American advocacy groups reject the label "America's model minority," insisting that Asian-Americans are disadvantaged and victimized. Even white males now portray themselves as victims. The new hate crime laws extend identity politics to the domain of crime and punishment. In effect, they redefine the crime problem as yet another arena for conflict between races, genders, and nationality groups.

We are certainly not saying that crimes motivated by bigotry do not occur. There is a long history of bigoted violence against Native Americans, African-Americans, Jews, Catholics, immigrants, Mexicans, Asians, women, homosexuals, and many other groups; indeed, even white males, typically characterized as the offender group, have often been the victims of racist violence. However, there is no reliable evidence from which to conclude that the incidence of such crimes is greater now than previously, or that the incidence is increasing. Indeed, behavior today, even that of criminals, is probably less prejudiced than in past generations. The current anti-hate crime movement is generated not by an epidemic of unprecedented bigotry but by heightened sensitivity to prejudice and, more important, by our society's emphasis on identity politics.

Hate Speech and Hate Groups Distinguished

The formulation of hate crimes as a new criminal law category must be compared to and distinguished from the drive to criminalize or otherwise prohibit and penalize "hate speech."[6] The attempt to outlaw racist, sexist, homophobic, and other genres of offensive speech has attracted a great deal of public attention and generated lively scholarly debates. Several incidents involving university students who were disciplined for using racist and sexist language have excited a lot of controversy, pitting advocates of multiculturalism against First Amendment purists. Proponents of university hate speech codes and similar laws argue that such odious and hurtful expression should enjoy no First Amendment protection. Nevertheless, state and federal courts have struck down hate speech codes as unconstitutional, and critics have assailed them as extreme examples of political correctness.[7]

Both hate speech and hate crime laws are components of a campaign against bigoted expression and conduct. However, constitutional challenges to hate crime laws have not been as successful because the majority of courts hold that hate crime laws seek to prohibit conduct, rather than pure speech. Despite this often repeated distinction, the line between conduct and pure speech is unclear. Hate crime laws *recriminalize* or *enhance the punishment* of an ordinary crime when the criminal's motive manifests a legislatively designated prejudice like racism or anti-Semitism. In effect, hate crime laws impose a more severe punishment for criminal conduct depending on whether the offender's prejudice falls within the list of legislatively designated prejudices. If the offender is motivated by a prejudice not covered by the hate crime law (e.g., gender bias, which is frequently excluded from hate crime laws), then punishment is not enhanced.

We also need to distinguish our inquiry from the study of organized "hate groups." In the last few years, especially since the conflagration at the Branch Davidian Compound in Waco, Texas, and the FBI's stand-off with the Freemen cult in Jordan, Montana, a great deal of attention has been paid to geographically isolated compounds or communes whose members profess strong, even intense, anti-government sentiments, and sometimes also espouse white separatist ambitions and anti-black and anti-Semitic prejudices. These groups and cults certainly deserve scholarly attention. Clearly, they are not all cut from the same cloth. Many are religious cults; others represent a new, virulent anti-government protest movement; still others may best be characterized as racist groups. Such cults, communes, and groups are often dominated by charismatic leaders and tend to be highly idiosyncratic. It is simplistic to label all these groups "hate groups." Although stories about their eccentric and confused ideologies and rejection of mainstream society generate a good deal of publicity and anxiety,[8] members of these groups have been linked to very few hate crimes.[9] In fact, because of their predilection for separation from society, such groups are infrequently involved in violence against members of the larger society.

Neo-Nazis, skinhead groups, and the Ku Klux Klan are, of course, relevant to our study. Unlike the "separatists" discussed above, their members are integrated with and engaged in the larger society. They generate literature and internet communications which encourage and applaud violence against minorities. They conjure up images of the Nazis and Fascists of the 1930s, as well as homegrown extremists. While skinhead and Neo-Nazi groups are more likely to collide with the larger society than the "separatists," surprisingly few hate crimes have been attributed to them either. The great majority of reported hate crimes under the new hate crime laws have been committed by "unaffiliated" individuals, many of them juveniles, who are not hard core ideologues.

The Socio-Political Consequences of a New Crime Category

In addition to providing more severe punishments for hate crime offenders, the states and the federal government have passed *hate crime reporting* statutes that seek to make collection and presentation of statistics on the number and type of hate crimes a regular feature of our national crime statistics. Some sponsors of these laws believe that hate crime statistics will aid law enforcement agencies. Other sponsors, however, believe that these statistics will dramatize and draw attention to "the problem." *But what problem?* How many hate crimes (or how high a hate crime rate) does it take to constitute a problem, much less an epidemic? Should we regard hate crimes as an indicator of something other than the activities of a small number of deviant bigots? Should we regard them as an indicator of overall prejudice in the United States, the tip of the iceberg? To state the question differently, are hate crimes to be taken as a limited problem involving a small number of bigoted criminals or as a *social indicator*, both of prejudice in the entire population and of the state of intergroup relations? If hate crime data are to be taken as an indicator of the overall state of intergroup relations, not just a limited crime problem, they must be approached very carefully, lest their very collection and presentation exacerbate the conflict they mean to prevent. Using the prejudices and conduct of criminals as a gauge of society's intolerances or as an indicator of the incivility of intergroup relations may be a grave mistake. The denunciation of crime may no longer serve to unite Americans; rather, highlighting criminals' racism, anti-Semitism, sexism, and homophobia may tend to redefine the crime problem along society's major fault lines.

The purpose of this book is to subject hate crime laws to critical examination. We argue that the well-intentioned attempt to strike out at designated prejudices with *criminal laws* raises a number of problems. First, the attempt to attribute crimes to a prejudiced motivation is fraught with difficulties because of the complexity of defining prejudice and establishing motivation for individual crimes. Second, should all prejudices (ageism, anti-gay bias, bias against the physically and mentally disabled, etc.) be included in hate crime laws or only a select few (racism, ethnic bias, and religious bias)? Inevitably, if some groups are left out, they will resent the selective depreciation of their victimization. However, if all victims are included, the hate crime category will be coterminous with "generic" criminal law.

Third, for reasons of socialization and education, criminals inherently are less amenable than other citizens to societal norms of tolerance and equality and to demands for higher levels of civility. It is one thing to purge our core political and social institutions of discrimination and bigotry and another to transform our criminals into equal opportunity offenders. Fourth, processing hate crimes through the criminal justice system poses challenges for the police, prosecutors, jurors, and criminal court judges; throughout the process, various audiences will be quick to see double standards and hypocrisy and to charge that those who bring hate crime charges are themselves racists, sexists, and so forth. Fifth, the splintering of criminal law into various offender/victim configurations based upon characteristics like race and gender may backfire and contribute to the balkanization of American society.

A Preview

Chapter 2 scrutinizes the concept of hate crime. At first blush it might seem relatively easy to define a species of crime based upon prejudice or bigotry. Upon inspection, that is not at all the case. What is hate? What is prejudice? Which prejudices transform ordinary crime into hate crime? How strong a motivating factor must the prejudice be? The answers to these questions determine the nature and extent of the problem.

Chapter 3 examines the various types of state and federal hate crime statutes. The state statutes differ substantially. In addition to the hate crime reporting laws, there are at least three types of hate crime laws: (1) statutes which define new low-level crimes like aggravated harassment; (2) statutes which enhance the maximum possible sentence for some or all crimes; and (3) statutes which are patterned after the federal criminal civil rights statutes.

Chapter 4 asks whether there is a hate crime epidemic. We believe there is not, despite a consensus to the contrary among journalists, politicians, and academics. Practically nothing is known about the actual incidence of hate crime because (1) there is no uniform and clear definition of hate crime; (2) in most cases, it is not possible to determine an offender's motivation(s); and (3) the data-gathering efforts by advocacy groups, states, and the federal government are unreliable.

In questioning the existence of a hate crime epidemic, we build upon a body of criminological research in which social problems have been shown to be inflated by those committed to mobilizing public reaction.[10] We know now, for example, that what was once touted as an *epidemic* of child kidnapping was in actuality no such thing.[11] Another prominent example is the consistent overstatement of the drunk driving problem.[12] And just recently, Christopher Jencks has brilliantly demonstrated the exaggeration of homelessness.[13]

Chapter 5 explains the passage of hate crime laws in terms of symbolic politics and, more important, identity politics. Who are the lobbyists for and against these laws? What arguments do they make? Why are these laws so popular with politicians?

Chapter 6 critiques the legal, philosophical, and social science rationales for hate crime laws. These justifications for hate crime laws include (1) greater culpability of hate crime offenders; (2) more severe emotional harm to hate crime victims; (3) more severe impact on the community; (4) greater potential to trigger retaliation and intergroup conflict; and (5) greater need for deterrence.

Chapter 7 deals with the enforcement of the hate crime laws. What problems do police departments and prosecutors face? What can police and prosecutorial hate crime units accomplish? Can the jury system withstand the strain of criminal trials focused on determining prejudice?

Chapter 8 takes up the question of the constitutionality of hate crime laws. Do these laws, like hate speech laws, in effect prescribe punishment for improper opinions? Are they distinguishable from hate speech laws that have run into serious First Amendment problems?

Chapter 9 speculates about the societal consequences of importing identity politics into the criminal law. Will the long-term effect of hate crime laws be to reduce the overall amount of social friction and conflict, or will splintering criminal law into offender/victim configurations based upon sociodemographic characteristics harden and exacerbate social divisions?

Chapter 10 presents our "bottom line" on what should be done about prohibiting and punishing prejudice-motivated crime.

2

What Is Hate Crime?

[C]rimes motivated by bigotry usually arise
not out of the pathological rantings and
ravings of a few deviant types in organized
hate groups, but out of the very mainstream
of society.
   Jack Levin and Jack McDevitt, *Hate Crimes:*
      The Rising Tide of Bigotry and Bloodshed

W E CANNOT TALK ABOUT how much hate crime exists in the United
States or what to do about it until we are clear about what a hate
crime is. This chapter shows that the concept of hate crime is loaded
with ambiguity because of the difficulty of determining (1) what is meant
by prejudice; (2) which prejudices qualify for inclusion under the hate
crime umbrella; (3) which crimes, when attributable to prejudice, become hate crimes; and (4) how strong the causal link must be between
the perpetrator's prejudice and the perpetrator's criminal conduct.

Complexity of Prejudice

"Hate" crime is not really about hate, but about bias or prejudice. As
we will see in chapter 3, statutory definitions of hate crime differ some-
what from state to state, but essentially hate crime refers to criminal
conduct motivated by prejudice. Prejudice, however, is a complicated,
broad, and cloudy concept. We all have prejudices for and against individuals, groups, foods, countries, weather, and so forth. Sometimes these
prejudices are rooted in experience, sometimes in fantasy and irrationality, and sometimes they are passed down to us by family, friends, school,
religion, and culture. Some prejudices (e.g., anti-Fascist) are considered
good, some (e.g., preference for tall people over short people) relatively

11

innocuous; but other prejudices provoke strong social and political censure (e.g., racism, anti-Semitism, misogyny). Even in this latter group,
as we shall see, there is a great deal of confusion about what constitutes
an acceptable opinion or preference (e.g., "I prefer to attend a historically black college," or "I oppose Zionism and a Jewish state," or "I
don't like men as much as women") and what constitutes unacceptable, abhorrent prejudice.

Though sociologists and social psychologists have long wrestled with
the concept of prejudice, they have been unable to agree on a single
definition. One point of consensus is that there are many kinds of prejudice. An individual can be prejudiced in favor of something (e.g., his
religion) or prejudiced against something (e.g., someone else's religion).

Some social psychologists have theorized that prejudice may be an
innate human trait. According to one theory:

> Because of various social pressures, we humans have a need to classify
> and categorize the persons we encounter in order to manage our inter-
> actions with them. We have a need to simplify our interactions with
> others into efficient patterns. This essential simplification leads natu-
> rally to stereotyping as a means to desired efficiency. The resultant
> stereotyping has as an unfortunate side effect, the bigotry and preju-
> dice that so frequently make social relations with others extremely
> difficult.[1]

Prejudice has also been explained as a "learned behavior." Abraham
Kaplan, a professor of philosophy, offers the following illustration: A
young child returning from his first day of school is asked, "Are there
any colored children in your class?" to which the child replies, "No, just
black and white."[2] Without instruction, the child has no concept of the
prejudice that gives meaning to the disparaging term "colored." (But
one might wonder how the child developed the constructs of "black"
and "white" rather than there just being children with different shades
of skin, hair, eyes, etc.)

In his classic book, *The Nature of Prejudice*, the late Harvard psychol-
ogist, Professor Gordon Allport, distinguished between hate-prejudice
and love-prejudice. With hate-prejudice, the hater "desires the extinc-
tion of the object of hate."[3] Allport characterizes hate as

> an enduring organization of aggressive impulses toward a person or
> toward a class of persons. Since it is composed of habitual bitter feel-
> ing and accusatory thought, it constitutes a stubborn structure in the
> mental-emotional life of the individual. By its very nature hatred is
> extropunitive, which means the hater is sure that the fault lies in the
> object of his hate. So long as he believes this he will not feel guilty
> for his uncharitable state of mind.[4]

Certain groups and individuals (e.g., Nazis, Ku Klux Klan) hold prejudices that amount to an ideology, a set of more or less elaborated assumptions, beliefs, and opinions that are espoused as a basis for policy or action. Love-prejudice occurs when "the very act of affirming our way of life" results in prejudice. It consists in "feeling about anyone [or anything] through love more than is right."[5] As an example, Professor Allport presents the case of a Southern woman who stated,

> Of course I have no such prejudice [hate-prejudice]. I had a dear old colored mammy for a nurse. Having grown up in the South and having lived here all my life I understand the problem. The Negroes are much happier if they are just allowed to stay in their place. Northern troublemakers just don't understand the Negro.[6]

Allport explained that this woman's love-prejudice was functional in allowing her to defend her position, privileges, and way of life. Although most people would label her a racist, she did not view herself as a racist because she did not hate blacks or northerners, but loved the way her life used to be.

Often groups and individuals reject the accusation that they are prejudiced or argue that their prejudices are justified because they amount to factually correct observations. For example, some white "separatists" and even white supremacists characterize themselves not as anti-black, but as pro-white. (One segment of the Afrikaner population in South Africa advocates a homeland for Afrikaners to preserve Afrikaner language and culture and insists that this is not an expression of racism toward blacks.) A white person who is persuaded by the evidence presented in Charles Murray's and Richard Herenstein's controversial book, *The Bell Curve*,[7] that the mean IQ of blacks is lower than the mean IQ of whites might object to being labeled a racist. Likewise, some blacks in the United States insist that Afro-centrism is not (or, at least, is not necessarily) an expression of anti-white prejudice. Resolving these claims, especially with respect to particular groups and situations, is no easy matter.

The apparent ease with which individuals develop prejudice has no single explanation. Professor Allport noted that "[t]he easiest idea to sell anyone is that he is better than someone else."[8] Accordingly, most prejudices have some "functional significance" for the individual—they make the individual feel secure, provide a source of self-esteem, or explain social or economic problems (i.e., scapegoating). For some individuals, prejudice may simply be "a matter of blind conformity with prevailing folkways."[9] In other words, a person may grow up *assuming* that members of another group are mean, stingy, dirty, weak, stupid, or inferior, because that is what she has always been told. Hatred may not be involved at all; indeed, some individuals holding such views may view themselves as well-intentioned paternalists.

Whether prejudice is innate or learned, it is generally agreed that

> Prejudice is not a unitary phenomenon . . . [I]t will take varying forms in different individuals. Socially and psychologically, attitudes differ depending upon whether they are the result of deep-seated personality characteristics, sometimes of a pathological nature, of traumatic experience, or whether they simply represent conformity to childhood socialization or to an established norm.[10]

Individuals vary in how conscious they are of their prejudices and, if conscious, in their willingness to admit to their prejudices. While only a small minority of individuals espouse their prejudices as ideologies, most deny that they hold any prejudices, sometimes in good faith and sometimes because they are ashamed of them.

As overt racism has become increasingly unacceptable over the past several decades, Americans often deny and repress their prejudices. Thus, psychoanalyst Joel Kovel speaks of the "aversive racist," who

> believes in white superiority, but her conscience seeks to repudiate this belief or, at least to prevent her from acting on it. She tries to avoid the issue by ignoring the existence of blacks, avoiding contact with them, or at most being polite, correct, and cold, whenever she must deal with them. Aversive racists range from individuals who lapse into demonstrative racism when threatened . . . to those who consider themselves liberals and, despite their sense of aversion to blacks (of which they are unaware), do their best within the confines of the existing social structure to ameliorate blacks' conditions.[11]

There remains a great deal of disagreement about who is prejudiced and what constitutes discrimination. For example, a 1993 Gallup Poll revealed starkly different attitudes between blacks and whites regarding civil rights and the amount of discrimination faced by minorities. One question asked: "[o]n average, blacks have worse jobs, income, and housing than white people. Do you think this is mostly due to discrimination against blacks, or is it mostly due to something else?"[12] Of the black respondents, 44 percent attributed the situation to discrimination, whereas only 21 percent of white respondents chose discrimination as the cause.[13]

Some writers assert that racial prejudice is nearly universal. Stanford Law School professor Charles R. Lawrence explains:

> Americans share a common historical and cultural heritage in which racism played and still plays a dominant role. Because of this shared experience, we also inevitably share many attitudes and beliefs that

attach significance to an individual's race and induce negative feelings and opinions about non-whites. To the extent that this cultural
belief system has influenced all of us, we are all racists. At the same
time, most of us are unaware of our racism. . . . In other words, a large
part of the behavior that produces racial discrimination is influenced
by unconscious racial motivation.[14]

Just as Professor Lawrence asserts that all whites harbor unconscious
feelings of prejudice and racism, Adam Jukes, counselor at the London
Men's Center and author of *Why Men Hate Women*, also writes: "Do all
men hate women? My central contention is that they do."[15] Jukes insists
that men harbor (at the very least) unconscious prejudice against women.

The hatred of women may be, in most cases, a deeply repressed fact of
the male character. At one extreme is the rapist or the sexual murderer;
at the other extreme is the apparently ordinary man who does not rape
or murder, and feels mild and hidden (at least socially) contempt for
women, or expresses it only in the privacy of his own home. . . . These
people, at these extremes, are expressing the same feelings, and that
the differences between them are quantitative rather than qualitative.[16]

Whether a particular individual or even a particular opinion should
be counted as prejudiced is sometimes debatable. For example, is a cab
driver who fears picking up young black males in New York City prejudiced, when young black males commit the majority of taxi robberies?
Some people argue that supporters of caps on welfare benefits and those
who question the wisdom of affirmative action are racists.[17] Sometimes
an individual need not say or do anything to warrant being labeled "prejudiced." For example, a women's studies professor at Brandeis University, Becky Thompson, explained that her teaching methods begin with
the premise that "it is not open to debate whether a white student is
racist or a male student is sexist. He/she simply is."[18] The word "prejudice" is often used so loosely that it can characterize the values, beliefs,
and attitudes of most Americans.

Consider this example. The National Conference (formerly the
National Conference of Christians and Jews) found that 55 percent of a
survey's respondents believe that Catholics "want to impose their own
ideas of morality on the larger society."[19] The National Conference concluded that this was proof of widespread anti-Catholic prejudice. A critic
might object that the survey respondents were giving an accurate response
based upon their perception that Catholics, or at least the Catholic
Church, had strong feelings and positions on matters on the social agenda
like abortion, homosexuality, government aid to parochial schools, and
assisted suicide.[20]

If practically everyone holds some prejudiced values, beliefs, and attitudes, every crime by a member of one group against a member of another group might be a hate crime; at least it ought to be investigated as such. Moreover, since criminals, as a group, are surely less tolerant and respectful of others than noncriminals, they are disproportionately likely to be motivated by prejudice. Indeed, in one sense, all (or at least most) violent crimes could be attributed, at least in part, to the offender's prejudice against the victim, based upon the victim's race, gender, age, size, looks, perceived wealth, perceived attitude, and so forth.

Which Prejudices Transform Crime Into Hate Crime?

Criminals probably have many conscious and unconscious prejudices, for example, against people who are (or appear to be) rich, poor, successful, unsuccessful, drunks, drug addicts, and so forth. These prejudices are not politically salient in contemporary American society, and would not, even if they are motivating factors, transform ordinary crime into hate crime. By contrast, racial, religious, and gender prejudices are widely and vigorously condemned. These prejudices are officially denounced in our laws and political discourse. Hate crime laws constitute a "next generation" effort. They condemn these traditionally and officially designated prejudices when they are held by and acted upon by criminals. By "officially designated prejudices," we mean to highlight that not all abhorrent prejudices are chosen by the federal and state legislatures for official censure. The legislatures choose which prejudices they want to officially condemn. In some states, sexual orientation bias is included in the hate crime laws, in other states it is not. The same goes for gender bias, bias based upon mental or physical disability, and bias based on age.

The civil rights paradigm that has condemned and outlawed certain prejudices in employment and housing does not apply easily to the world of crime. The first problem is that some of the groups that are the classic targets of prejudice serve as active perpetrators of prejudice-motivated crime. It is true that anti-discrimination laws protect white job applicants from being discriminated against by black employers, but that scenario rarely arises and, for that reason, does not have to be dealt with in considering the desirability of anti-discrimination legislation. Many commentators continue to portray the United States as a nation of two races, a dominant and oppressive white race and a subjugated and victimized black race.[21] That picture, while a caricature, is more accurate in the context of employment and housing than with respect to crime. The majority of crimes are intraracial (i.e., the perpetrator and victim are members of the same racial group). Eighty percent of violent crimes involve an offender and victim of the same race.[22] Ninety-two percent of black murder victims and 66.6 percent of white murder victims are killed by murderers of the same race.[23] For the 20 percent of violent crimes that are interracial, 15 percent involve black offenders and white victims; 2 percent involve white offenders and black victims; and 3 percent involve other combinations.[24] Robbery is the crime with the highest interracial percentage; 37 percent involve victims and offenders of different races: 31 percent involve black offenders and white victims, 4 percent involve other-race offenders and white victims, and just 2 percent involve white offenders and nonwhite victims.[25]

The number of black offender/white victim crimes has made some strong proponents of hate crime laws uncomfortable. Some argue that black offenders who attack white victims are motivated by economics not prejudice.[26] A few have proposed removing crimes based upon antiwhite prejudice from the definition of hate crime. After the shootings (black perpetrator, white victims) and arson at Freddy's clothing store in Harlem in 1995, which resulted in the death of eight people, a number of politicians argued that the crime should not be seen as a racial incident, but rather as a business dispute over a lease between the owner of Freddy's, who was Jewish and the owner of the adjacent store, who was black.[27] The crime was committed by a black man, who previously had participated in demonstrations outside Freddy's that involved racial insults against customers, and threats against the owner and employees.

Jill Tregor, executive director of San Francisco's Intergroup Clearinghouse, which provides legal services and counseling to hate crime victims, claims that white crime victims are using hate crime laws to enhance penalties against minorities, who already experience prejudice within the criminal justice system.[28] One law review author proposes that in cases of interracial assault by a white offender, *prejudice should be presumed,* and the burden placed on the defendant to prove the absence of a prejudiced motivation.[29] No such presumption would apply in interracial attacks by black perpetrators.

In theory, it would be possible to exclude from the definition of hate crime those crimes motivated by minority group members' prejudice against whites on the ground that such prejudices are more justified or understandable, and the crimes less culpable, or less destructive to the body politic than crimes by whites against minorities. But such an argument would be difficult to construct, and might well violate the Fourteenth Amendment's Equal Protection Clause.

Just as it makes no sense to presume the prejudice of white offenders against black victims, it makes little sense to argue that black offend-

ers cannot ever be prejudiced against their white victims. Black prejudice and even hatred of whites, and especially Jews, is well documented.
When the Reverend Louis Farrakhan, Nation of Islam leader, mentioned
Colin Ferguson, the Long Island Railroad mass murderer, at a rally in
New York City, the audience cheered.[30] In a speech before an audience
of 2,000 at Howard University, Nation of Islam spokesman Khalid
Muhammad drew loud applause when he stated, "I love Colin Ferguson,
who killed all those white folks on the Long Island train."[31] Louis
Farrakhan is probably the best-known avowedly racist and anti-Semitic
black leader, but examples of such prejudice are common in the black
press and radio, at least in the New York City area. On April 19, 1989,
a white female jogger was beaten and gang-raped by a group of black
youths. After months of rehabilitation, she still suffered from vision,
balance, and olfactory problems.[32] Attorney Alton Maddox, Jr., during
a program on black radio station WLIB, claimed that the gang rape of
the "Central Park jogger" was a racist hoax and questioned whether the
victim had really been hurt. "Who," he asked, "had seen the victim before her suspiciously 'miraculous recovery?'"[33] The *Amsterdam News*, a
black newspaper, published the victim's name and labeled the prosecution a racist conspiracy.

   A second problem in importing the basic civil rights paradigm from
the employment and housing contexts to the crime context is the sheer
pervasiveness of prejudice, of one type or another, that plays a role of
some kind in a large percentage of crimes. Because of that pervasiveness
it will be difficult to prevent the category of hate crime, if defined broadly,
from expanding to be coextensive with the entire criminal law.

   Our basic civil rights paradigm does not deal extensively with prejudice among European ethnic groups. However, such prejudices are a salient
feature of American history and still are apparent in some criminality.
Should the criminal law and the criminal justice apparatus begin hunting
out these prejudices in "white-on-white" personal and property crimes?

   Perhaps some percentage of black-on-black, Hispanic-on-Hispanic,
and Asian-on-Asian crime could also be attributed to prejudice if we scour
every crime for evidence. The contemporary multicultural discourse refers
to "Hispanics," "Asians," and "Africans" as if they were single homogeneous groups without divisive ethnicities. Only a moment's reflection
is needed to dispel that misconception. These classifications disguise
enormous differences, historic animosities, and prejudices.

   Asian-American is perhaps the most distortive term. Asia, the world's
largest continent, includes nationality, ethnic, tribal, and religious groups
whose prejudices against one another are every bit as palpable as European ethnic prejudices. Consider the animosities between Sunni Mus

lims and Shiite Muslims and between Muslims and Hindus, between Muslims and Sikhs, and between Pakistanis and Indians. Consider the animosities and hatreds between Chinese and Tibetans, between Japanese and Chinese, and between Koreans and Japanese. There are intense, centuries-old hatreds held in Vietnam by minority ethnic groups against the majority and in Cambodia by the Khem against the Vietnamese minority. Therefore, if hate crime is to become a basic category for defining crime, it will be necessary to get beyond thinking of "Asians" as a homogeneous group among whose members only nonhate crimes exist. Once we begin hunting down prejudices in criminals' motivations, we will find them in abundance.

In the last decade, there has been an increasing amount of attention to the nationality and ethnic differences masked by the blanket term "Hispanic."[34] But anyone familiar with Latin America and the Caribbean Islands knows that there are great differences among the peoples and cultures of this area. Just as European nationality groups have their own cultures, foods, myths, and histories, so too do Argentineans, Colombians, Cubans, Mexicans, Nicaraguans, Puerto Ricans, and so forth. There is no reason to exclude prejudices among and between these peoples from the hate crime concept.

Sub-Sahara Africa is plagued by ethnic and tribal hatreds. Only recently, the world has been appalled by massacres of the Tutsis and Hutus in Rwanda, the Ibo and Hausa in Nigeria, and the Zulu and Xhosa in South Africa. If members of these groups immigrate to the United States and commit crimes against one another, we will have yet another potential species of hate crime. Even the category "African American" disguises ethnic or national prejudices, for example, between American blacks and blacks of Caribbean descent. Intrablack prejudice also extends to what is called, "colorism," or prejudice based on the darkness or lightness of skin color.[35] Are all of these ethnic or color prejudices the proper subject of hate crime laws? If not, what principle enables us to impose extra punishments for offenders who act out only certain prejudices, but not others?

The women's movement emerged as a political force later than the black civil rights movement, but today it is equally well entrenched. Sexism is widely seen as racism's counterpart, and denunciations of racism and sexism are frequently uttered in the same breath. Thus, as a matter of first impression, it would be natural to include gender prejudice under the hate crime umbrella, especially in light of the extent to which women as a group are victimized by men. Indeed, crimes against women would seem to be the most obvious candidate for recognition as hate crime. For women, crime is overwhelmingly an intergroup phenomenon. In 1994, women reported approximately 500,000 rapes and sexual assaults, almost 500,000 robberies and 3.8 million assaults.[36] The perpetrator was male in the vast majority of these offenses.

There is every reason to believe that a high percentage of male violence against women is motivated, at least in part, by anti-female prejudice, especially if prejudice is broadly defined. Practically every act of male violence and intimidation against women is a potential hate crime. Should all crimes by men against women be counted twice, first as generic crimes (murder, assault, rape) and second as hate crimes? And should every crime by a male against a female receive a harsher penalty than the same crime when committed by a male against a male? Surprisingly, as we shall see in chapter 5, there has been strong political resistance to treating crimes by men against women as hate crimes.

Discrimination and prejudice based on sexual orientation is the most recent addition to the civil rights movement, but it has not yet been fully accepted as an equal. During the last two decades, gay men and lesbians have demanded the same protection against discrimination as blacks, Jews, women, and other groups;[37] they have demanded recognition as a victimized minority. Although some states and municipalities have enacted laws prohibiting discrimination against homosexuals, many states and the federal government do not have any laws extending civil rights protection to homosexuals. The Supreme Court has held that states can make it a crime for adult homosexuals to engage in voluntary sexual relations. The president of the United States has ordered that military personnel who are open about their homosexuality be dismissed from the armed forces for that reason alone.

So how should criminal law react to the ambivalence of American political institutions? How should the criminal law regard crime by prejudiced heterosexuals against homosexuals? If that is a hate crime, then is it also a hate crime whenever one person attacks another because he or she dislikes (hates) that person's sexual practices?

Considering all the different contexts where discrimination against gays and lesbians occurs, none is more compelling than the criminal context, with its bloody legacy of "gay bashing."[38] Whatever arguments might be made to deny gays and lesbians protection against discrimination in housing and employment, it is hard to imagine any coherent argument in favor of their exclusion from the hate crime umbrella. Indeed, such exclusion would rightly be perceived by gays and lesbians as a case of blatant governmental discrimination.

There are many other prejudices toward which American society has become more sensitive in the past several decades. One prominent example is ageism—prejudice and discrimination against the elderly. Senior citizens, through their lobbying organization, the American Association of Retired Persons, have become a powerful political force, and they have achieved considerable success in having age discrimination prohibited.[39] If crime based upon race discrimination is an especially heinous crime, then many people will no doubt conclude that crime based upon ageism ought also to be a hate crime trigger. The same kind of logic no doubt will lead advocates for the physically and mentally handicapped, undocumented aliens, HIV positive persons, and others to demand special condemnation and extra punishment for criminals who victimize them. Thus, the creation of hate crime laws and jurisprudence will inevitably generate a contentious politics about which prejudices count and which do not. Creating a hate crime jurisprudence forces us to proclaim which prejudices are worse than others, itself an exercise in prejudice. This controversy will really have little to do with appropriate sentencing for criminals and everything to do with the comparative symbolic status of various groups.

The Causal Link

For criminal conduct to constitute a hate crime, it must be motivated by prejudice and there must be a *causal relationship* between the criminal conduct and the officially designated prejudice. Must the criminal conduct have been totally, primarily, substantially, or just slightly caused by prejudiced motivation? If the criminal conduct must be motivated by prejudice to the exclusion of all other motivating factors, there will not be much hate crime. Contrariwise, if the hate crime designation is satisfied by a showing of merely a slight relationship between prejudice and criminal conduct, a great deal of crime by members of one group against members of another group will be labeled as hate crime.

Which Crimes, When Motivated by Prejudice, Constitute Hate Crimes?

Vandalism or criminal mischief involving the defacement of public and private property presents another complicated problem. A great deal of graffiti, in public and private, expresses disparaging opinions of women, gays and lesbians, Jews, blacks, and other minorities, whites, and other social categories. Should the act of scrawling such graffiti be included in the hate crime accounting system and trigger special condemnation and extra punishment? For example, should anti-homosexual graffiti scrawled on a bathroom wall be counted as a hate crime, or should it only count as hate crime if the graffiti is directed at an individual, institution, or place identified with a particular group (e.g., anti-homosexual graffiti on a gay man's home, anti-homosexual vandalism on an AIDS center, or anti-Semitic graffiti in a Jewish cemetery)?

Should hate crimes include the use of racist, sexist, homophobic, and other disparaging epithets combined with in-your-face shouting, gesticulating, and threatening conduct that occurs all too often in the context of ad hoc arguments and fights on playgrounds, streets, and in the workplace? Consider the following incident involving two neighbors, a white woman and a Hispanic woman, which was reported to the New York City Bias Incident Investigation Unit. According to the Hispanic woman, her white neighbor insulted and harassed her with anti-Hispanic epithets. After investigating, the police declined to label the incident a "bias crime" because the neighbors had been engaged in an on-going dispute over building code violations and the epithets had been uttered during a heated argument on this same subject. In Queens, New York, the following incident was treated as a bias crime. A gay male couple knocked on their neighbor's door and asked him to turn down the music, which was so loud it shook the walls. The neighbor refused and hurled anti-gay epithets.[40] Is this a hate crime?

Some instances like this do not qualify as crimes at all because they do not pass the threshold that separates offensive speech from criminal conduct. But other instances could be classified as criminal harassment or intimidation. Does hate crime include or exclude mixed speech/conduct?

The Many Faces of Hate Crime

Hate crime is a potentially expansive concept that covers a great range of offenders and situations. We can see this more clearly with the aid of Table 1. On the horizontal axis we classify the offender's prejudice (high/low) and on the vertical axis the strength of the causal relationship between the officially designated prejudice and the criminal conduct (high/low). The table shows that a broad definition of hate crime includes many run-of-the-mill crimes that look far different from the ideologically driven acts of extreme violence that often color thinking about this subject.

High Prejudice/High Causation

When we think about clear-cut, unambiguous hate crimes, we call to mind the Ku Klux Klan's 1963 assassination of Medgar Evers or the June 1984 assassination of Colorado Jewish radio show host, Alan Berg, by five members of *Bruder Schweigen* ("the Silent Brotherhood"), a neo-

Table 1   Labeling Hate Crime: The Prejudice and Causal Components

		High	Low
	High	High Prejudice/ High Causation I	Low Prejudice/ High Causation III
Strength of Causal Relation			
	Low	High Prejudice/ Low Causation II	Low Prejudice/ Low Causation IV

High   Low
Degree of Offender's Prejudice

Nazi group.[41] If hate crimes included only cases like these, the concept would not be ambiguous, difficult to understand, or controversial. But it would also not cover many cases and would have little, if any, impact on case outcome, because such crimes are already punished with the most severe possible sentences.

Cell I on our table also includes hate crimes by individuals whose prejudices are emotionally intense, but who are not part of any organized group. Consider Colin Ferguson, the black man who murdered six white commuters and wounded 19 others on the Long Island Railroad in December 1993.[42] After the shooting, police found a note in his pocket explaining that he chose Long Island as the venue because it was predominantly white. In the note Ferguson expressed hatred for Asians, whites, and "Uncle Tom Negroes."[43] Some commentators said Ferguson's murders were not hate crimes because he was mentally ill or because he was prejudiced against "Uncle Tom Negroes" as well as whites and Asians. According to Bob Purvis, legal director of the University of Maryland's Center for the Applied Study of Ethnoviolence, the Ferguson rampage was not a hate crime: "By its nature, a mass murder is a crime born of immense psychiatric disturbance. . . . Mass murder is mass murder; it's not a hate crime."[44] This argument, in effect, says that bona fide prejudice is irrational but not so irrational as to lead to crimes of grand scale. Such reasoning might lead to the bizarre conclusion that Hitler was not prejudiced and the Holocaust not the ultimate hate crime. In short, we are quite prepared to accept that prejudice often includes extreme irrationality and even mental instability.

Here are some other cases that we think fall easily into cell I of the table.

- In November 1995, Robert Page, a white man, attacked Eddy Wu, an Asian man, stabbing him twice in the back, puncturing a lung, in the parking lot of the Lucky Food Center. In a statement to police, Page said, "It all started this morning. I didn't have anything to do when I woke up. . . . So I figured, what the fuck, I'm gonna go kill me a Chinaman."[45]
- In September 1990, a group of Kentucky youths beat a gay man with a tire iron, locked him in a car trunk containing snapping turtles and then tried to set the car on fire. The victim suffered severe brain damage.[46]
- In December 1995, Roland Smith, a protester who participated in a boycott of Freddy's, a Jewish-owned clothing store, entered the store, shot four white people, and set the store on fire, killing the owner and six other white and Hispanic people. Smith also died in the fire.[47] Before the attack, he reportedly said that he would "come back and burn and loot the Jews."[48] Upon entering the clothing store, Smith ordered all blacks to leave and started shooting the whites.
- Serial killer Joel Rifkin admitted to killing at least seventeen women from the late 1980s until 1993.[49] According to psychiatrists who testified at his trial, since childhood Rifkin was obsessed by violence against women.[50]

Some commentators would not label Rifkin a hate criminal, because of his mental instability or because they believe misogyny should not be a hate crime trigger. It seems to us that psychosis or mental pathology cannot negate prejudice without stripping the concept of some of its meaning. Moreover, it is very difficult to imagine an intellectually coherent hate crime category that would include crimes motivated by racism but not crimes motivated by sexism/misogyny.

High Prejudice/Low Causation

In cell II, we find crimes committed by extremely prejudiced offenders whose crimes are not solely or strongly motivated by prejudice. Generally, these crimes, including the following examples, are not classified as hate crimes. However, we include this category to present a more complete picture of the configurations that prejudice, crime, and causation can take. It should not be presumed that every law violation committed by highly prejudiced individuals is a hate crime and it is not sound to use the hate crime laws to persecute persecutors. Suppose that the neo-Nazi leader, Tom Metzger, was to shoplift merchandise from a store owned by Jews? He might contest the hate crime designation by saying that although he abhors Jews, his primary motivation was to acquire some goods for free and that had a Jewish store not been available he would have stolen the merchandise from a non-Jewish store. The fact that the victims were Jewish was only of secondary importance.

- In 1986, David Dawson escaped from a Delaware prison. Dawson, while burglarizing the home of Richard and Madeline Kisner, murdered Mrs. Kisner. After a conviction for first-degree murder, the prosecution attempted at the capital punishment sentencing stage to introduce evidence of Dawson's membership in the White Aryan Brotherhood. The Supreme Court held that introduction of this evidence violated the First and Fourteenth Amendments because "the Aryan Brotherhood evidence was not tied in any way to the murder of Dawson's victim."[51]

- In 1996, federal agents arrested a gang of four men, who committed 22 bank robberies throughout the Midwest during a two-year period. Law enforcement officials dubbed the gang, "the Midwestern bank bandits," but the men called themselves the "Aryan Republican Army." The Aryan Republican Army used money from the bank robberies to finance their revolution against the federal government and the extermination of all Jews.[52]

Low Prejudice/High Causation

Cell III includes the majority of hate crimes covered by the new wave of American hate crime laws. The offenders in this category are not ideologues or obsessive haters; some may be professional or at least active criminals with short fuses and confused psyches; some may be hostile and alienated juvenile delinquents; others may be ignorant, but relatively law-abiding Archie Bunker types. The prejudices of such individuals are to some extent unconscious. Whether or not the authors of hate crime legislation meant to cover these offenders, these are the individuals who dominate the statistics. The following cases are good examples:

- During a two-year crime spree, which culminated in a 1993 conviction for kidnapping, murder, and attempted murder, Dontay Carter targeted white men as his favorite robbery victims. Carter used his victims' credit cards to rent expensive hotel rooms and purchase jewelry and other luxury items for himself and his friends. No racial epithets were uttered during the crimes. According to Carter, who characterized himself as a victim of white oppression, he targeted white men because they are all rich.[53]

- In May 1991, in Rumson, New Jersey, a 19-year-old male who had been drinking and smoking marijuana painted a swastika and the words "Hitler Rules" on a synagogue, and then proceeded to paint a satanic pentagram on the driveway of a Christian church. During the sentencing hearing, the defendant, Steven Vawter, told the judge, "I want to apologize. This is not the crime you think it is. I don't have a racist bone in my body. I don't hate anybody." The judge sentenced Vawter to four months imprisonment, but stated that Vawter's behavior was an aberration. The judge explained that during the trial evidence about Vawter's character and letters of support from "people of all walks of life" showed he was not a hatemonger.[54]

- In December 1995, in Fayetteville, North Carolina, Randy Lee Meadows, a soldier stationed at Fort Bragg, was charged with conspiracy to commit murder in the shooting deaths of a black couple. Meadows joined fellow soldiers Malcolm Wright and James Burmeister, both avowed white supremacists, at a local bar. According to the police, Meadows drove the car and "was apparently just along for the ride and did not share the racist views of the other two men." When he heard the gun shots, Meadows ran out of the car to where the victims lay on the ground.[55]

Low Prejudice/Low Causation

Many crimes which fall into cell IV are "situational"; they result from ad hoc disputes and flashing tempers. Sometimes these incidents are counted as hate crimes, but sometimes they are not.

- In 1993, an on-going dispute over grass clippings in San Jose, California culminated in a hate crime conviction. William Kiley, a gay man, lived across the street from the H. family and also owned the house next door to the H's, which he rented to a tenant. The trouble began in 1988 when Kiley's tenant's dog bit Mrs. H. She sued and Kiley was forced to pay damages; his tenant had to have the dog destroyed. Three years later, animosity between the H's and Kiley came to a head after Kiley purchased a lawnmower that had no grass catcher. When Kiley mowed the tenant's lawn, grass clippings blew onto the H.'s driveway. The H's frequently complained about the grass clippings. After six months, arguments over the grass clippings became so unpleasant that Kiley stopped mowing the lawn. The first time Kiley resumed mowing the lawn Mr. H. yelled at Kiley, "You cocksucker, I'm tired of your fucking games." Kiley interpreted this as harassment because of his sexual orientation. Later that day, Joshua, the H's son, asked Kiley to clean the grass off the driveway. Kiley agreed and swept the grass clippings into the street. Later in the day, Kiley discovered a pile of dirt and grass clippings on his front porch. When Mrs. H. saw Kiley throwing the clippings back in their driveway, Mrs. H. said that all she wanted was for him to be "a reasonable neighbor." Yelling ensued and Mr. H. called the police. Joshua H. started shouting at Kiley to clean up the grass, calling him a "faggot," a "queer," and a "punk." Joshua, with his fists in the air, challenged Kiley to "come on, let's get it on you faggot queer." When Kiley ordered Joshua to get off his property, Joshua hit him. In retaliation, Kiley squirted Joshua with a hose. Enraged, Joshua hit and kicked Kiley several times. Joshua was convicted of bias-motivated assault—a felony.[56]

- On December 23, 1993, the theft of a winter solstice banner depicting a yellow sun that said "Solstice is the reason for the season" was investigated by Wycoff, New Jersey police as a hate crime against atheists. The banner, erected by the New Jersey Chapter of American Atheists, was part of a holiday display open to all groups—Christian, Jewish, atheist, or any other group that wished to put up holiday decorations. A spokesperson for the American Atheists stated that the theft sends a message that "atheists will not be tolerated in Wycoff. It's like burning a cross on an African-American's lawn."[57] No anti-atheist graffiti or other evidence indicating prejudice accompanied the theft.

Conclusion

"Hate crime" is a social construct. It is a new term, which is neither familiar nor self-defining. Coined in the late 1980s to emphasize criminal conduct motivated by prejudice, it focuses on the psyche of the criminal rather than on the criminal's conduct. It attempts to extend the civil rights paradigm into the world of crime and criminal law.

How much hate crime there is and what the appropriate response should be depends upon how hate crime is conceptualized and defined. In constructing a definition of hate crime, choices must be made regarding the meaning of prejudice and the nature of the causal link between the offender's prejudice and criminal conduct.

"Prejudice" is an amorphous term. If prejudice is defined narrowly, to include only certain organized hate-based ideologies, there will be very little hate crime. If prejudice is defined broadly, a high percentage of intergroup crimes will qualify as hate crimes. If only a select few crimes, such as assault or harassment, can be transformed into hate crimes, the number of hate crimes will be small. If vandalism and graffiti, when motivated by prejudice, count as hate crimes, the number of hate crimes will be enormous. If criminal conduct must be completely or predominantly caused by prejudice in order to be termed hate crime, there will be few hate crimes. If prejudice need only *in part* to have motivated the crime, hate crime will be plentiful. In other words, we can make the hate crime problem as small or large as we desire by manipulating the definition.

There are many different types of prejudices that might qualify for hate crime designation. Some civil rights and affirmative action legislation speaks in terms of "protected groups," but this does not easily apply in the hate crime context because when it comes to crime, all victims are a protected group. Why should some victims be considered more protected than others?

3

Hate Crime Laws

[O]ur single most effective weapon is the law.
I implore you to support the Bias Related
Violence and Intimidation Act I have
proposed, and make it clear to the people of
this state that behaviour based on bias will
not be ignored or tolerated.

> Letter from New York State Governor
> Mario M. Cuomo to the New York State
> Legislature, August 16, 1991

*B*Y 1995, THE FEDERAL GOVERNMENT, thirty-seven states, and the District of Columbia had passed hate crime laws that fall into four categories: (1) sentence enhancements; (2) substantive crimes; (3) civil rights statutes; and (4) reporting statutes. The diversity of these laws demonstrates the plasticity of the hate crime concept.

Sentence Enhancements

The majority of hate crime statutes are of the sentence enhancement type. Typically, these laws bump up the penalty for a particular crime when the offender's motivation is an officially designated prejudice. The Montana and Alabama sentence enhancement statutes are typical. Montana provides that

> a person who has been found guilty of any offense . . . that was committed because of the victim's race, creed, religion, color, national origin, or involvement in civil rights or human rights activities . . . *in addition to* the punishment provided for commission of the offense, *may be* sentenced to a term of imprisonment of not less than two years or more than 10 years.[1]

Alabama provides a mandatory minimum sentence for violent crimes motivated by an officially designated bias.

> On a conviction of a Class A felony that was found to have been motivated by the victim's actual or perceived race, color, religion, national origin, ethnicity, or physical or mental disability, the sentence shall not be less than 15 years.[2]

The size of the penalty enhancement varies from state to state. In Vermont, a hate crime is subject to *double* the maximum prison term.[3] Under Florida's enhancement provision, the maximum possible sentence is tripled.[4] The hate crime statute challenged before the Supreme Court in *Wisconsin v. Mitchell*[5] provided for a two-year maximum prison term for aggravated battery, but if the perpetrator was motivated by bias, the maximum punishment jumped to seven years.

On the federal level, the Violent Crime Control and Law Enforcement Act of 1994[6] mandated that the U.S. Sentencing Guidelines provide a sentence enhancement of three "offense levels" above the base level for the underlying federal offense, if the sentencing court finds

> beyond a reasonable doubt that the defendant intentionally selected any victim or any property as the object of the offense because of the actual or perceived race, color, religion, national origin, ethnicity, gender [but not in the case of a sexual offense], disability, or sexual orientation of any person.[7]

Applying the Sentencing Guidelines in the case of an aggravated assault, for example, the ordinary base level offense score of 15 is increased to 18, elevating the sentencing range from 18–24 months to 27–33 months.

The Enumerated Prejudices

The various state substantive and sentence enhancement hate crime laws differ from one another with respect to which prejudices transform ordinary crime into hate crime. All hate crime laws are designed to punish criminals motivated by prejudice based on race, color, religion, and national origin,[8] but all uniformity ends there. Only eighteen states and the District of Columbia include gender and/or sexual orientation bias as hate crime triggers. Prejudice against Native Americans, immigrants, the physically and mentally handicapped, union-members, nonunion members, right-to-life and pro-choice groups are included in some hate crime laws.[9] Vermont's law applies to offenders motivated by prejudice against service in the armed forces.[10] Montana condemns prejudice against "involvement in civil rights or human rights activities."[11] The

District of Columbia statute is the most inclusive; in addition to race, color, religion, national origin, gender, and sexual orientation, it prohibits targeting an individual or group by reason of physical disability, age, personal appearance, family responsibility, marital status, political affiliation, and matriculation.

Predicate Offenses

State hate crime laws also differ with respect to which predicate offenses, when motivated by prejudice, qualify as hate crimes. The Anti-Defamation League (ADL) model statute, which many states used as a prototype for their statutes, covers only harassment or intimidation. By contrast, in Pennsylvania, Vermont, and Alabama, *any offense* is a hate crime if the offender was motivated by race, religion, national origin, or other selected prejudices.[12] The Alabama statute, which covers all misdemeanors and felonies provides:

> The purpose of this section is to impose additional penalties where it is shown that a perpetrator committing the underlying offense was motivated by the victim's actual or perceived race, color, religion, national origin, ethnicity, or physical or mental disability.[13]

Other states limit hate crimes to certain predicate offenses. Some states reserve hate crime designation for low-level offenses, such as harassment, menacing, or criminal mischief. The Ohio hate crime statute covers only menacing, aggravated menacing, criminal damage or endangering, criminal mischief, and phone harassment.[14] Similarly, in New Jersey, only simple assault, aggravated assault, harassment, and vandalism can be classified as hate crimes.[15] New York has a single hate crime offense—aggravated harassment. Illinois designates nine predicate offenses: assault, battery, aggravated assault, misdemeanor theft, criminal trespass to residence, misdemeanor criminal damage to property, criminal trespass to vehicle, criminal trespass to real property, and mob action.[16] Washington, D.C. includes arson, assault, burglary, injury to property, kidnapping, manslaughter, murder, rape, robbery, theft, or unlawful entry as possible hate crimes.[17]

Defining and Proving Prejudiced Motivation

Most state hate crime laws do not use the word "motivation," rather, they prohibit *choosing* the victim "by reason of"[18] or "because of"[19] certain characteristics. Other states prohibit choosing the victim "maliciously and with specific intent."[20]

The hate crime statutes differ on whether the offender's prejudice has to be "manifest" in the commission of the crime itself, or whether prejudice can be based on character evidence and evidence of the defendant's actions or words prior to the crime. In Washington, D.C., an ordinary crime becomes a hate crime when the conduct "*demonstrates an accused's prejudice.*"[21] Florida requires that the crime "evidences prejudice." One would think that what has to be demonstrated is (1) that the defendant harbors prejudiced beliefs, and (2) that this particular crime, in the way it was committed, demonstrates or reaffirms the existence of such prejudice.

But some juries and/or courts, perhaps hostile to the idea of hate crimes or wary of applying the statutes in an unconstitutional manner, seem to require that the crime demonstrate hard core prejudice.

In interpreting Florida's hate crime statute, which requires that the crime "evidences prejudice," the Florida Supreme Court held that

> [t]he statute requires that it is the commission of the crime that must evidence the prejudice; the fact that racial prejudice may be exhibited during the commission of the crime is itself insufficient.[22]

The court explained that the statute was not meant to cover disputes, such as arguments over a parking space, which escalate into fist fights accompanied by racial or other slurs. If that restricted interpretation of hate crime law prevailed, hate crime laws would be reserved for hard core ideologues like neo-Nazis and thus rarely used.

Other states, such as Wisconsin and California, deal with the motivation element by requiring that the offender have "intentionally selected" the victim "because of" or "by reason of" race, color, religion, and so forth.[23] Read literally, this type of statute would not require proof of *prejudice*, but merely color consciousness in the selection of a victim. For example, it would be a hate crime for a white defendant to attack and rob only Asian women because he perceived them as more vulnerable and less likely to resist. The defendant, although not prejudiced against Asians, would be a hate criminal for selecting the victim by reason of race. However, it is doubtful that prosecutors and judges would interpret the hate crime statute this way, because they recognize the legislative intent to penalize prejudice.[24] Despite differences in the language used to set forth motivation requirements (manifest, evidences, motivated in whole, or in part, because of, etc.), the majority of courts hold that prejudice must be a *substantial* motivating factor.[25]

In Pittsburgh, Pennsylvania, Emmitt Harris, a black male, and Matthew Chapman, a white male, were throwing trash in a dumpster behind the deli where Harris worked. The defendant, Theresa Ferino, a white woman whom Harris and Chapman knew as a deli customer, walked up the alley to the rear of the deli, pointed a gun at Harris and Chapman, and stated, "I'm going to kill you, you fucking nigger." Ferino fired the gun in the direction of both Harris and Chapman, but injured no one. The state supreme court, in less than straight-forward language, reversed the conviction for ethnic intimidation on the grounds that

> the singularity of the act committed by the [defendant], directed as it was against both Harris [a black man] and his companion (a Caucasian), the antecedent of which was neither a harsh word, gesture nor conduct exhibited between the victim and the [defendant], we do not believe rises to the proof-level sufficient to constitute a contravention of the ethnic intimidation statute.[26]

In other words, use of the word "nigger," plus the firing of the gun, was not sufficient to sustain a hate crime conviction, when a second possible victim was someone of the same race as the defendant.

Substantive Offenses

ADL Model Hate Crime Law

Some hate crime statutes define new substantive offenses. They redefine conduct that is already criminal as a new crime or as an aggravated form of an existing crime. The ADL model statutes, which many states have adopted, provide for new substantive offenses of "intimidation" and "institutional vandalism."

> A person commits the crime of intimidation if, by reason of the actual or perceived race, color, religion, national origin or sexual orientation of another individual or group of individuals, he violates Section _____ of the Penal Code (insert provision for criminal trespass, criminal mischief, harassment, menacing, assault and/or other appropriate statutorily proscribed criminal conduct).
>   Intimidation is a _____ misdemeanor/felony (the degree of liability should be at least one degree more serious than that imposed for commission of the offense).[27]

Intimidation, a new substantive offense, recriminalizes several existing low-level offenses, in effect *enhancing the maximum possible sentence* when the offender is motivated by one of the enumerated biases. Whether a hate crime law takes the form of a new substantive offense, or a sentence enhancement, the end result is the same—a more severe punishment. Hate crime laws in general, and this statute in particular, do not seem aimed at the archetypical racists, anti-Semites, misogynists, and homophobes. Instead, they seem aimed at the ad hoc disputes, arguments, and fights that frequently erupt in a multiracial, multiethnic, multireligious society. The following case is typical:

- In 1989, David Wyant and his wife, both white, were playing loud music at their campsite in Ohio's Alum Creek State Park. Two black campers at the adjoining campsite, Jerry White and Patricia McGowan, complained to park officials. When asked by park officials to turn off the music, Wyant complied, but fifteen minutes later turned on the radio again. White and McGowan then overheard Wyant shouting that "[w]e didn't have this problem until those niggers moved in next to us. I ought to shoot that black motherfucker. I ought to kick his black ass." Wyant was convicted of ethnic intimidation, a fourth degree felony, and sentenced to one and one-half years imprisonment,[28] *triple* the maximum sentence for the underlying offense of aggravated menacing, a first degree misdemeanor, with a sentence range of 0–6 months imprisonment or a fine.

- In 1991, a white police officer, Stephen Keyes, responded to a domestic disturbance call at the Florida home of Michael Hamm, an African-American. When Officer Keyes attempted to arrest him, Hamm shouted, "I'll shoot you white cracker motherfucker." Believing that Hamm was armed, Keyes radioed for back-up. In the meantime, Hamm escaped, but was later apprehended. No gun was found. Hamm was charged with aggravated assault for "evidenc[ing] prejudice based on race, color, [etc.]."[29] All charges were later dropped because there was not enough evidence (primarily, the lack of a weapon) that Hamm intended to assault Officer Keyes.

- In 1994, Herbert Cohen accompanied Denise Avard to Richard Stalder's Florida home to retrieve Avard's earrings; allegedly, Avard had some sort of a dispute with Stalder. Stalder pushed Cohen and called him a "Jew boy," "Jewish lawyer," "you fat Jewish lawyer, get off my property," "Jewish kike, come on Jewish lawyer . . . I'm going to kick your ass." Stalder was charged with battery subject to a hate crime sentence enhancement.[30]

ADL Model Institutional Vandalism Statute

The ADL recommends a second substantive hate crime statute for the destruction of property that belongs to religious groups. Its "Institutional Vandalism" law provides:

A person commits the crime of institutional vandalism by knowingly vandalizing, defacing or otherwise damaging:

    i. Any church, synagogue, or other building, structure or place used for religious worship or other religious purposes;

    ii. Any cemetery, mortuary or other facility used for the purpose of burial or memorializing the dead;

    iii. Any school, educational facility or community center;

    iv. The grounds adjacent to, and owned or rented by any institution, facility, building, structure or place described in subsections (i), (ii) or (iii) above.[31]

This statute increases penalties for vandalism of sacred buildings. "It is critical . . . that the enhanced penalties be sufficiently severe for the new statute to have its desired deterrent impact."[32]

Some states combine the ADL intimidation and institutional vandalism model statutes. For example, Connecticut's hate crime statute provides:

A person is guilty of intimidation based on bigotry or bias if such person maliciously, and with specific intent to intimidate or harass another person because of such other person's race, religion, ethnicity or sexual orientation does any of the following: (1) causes physical contact with such other person; (2) damages, destroys or defaces any real or personal property of such other person; or (3) threatens, by word or act, to do an act described in subdivision (1) or (2).[33]

Under this statute, a hate crime prosecution could be brought if an offender spray paints anti-gay graffiti on the facade of a gay bar, but not if the offender spray paints misogynistic graffiti on *Ms. Magazine*'s headquarters. While both hypothetical acts of vandalism express prejudice, gender-based prejudice is not covered by Connecticut's statute. In contrast, the Alaska and Michigan hate crime laws would produce the opposite result; the definition of hate crime includes gender bias, but not sexual orientation bias.[34]

In New York, the substantive hate crime statute is called "aggravated harassment." It provides:

A person is guilty of aggravated harassment . . . when with intent to harass, annoy, threaten, or alarm another person, he: Strikes, shoves, kicks, or otherwise subjects another person to physical contact, or attempts or threatens to do the same, because of the race, color, religion or national origin of such person.[35]

Essentially, when a crime is motivated by bias, the defendant is charged with the underlying crime, assault for example, plus an added count of aggravated harassment. If convicted of aggravated harassment, the defendant faces a significantly more severe sentence. For example, in *People v. Grupe*,[36] the defendant was convicted of aggravated harassment for striking a Jewish man while shouting anti-Semitic epithets, such as "Is that the best you can do? I'll show you Jew bastard." The maximum sentence under the aggravated harassment statute is one year imprisonment, whereas the maximum sentence for the same conduct, absent the anti-Semitic epithets, is 15 days imprisonment. Such significant differences in sentencing based on the words uttered during the crime have led some critics to call hate crime statutes "thought crime laws."[37]

The Federal Civil Rights Acts

Some commentators refer to the federal criminal civil rights laws as hate crime statutes. However, they are actually quite different in intent, formulation, and operation—especially the post-Civil War statutes. They do not deconstruct criminal law into various offender/victim configurations based upon race, religion, sexual orientation, and the like; neither do they politicize "the crime problem" in the manner of the contemporary state hate crime laws.

Post-Civil War Civil Rights Acts

After the Civil War, in many places within the former Confederacy, local law enforcement agencies would not prosecute crimes committed by whites against blacks, nor would local governments permit blacks to exercise rights guaranteed by the Fourteenth Amendment.[38] So, Congress passed laws to authorize federal prosecution of the Ku Klux Klan and others, including law enforcement and government officials, who denied the newly freed slaves their civil rights.[39] The authority for these statutes was Congress's power to enforce the Thirteenth and Fourteenth Amendments.

The federal statutes did not aim to enhance punishment or to *recriminalize* conduct already covered by criminal law. At the time, these statutes provided the only de facto law enforcement option. If local law enforcement officers had investigated and prosecuted those who victimized the former slaves, there would have been no need for the federal laws. The federal criminal civil rights statutes are not directed exclusively at hate crimes (although they can be used for that purpose), but at what law professor Frederick Lawrence calls "rights interference crimes."[40] The civil rights statutes and hate crime laws both respond to issues of race and discrimination, but any similarity ends there. The civil rights statutes are not framed in terms of identity politics and group rights, but in terms of everyone's *individual* civil rights.

The first of the two post-Civil War statutes, 18 United States Code § 241, provides punishment for conspiracies to violate federally guaranteed rights. It provides that

[i]f two or more persons conspire to injure, oppress, threaten, or intimidate any person . . . in the free exercise or enjoyment of any right or privilege secured to him by the Constitution or laws of the United States . . . or;

If two or more persons go in disguise on the highway [i.e., the Ku Klux Klan], or on the premises of another, with intent to prevent or hinder [the] free exercise or enjoyment of any right or privilege so secured . . .[41] They shall be fined not more than $10,000, or imprisoned not more than 10 years or both. . . .

The second post-Civil War statute, 18 U.S.C. § 242, is explicitly concerned with federal, state, or local government officials who deprive private citizens of their federally guaranteed rights on the basis of certain characteristics. Its purpose is to guarantee even-handed, color-blind law enforcement:

Whoever, under color of any law, . . . willfully subjects any person . . . to the deprivation of any rights, privileges, or immunities secured or protected by the Constitution or laws of the United States, or to different punishments, pains, or penalties, on account of such person being an alien, or by reason of his color, or race, than are prescribed for the punishment of citizens, shall be fined . . . or imprisoned . . . .[42]

Neither of these statutes was meant to single out the prejudices of common criminals for special condemnation and more severe punishment; rather, their purpose was to ensure that laws were enforced equally on behalf of all victims, no matter what race, and against all offenders, whatever their race, prejudice, or criminal motivation. Unlike modern-day state hate crime statutes, which cover only those victims who fall within the groups listed in the hate crime statute, the post-Civil War statutes apply to everyone.

Sections 241 and 242 have been used to prosecute a wide variety of conduct, including ballot tampering,[43] extortion by a public defender,[44] unlawful searches,[45] obstruction of federal witness's testimony,[46] and the abuse of a state hospital patient by hospital staff.[47] When the federal civil rights statutes have been used to prosecute cases of racially motivated violence, the crimes have almost always been committed "under color of law" as, for example, the 1964 murders by Mississippi police of civil rights workers Michael Henry Schwerner, James Earl Chaney, and Andrew Goodman,[48] or the 1992 attack of black motorist Rodney King by a group of Los Angeles police officers.[49]

The 1968 Civil Rights Act

Passed as part of the Civil Rights Act of 1968, 18 United States Code § 245, might be considered a precursor to the modern state hate crime laws. Indeed, § 245 was one component of the legislation that marks the beginning of the modern civil rights movement. Entitled "Federally Protected Activities," § 245 was designed to provide a remedy for the violence resulting from opposition to civil rights marches, voter registration drives and other voting issues, enrollment of black students in formerly all-white schools and universities, and efforts to abolish Jim Crow laws.[50]

The first subsection of Section 245 mirrors §§ 241 and 242 by specifically enumerating federal activities, the enjoyment of which the Act seeks to protect against infringement by anybody for any reason. The second subsection specifically protects a broad category of "state and local activities" from interference motivated by certain prejudices.[51] It protects participants in state and local activities from victimization based on race, color, religion, and national origin. The prosecution must prove that the defendant, motivated by bias, attacked a victim who was participating in a state or local activity. The offender's prejudice need not have been the sole motivating factor.[52] Subsection (b)(2) provides that

> Whoever, whether or not acting under color of law, by force or threat of force willfully injures, intimidates or interferes with, or attempts to interfere with . . . any person because of his race, color, religion, or national origin and because he is or has been . . . enrolling in or attending a public school or university; participating in any benefit, program, service or facility provided by a state or local government; applying or working for any state or local government or private employer; serving as a juror; traveling in or using any facility of interstate commerce, or using any vehicle, terminal, or facility of any common carrier; or using any public facility, such as a bar, restaurant, store, hotel, movie theater, or stadium[53] shall be punished . . . . [The statute provides a range of different punishments depending on the conduct, whether firearms or explosives are used, and the degree of injury to victims.]

Perhaps because of its complexity and abstruseness, this statute has rarely been used. The Department of Justice estimates that it "seeks indictments [for violations of §§ 241, 242, and 245] in 50–60 cases per year."[54] These statutes were never intended, and have never served, as all-purpose federal hate crime statutes.[55] Rather, they function as insurance which can be called upon if, for discriminatory or other improper reasons, state and local law enforcement officers fail to prosecute violations of civil rights.[56]

State Civil Rights Offenses

At least ten states have civil rights-type statutes, patterned on the federal laws. These statutes are quite justifiably referred to as hate crime laws, since they aim at criminals who are prejudiced. West Virginia's statute, titled "Prohibiting Violations of an Individual's Civil Rights," provides:

> All persons within the boundaries of the state of West Virginia have the right to be free from any violence, or intimidation by threat of violence, committed against their persons or property because of their race, sex, color, religion, ancestry, national origin, political affiliation, or sex.
>
> If any person does by force or threat of force, willfully injure, intimidate or interfere with, or attempt to injure, intimidate or interfere with, or oppress or threaten any other person in the free exercise or enjoyment of any right or privilege secured to him or her by the Constitution or laws of the state of West Virginia or . . . of the United States, because of such other person's race, color, religion, ancestry, national origin, political affiliation, or sex, he or she shall be guilty of a felony, and upon conviction, shall be fined not more than five thousand dollars or imprisoned not more than ten years or both.[57]

Since every violent crime is committed with the intent to deprive the victim of "the right to be free from any violence, or intimidation by threat of violence," West Virginia's statute transforms practically every violent crime into a possible hate crime, if prejudice can be found to have played some causal role.

Reporting Statutes

The Hate Crime Statistics Act of 1990

The Hate Crime Statistics Act (HCSA), enacted by Congress in 1990, mandated federal compilation and reporting of hate crime statistics and publication of an annual report. The HCSA directed the Attorney General to collect data on predicate crimes which demonstrate "manifest evidence of prejudice based on race, religion, sexual orientation, or ethnicity" and instructed the Attorney General to establish guidelines for data collection and to determine the "necessary evidence and criteria that must be present for a finding of manifest evidence [of the enumerated prejudices]." Attorney General Richard Thornburgh delegated authority for data collection and creation of guidelines to the Federal Bureau of Investigation.[58] The FBI passed the assignment along to its Uniform Crime Reports (UCR) Section, which is responsible for compiling crime data.

In devising a data collection plan, the UCR Section surveyed twelve states and a number of cities that were already compiling hate crime statistics, and turned to private groups like the National Institute Against Prejudice & Violence, the Anti-Defamation League of B'nai B'rith, and the National Association for the Advancement of Colored People. In 1991, the UCR Section issued its *Training Guide for Hate Crime Data Collection*, which set forth definitions and criteria for use by local law enforcement officials in classifying incidents as bias motivated.

HCSA Predicate Crimes

The Act names eight predicate crimes—murder; nonnegligent manslaughter; forcible rape; aggravated assault; simple assault; intimidation; arson; and destruction, damage, or vandalism of property—which, if motivated by any one of the prejudices enumerated in the law, count as hate crimes. Congress apparently chose these crimes not because they might be more likely than others to be motivated by officially designated prejudice, but because the UCR already gathers national data on them. The limitation of hate crime reporting to these eight crimes—later supplemented by robbery, burglary, and motor vehicle theft—still seems arbitrary since the UCR has long provided uniform definitions of dozens of other criminal offenses. One might ask, for example, why prejudice-motivated kidnapping does not count as a hate crime.

HCSA Types of Bias

The Act defines bias as "a preformed negative opinion or attitude toward a group of persons based on their race, religion, ethnicity/national origin, or sexual orientation." According to the *Training Guide*, an offender commits a bias crime when the crime is "motivated, *in whole or in part*, by racial, ethnic, national origin [or] sexual orientation prejudice." This loose definition could transform virtually any intergroup crime into a hate crime. An example mentioned earlier, involving a white offender who robs and attacks only Asian women based on his belief that they are more vulnerable and less likely to resist, highlights the broad scope of the HCSA definition. Surely, the above offender's opinion about Asian women could be classified as "a preformed negative opinion or attitude toward a group." Read literally, the *Training Guide* categorizes as hate crimes, for example, car thefts by offenders motivated to any extent by the belief that Jews are stingy, blacks are noisy, or gays promiscuous.

The HCSA's most glaring omission is gender prejudice. The picture of hate crime that Congress promised to create through the HCSA ignored all forms of male violence against females, including serial murder, rape, spousal abuse, and child sexual abuse. It also ignored crimes against the mentally and physically disabled and against proponents of controversial political and social causes. There is no mention in HCSA of prejudice against children, which must account, at least in part, for some percentage of the enormous amount of violence perpetrated against children each year. Nothing could more poignantly demonstrate what we mean by "the social construction of hate crime."

HCSA Motivation

The Act specifies that where an officially designated prejudice is involved, any of the enumerated predicate crimes will be defined as a hate crime as long as the prejudice was responsible for the offender's conduct. The *Training Guide* instructs police officers to label a crime as a suspected bias incident when there is *some evidence* that the offender was *in part* motivated by one of the prejudices. One may, of course, think that all or practically all criminals harbor conscious or unconscious prejudice against members of other groups. Otherwise, one is faced with the formidable challenge of determining which intergroup crimes involve—even in part—a prejudiced motive.

Variation in Defining and Reporting Hate Crimes

Differences between state and local hate crime reporting and the HCSA complicate the development of an accurate hate crime reporting system. Laws in at least eighteen states mandate the collection of hate crime statistics.[59] A few large police departments, such as New York City's, collect hate crime statistics without a statutory mandate. The state reporting statutes differ widely from the HCSA in the designated predicate crimes and prejudices. For instance, Oregon's statute defines hate crimes much more broadly than federal law:

> All law enforcement agencies shall report to the Executive Department statistics concerning crimes: . . . (c) Motivated by prejudice based on the perceived race, color, religion, national origin, sexual orientation, marital status, political affiliation or beliefs, membership or activity in or on behalf of a labor organization or against a labor organization, physical or mental handicap, age, economic or social status or citizenship of the victim.[60]

In effect, Oregon law enforcement personnel must scrutinize crimes twice, once to see if they qualify as state hate crimes, and once to see if they qualify as federal hate crimes.

To take another example, Virginia's reporting statute mandates "the collection and analysis of information on terrorist acts and groups and individuals carrying out such acts." Terrorist acts are defined as:

> (i) a criminal act committed against a person or his property with the specific intent of instilling fear or intimidation in the individual against whom the act is perpetrated because of race, religion or ethnic origin or which is committed for the purpose of restraining that person from exercising his rights under the Constitution or laws of this Commonwealth or of the United States, (ii) any illegal act directed against any persons or their property because of those persons' race, religion or national origin, and (iii) all other incidents, as determined by law-enforcement authorities, intended to intimidate or harass any individual or group because of race, religion or national origin.[61]

In Virginia, "gay-bashing" is a hate crime for federal reporting purposes, but not for state reporting purposes.

Conclusion

In the mid-1980s, Congress and a majority of state legislatures passed hate crime laws that do not criminalize previously *noncriminal* behavior, but enhance punishment for conduct that was already a crime. The well-known federal criminal civil rights statutes are often assumed to be the model for these new laws, but they are quite different. They do not recriminalize prohibited behavior, enhance sentences, or designate a finite list of prejudices. They protect the federal, constitutional, and statutory rights of all citizens by making it a criminal offense to interfere with those rights. They provide federal insurance that crime will be prosecuted if state and local law enforcement authorities default in carrying out their responsibilities.

There are significant differences in the ways that federal and state legislatures define hate crimes.[62] A number of states, following the ADL's lead, treat hate crime as a low-level offense, such as intimidation or harassment. Other states have more general hate crime laws and sentence enhancements that mandate higher sentences for most or all crimes when motivated by prejudice. The statutes also differ as to which prejudices transform ordinary crime into hate crime and as to whether those prejudices must be manifest in the criminal conduct itself or can be proved by evidence concerning the defendant's beliefs, opinion, and character. The diversity of hate crime laws means that we cannot assume that people are talking about the same thing when they discuss "hate crime" or that

Table 2 Prohibited Prejudices in State Statutes

Category	States
No Statute	Arizona, Arkansas, Georgia, Hawaii, Indiana, Kansas, Kentucky, Louisiana, Nebraska, New Mexico, South Carolina, Wyoming
Race, Color, Religion, National Origin/Ancestry	Alabama, Alaska, California, Colorado, Connecticut, Delaware, Washington, D.C., Florida, Idaho, Illinois, Iowa, Maryland, Massachusetts, Michigan, Minnesota, Mississippi, Missouri, Montana, Nevada, New Hampshire, New Jersey, New York, North Carolina, North Dakota, Ohio, Oklahoma, Oregon, Pennsylvania, Rhode Island, South Dakota, Tennessee, Vermont, Virginia, Washington, West Virginia, Wisconsin
Physical Disability	Alabama, Alaska, California, Connecticut, Delaware, Washington, D.C., Illinois, Iowa, Minnesota, New York, Oklahoma, Vermont, Washington, Wisconsin
Gender	Alaska, California, Washington, D.C., Florida, Illinois, Iowa, Michigan, Minnesota, Mississippi, New Hampshire, North Dakota, Vermont, Washington, West Virginia
Sexual Orientation	California, Connecticut, Washington, D.C., Illinois, Iowa, Minnesota, Nevada, New Hampshire, New Jersey, Oregon, Vermont, Washington, Wisconsin
Blindness	Connecticut
Mental Disability*	Alabama, California, Illinois, Iowa, Minnesota, New York, Oklahoma, Vermont, Washington, Wisconsin
Age	Washington, D.C., Iowa, Minnesota, Vermont
Marital Status	Washington, D.C., New York
Personal Appearance	Washington, D.C.
Family Responsibility	Washington, D.C.
Matriculation	Washington, D.C.
Political Affiliation	Washington, D.C., Iowa, West Virginia
Association with "Person of Certain Protected Status"	Iowa
Interference with Civil Rights—No Group	Maine, Texas, Utah
Involvement in Civil or Human Rights Activities	Montana
Service in U.S. Armed Forces	Vermont
Sensory Handicap	Washington

*Includes states that specify only "disability."

hate crime reports and statistics from one jurisdiction can be compared with reports and statistics from other jurisdictions.

Because it deals with labeling, counting, and thus, shaping reality, the HCSA may turn out to be more important than the substantive hate crime laws and sentence enhancements. After several years of operation, the federal hate crime reporting system presents a highly inaccurate and distortive picture of hate crime in the United States and is viewed as a major disappointment, even by its once erstwhile proponents. The HCSA held out the promise of a data collection effort that would reveal the rate of hate crime and permit comparison of various groups' hate offending and hate victimization rates. That promise has definitely not been fulfilled.

4

Social Construction of a Hate Crime Epidemic

It has become nearly impossible to keep track
of the shocking rise in brutal attacks directed
against individuals *because* they are black,
Latino, Asian, white, disabled, women, or
gay. Almost daily, the newspapers report new
and even more grotesque abominations. . . .
As ugly as this situation is now, it is likely to
worsen throughout the remainder of the
decade and into the next century as the forces
of bigotry continue to gain momentum.
     Jack Levin and Jack McDevitt, *Hate Crimes:*
          The Rising Tide of Bigotry and Bloodshed

IT IS WIDELY BELIEVED that since the mid-1980s the United States has
been experiencing a *hate crime epidemic.* This belief has been expressed over and over again by politicians, journalists, scholars, and
spokespersons for racial, religious, gay and lesbian, and other advocacy
groups. Leo McCarthy, lieutenant governor of California, declared that
"[t]here is an epidemic of hate crimes and hate violence rising in California";[1] Mississippi State Senator Bill Minor warned, "this is the type
of crime that easily spreads like an epidemic."[2] The District Attorney
for St. Paul, Minnesota claimed that state and local governments faced
a "massive increase in hate crimes."[3] A journalist for the *San Francisco
Chronicle* wrote that "hate-motivated violence is spreading across the
United States in 'epidemic' proportions."[4] Dr. Arthur Caliandro, cochair
of the religious group, Partnership of Faith, termed hate crimes "a virus
that has turned into a disease that has grown into an epidemic."[5] A
New York Times journalist characterized the incidence of hate crime

as "rain[ing] down hard and heavy," and as "a recent explosion."[6] The *Boston Globe* claimed that "incidents of racial and religious harassment or intimidation have skyrocketed."[7] An article in the *National Law Journal* characterized the 1990s as "the decade of hate—or at least, of hate crime."[8]

This chapter explains how the hate crime epidemic has been socially constructed. We identify the leading proponents of the epidemic claim—advocacy groups, the media, politicians, and academic commentators—and show that this claim lacks any empirical basis. We then show how the effort to create a reliable governmental accounting system for hate crimes has failed. Finally, we offer some historical observations in order to place the hate crime problem in perspective.

Advocacy Groups

Spokespersons for gays and lesbians have been among the most vocal proponents of the hate crime epidemic theory. Kevin Berrill, Director of the National Gay and Lesbian Task Force (NGLTF), explained that "[t]he problem [of bias crime] is alarmingly pervasive. The real message is not whether the numbers are up or down, but rather that we have an epidemic on our hands, one that is in dire need of a remedy."[9] Upon release of its 1993 survey report showing that violence against gays and lesbians had *decreased* by 14 percent in the six cities surveyed, a NGLTF spokesperson stated, "all the anecdotal evidence tells us this is still an out-of-control epidemic."[10] Despite the apparent good news indicated by the declining numbers, NGLTF spokesperson Tanya L. Domi told a U.S. House of Representatives Committee that "anti-gay violence clearly remains at epidemic proportions."[11] Robert Bray, another NGLTF spokesperson, stated that "[t]he gay community is under siege in this country. We are fighting an epidemic of violence."[12] Michael Petrelli, a spokesperson for Gay and Lesbian Americans, has made similar statements: "[A]ny time there's a murder of a gay or lesbian person, I am concerned because our group . . . believes there is an epidemic of this kind of anti-gay violence."[13]

The Anti-Defamation League (ADL) has been lobbying for hate crime legislation and data collection longer than any other advocacy group. Since 1979, the ADL has compiled and published an "Annual Audit" of "overt acts or expressions" of anti-Jewish bigotry or hostility (an incident may be included in the Audit regardless of whether the police label it bias-motivated).[14] According to the ADL, "[t]he pervasiveness of bias-motivated criminal conduct in a country conceived as a bastion of freedom is both tragic and ironic. . . . All indications are that such crimes are on the rise."[15]

In compiling its data, the ADL relies upon victim and community group reports, newspaper articles, and local law enforcement agencies' information. Individuals and community groups who believe they have been the victims of an anti-Semitic incident fill out a standard ADL form which the ADL attempts to verify by reviewing police reports, interviewing witnesses, or examining the property damage or vandalism. If the incident is a noncriminal event, like the mailing of literature or an anti-Semitic message left on an answering machine, the ADL will examine the literature or listen to the recorded message to determine whether it meets the Audit's definition of harassment.

A large number of the anti-Semitic overt acts or expressions included in the Audit do not constitute crimes. For example, anti-Semitic verbal and written expressions do not violate the criminal code. The 1993 ADL Audit of Anti-Semitic Incidents lists a "representative sampling" of anti-Semitic incidents such as:

> *In Connecticut:* A high school hockey coach yelled an anti-Semitic slur, "Get the Jew Boy," at an opposing player.
> *In Georgia:* A business owner accused a Jewish woman who questioned the price increase of service of "trying to Jew me down."
> *In Massachusetts:* "Jew!" was yelled by a man in a passing truck at a Jewish mourner leaving a cemetery.
> *In California:* University of San Diego, anti-Semitic literature left on lawn of university.
> *In Florida:* Florida Atlantic University, JAP (Jewish American Princess) jokes told on university radio station.
> *In Georgia:* Georgia State University faculty member made Holocaust denial statements.[16]

These examples show that the ADL Audit really counts anti-Semitic *incidents*, not hate *crimes*. Nevertheless, it is often cited as a hate crime index.[17]

Klanwatch, a project of the Southern Poverty Law Center, was created to monitor the activities of white supremacist groups. It has expanded its activities to include a hate crime data collection program patterned after the ADL's, but covering crimes motivated by racial and ethnic prejudice. Klanwatch monitors newspapers and electronic media and applies the hate crime label to any crime "if its motivation seemed to be race-related."[18]

One Klanwatch report, "Campus Hate Crime Rages in 1992,"[19] illustrates how the hate crime epidemic theory has been constructed on the foundation of dubious statistics. The report claims that there is a "raging hate epidemic" on college campuses. Two types of data are offered to support this claim. First, Klanwatch cites a 1990 report by the National Institute Against Prejudice and Violence[20] (NIAPV) which states that "25% of minority students will becomes victims of violence based on prejudice. And 25% of those students will be revictimized, according to a survey conducted by the NIAPV at the University of Maryland at Baltimore."[21] Second, Klanwatch cites a survey of 2,823 junior and senior high school students by the New York State Governor's Task Force on Bias-Related Violence, which found that the majority of respondents held biased views against gays and lesbians.[22] The extent to which this bias translates to violence is left to the imagination. It also remains unclear where the NIAPV's 25 percent figure comes from. What qualifies as an act of violence? How is a perpetrator identified and his or her prejudice confirmed?

The reported NIAPV findings cannot be reconciled with standard criminal justice statistics. For example, the FBI statistics on campus crimes for 1990 at the University of Maryland in Baltimore county show that of its 9,868 students, only 12 incidents of violent crime were reported; of 4,563 students at the University of Maryland at Baltimore City, 25 incidents of violence were reported.[23] Even if the FBI's statistics significantly underreport crime, Klanwatch's and NIAPV's claim seems grossly exaggerated.

Klanwatch also neglects to explain the link between the New York State Governor's Task Force finding of *biased feelings* among New York high school students and acts of hate violence on college campuses.

The more that the NIAPV's data are examined, the less reliable they appear. The 1990 NIAPV report on campus "ethnoviolence" claimed that "the number of college students victimized by ethnoviolence is in the range of 800,000 to one million students annually."[24] The report offers no explanation for how NIAPV came up with this incredible figure. The report also found that from 1986 to 1990, 250 colleges and universities reported racist incidents. Should we regard this statistic with alarm? Nationwide, there are approximately 3,500 colleges and universities. If 250 of them reported racist incidents during a one-year period (as opposed to the four years covered by NIAPV) that would mean that 90 percent of colleges and universities reported no racist incidents.

Richard Bernstein, a journalist critical of the NIAPV report, stated that "[c]ollecting figures on their total numbers does not prove the alarming increase in hatred so commonly reported. It only proves that the

United States has not reached that state of perfection in which all racism and all racial conflict are eliminated."[25] Indeed, NIAPV director, Howard Ehrlich, admits that "there is no way of knowing whether any upsurge of racial harassment at colleges is actually occurring. It may simply be that minority students are showing strength and courage in filing more reports and demanding changes."[26]

Examining NIAPV's definition of ethnoviolence and victimization sheds some light on why their numbers are so high. According to the NIAPV, ethnoviolence includes more than *crimes* motivated by bias, and more than verbal *harassment*. NIAPV defines ethnoviolence to include biased or even insensitive speech and literature. Further, NIAPV's definition of ethnoviolence includes "psychological violence"[27] and can encompass *any actual or perceived expression of insensitivity*. Two instances of ethnoviolence reported at the Massachusetts Institute of Technology were: (1) a student's statement that "[i]n one of my courses in freshman year, the professor would rarely call on any black student and the few times he did he asked embarrassingly easy questions;" and (2) a student's statement that "[a]t times professors would ask me to drop a course when I didn't think it was appropriate. I was outraged."[28] Other incidents of ethnoviolence included:

- *University of California, Los Angeles:* denial of tenure to an Asian-American faculty member.

- *Oberlin College:* guest speaker criticized Israel and Zionism as immoral, which caused 50 students in the audience to stand up and turn their backs, which caused black students in the audience to applaud. (The report doesn't specify whether the ethnoviolence was the speaker's remarks, the offended Jewish students' protest, or the applause by black students.)

- *Brigham Young University:* during a basketball game against Wyoming University, one of the players from Wyoming said to a BYU player, "Get off the floor and quit crying you *&#$@* [*sic*] Mormon."

- *California State University:* the campus newspaper published a piece critical of affirmative action.

Ought we to infer from such incidents that there is a campus hate crime epidemic or a campus atmosphere boiling with hatred?

And who are the victims of this ethnoviolence? Is the NIAPV counting as victims those who attended the lecture or read the newspaper? According to NIAPV,

> Victimization is more than a matter of counting bodies. Every person victimized has family and friends, and every active victimization has either direct witnesses or people who hear about it from the victim or others. Many of these people are also victims. We call them co-victims.[29]

Other advocacy groups also claim unprecedented levels of victimization. Asian-American advocacy groups lobbying for passage of the federal Hate Crime Statistics Act claimed that Asian Americans were experiencing increased hate violence. In a letter to the United States Senate, the Asian National Democratic Council of Asian and Pacific Americans stated, "[o]ur members in California, Texas, Massachusetts and New York are aware of an increase in violent crimes against Asian and Pacific Americans, most frequently new arrivals from Southeast Asia and Korea, often elderly."[30] William Yoshimo of the Japanese American Citizens League added, "[t]here has been a dramatic upward trend in violence toward Asians since 1980."[31] Likewise, Karen Kwong of the Asian American Bar Association of the Greater Bay Area wrote, "we believe in California, as well as throughout the nation, there has been an increase in crimes committed against Asians and other minorities which are motivated by racial, ethnic, or religious prejudice."[32] No numbers are cited. Even when the state of New Jersey reported a 22 percent drop in the number of bias crimes, Asian American organizations continued to proclaim an epidemic.[33]

The Media's Role

The media have accepted, reinforced, and amplified the image of a nation besieged by hate crime, despite the absence of any reliable evidence to support that claim and in the face of much evidence to contradict it. Headlines like these are typical: "A Cancer of Hatred Afflicts America,"[34] "Rise in Hate Crimes Signals Alarming Resurgence of Bigotry,"[35] "Black-on-White Hate Crimes Rising,"[36] "Decade Ended in Blaze of Hate,"[37] and "Combatting Hate: Crimes Against Minorities are Increasing Across the Board."[38] These alarmist articles claim that "across the nation, hate crimes . . . are on the increase after years of steady decline"[39] and "[t]hroughout the country, there are increasing numbers of shootings, assaults, murders and vandalism that are motivated by bias and hatred."[40] Intergroup conflict is "news," but intergroup cooperation is not. A *Newsday* headline states "Bias Crimes Flare Up in City's Heat";[41] five paragraphs later we find out that "the number of bias-related incidents in the city *dropped* in the first half of this year from the same period last year."[42]

The media seem enthusiastically to embrace the most negative interpretation of intergroup relations. For example, a Florida newspaper portrayed a deadly attack by a group of whites on a black tourist as "a dramatic example of the growing problem of hate crime."[43] Why "growing"? The article gave no explanation.[44]

When an alleged hate crime turns out to be a hoax, that fact often goes unnoted. One widely-reported incident that triggered an outpouring of outrage and theorizing involved a report that two black children, ages 12 and 14, were attacked in the Bronx by a group of whites who smeared white shoe polish on their faces and stole their lunch money.[45] Civil rights and advocacy groups, as well as church leaders, demanded action. New York City's first black mayor, David Dinkins, announced that he "would leave no stone unturned" to bring the perpetrators of this "dastardly deed" to justice.[46] The police launched a massive investigation, at one point assigning 200 detectives to the area. They offered a $20,000 reward for information leading to arrest of the offenders, and created a telephone hot line for anonymous tips.[47] Despite the reward and hundreds of interviews, no witnesses were found. A month into the investigation, police began considering the possibility that they were dealing with a hoax. This infuriated some politicians and community spokespersons, who demanded that the investigation continue. New York State Assembly member Roberto Ramirez stated, "Based on statements to us, these incidents did take place."[48] Police Commissioner Lee Brown, an African American, announced that the incident was "being fully investigated."[49]Clearly, political pressure prevented the department from labeling the incident a hoax. Even labeling or refusing to label hate crime has become a divisive issue for communities.

The media typically accept at face value advocacy organizations' assertions about epidemics of hate violence.[50] In fact, that is exactly how the media reported the NIAPV's claim that 800,000 to one million students are the victims of ethnoviolence. *Time Magazine* published an article summarizing that report and concluding:

> [i]n the heat of such boiling hatreds, it is hard to sustain any notion of the university as a protected enclave devoted to opening minds and nurturing tolerance. Instead, many campuses seem to distill the free-floating bigotries of American society into a lethal brew. . . . Virtually every minority group finds itself under fire.[51]

The *San Francisco Chronicle* reported that there is a "new trend of increasingly violent acts against Asian Americans."[52] The *Chronicle* stated that anti-Asian incidents increased from 335 in 1993 to 452 in 1994; "[i]n Northern California, the increase was sharper, from 39 to 83." In a nation with 7.3 million Asian Americans, and 207,155 Asians in San Francisco county (which the *Chronicle* did not report), do attacks on 452 and 83 Asians, respectively, constitute a "new trend of increasingly violent attacks"? One magazine article proclaimed that hate crimes against Asian Americans have "increased dramatically," and are "a serious national problem,"[53] but neglected to say how many hate crimes were directed at Asians, apparently leaving it to readers' imaginations.

Politicians

Politicians have fully endorsed the existence of a hate crime epidemic. Passing laws denouncing hate crime provides politicians with an opportunity to decry bigotry. They can propose hate crime legislation as a quick-fix solution that is cheap and satisfying to important groups of constituents. Recognizing the political and symbolic importance of legislation, politicians, both Democrats and Republicans, embrace anti-bias laws, routinely citing advocacy groups' statements and statistics. Representative Charles Schumer (D-N.Y.) proclaimed that "[t]he menace of bias crimes is spreading like a cancer across this country."[54] Senator Alan Cranston (D-Cal.), sponsor of the federal Hate Crime Statistics Act, referred extensively to the 1987 NGLTF statistics, stating "the number of hate crimes increased substantially, . . . representing a 42% increase from 1986."[55] Cosponsor John Kerry (D-Mass.) similarly explained:

> "[h]earings which have been held in the House Judiciary Committee indicate that there is a serious problem in America with hate crimes of all types, including violence against Blacks, Hispanics, Asian-Americans, Jews, Arab-Americans and gays. A recent report by the National Gay and Lesbian Task Force [asserts] that hate crimes directed against gays and lesbians are increasing. Legislation is needed to address the serious problem of anti-gay violence."[56]

The claim that the country is beset by an epidemic of violent bias crime led to passage of the Hate Crimes Statistics Act of 1990.[57] Sponsors of the HCSA favored a data collection effort to confirm what they claimed to know already: that every category of hate crime is rampant and getting worse. In 1992, the United States House of Representatives held hearings on a federal hate crime sentence enhancement bill. The hearings opened with witnesses stating as fact that "a veritable epidemic of hate crime is sweeping through our country at an alarming rate," and pointing to reports generated by the ADL and the National Gay and Lesbian Task Force.[58]

Scholars Weigh In

Academic writers, almost without exception, have accepted the existence of a hate crime epidemic and thus have lent their imprimatur to it. In *Hate Crimes: The Rising Tide of Bigotry and Bloodshed*, sociologists Jack Levin and Jack McDevitt claim that America is experiencing a "rising tide" of hate crimes. This assertion is based upon reports of advocacy groups like the ADL, Klanwatch, and the National Institute Against Prejudice and Violence. Much of the book is devoted to descriptions of horrific hate crimes.[59] But conspicuously absent are the data to support the claim that hate crime is increasing.

Levin and McDevitt attribute the supposed increase in hate crime to economic decline and attendant social-psychological malaise. They believe that "resentment" is at the root of most hate crime offenses: as Americans cope with dwindling economic opportunities, they blame others for taking opportunities away from them. This resentment and frustration, coupled with extant biases and stereotypes, expresses itself through hate crimes. This explanation is not based on any empirical studies or evidence. In short, the authors have a theory in search of a problem.

Bias Crime: American Law Enforcement and Legal Responses, is a collection of essays by law enforcement officials, social scientists, activists, and government officials, mostly documenting how law enforcement agencies have dealt with hate crimes. All of the essays assume that hate crimes are on the rise. Joan Weiss, executive director of the Justice Research and Statistics Association, acknowledges that the extent of the problem is unknown, but then claims that "[t]*he problem is so pervasive that, even without accurate data, we know that thousands upon thousands of incidents occur throughout the country every year.*"[60] In another essay, Allen Sapp, Richard Holden, and Michael Wiggins begin by stating, "[i]n recent years, bias-motivated activities directed at members of minority groups have occurred with increasing frequency. The escalating rate of these crimes is proving to be a major source of concern."[61]

In *Hate Crimes: Confronting Violence Against Lesbians and Gay Men*, Gregory Herek and Kevin Berrill begin with the premise that violence against homosexuals, while not a new problem, has *increased dramatically*. A large portion of the book presents brutal incidents of anti-gay violence. The authors state that surveys of victimization among gays and lesbians may not present an accurate picture of the magnitude of the anti-gay hate crimes due to an unwillingness by some individuals to "come out," and to general underreporting of incidents.

The most inflammatory of the recent books on hate crimes is Alphonso Pinkney's, *Lest We Forget: White Hate Crimes*. Pinkney argues that the conservative politics that prevailed in the 1980s created an atmosphere which allowed hostility against minorities to thrive. Pinkney states, "[t]he most alarming trend was the resurgence of overt racist behavior. . . . racial violence was rampant."[62] In one chapter, entitled "Recent Surge of Racial Violence," Pinkney points the finger of blame at former President Ronald Reagan: "the point is that Ronald Reagan set the tone and created the environment in which acts of racial violence thrived. . . . Thus, the widespread physical attacks on Blacks and other minorities went unchecked."[63] The bulk of the book is devoted to describing highly publicized incidents of violence, many of which are not clearly attributable to racism. For example, Pinkney labels as race-based violence an incident in which a New York City police officer shot a mentally unstable black woman, as she lunged at another police officer with a knife.

Most academic articles dealing with hate crime assume the existence of an across-the-board hate epidemic and go on to argue for new substantive laws, enhanced sentences, and increased enforcement. These scholarly commentators consistently cite data which do not support their conclusions. For example, Professor Abraham Abramovsky, in a 1992 law journal, claims an "urgency of the escalating problem [of bias crime]."[64] He states that "categories of bias crime are rapidly growing along with the reported number of instances." The proliferation of bias crime "categories" (e.g., anti-gender prejudice, anti-disability prejudice, etc.) is real, but it does not indicate more bias crime overall; rather, it indicates the willingness of lawmakers to accommodate more advocacy groups' demands for inclusion under the hate crime umbrella.

Professor Abramovsky was alarmed by the New York City Police Department's statistics showing that for the first four months of 1990 there was a 12 percent increase in the number of bias-related crimes over [the same period] in 1989.[65] "The most alarming statistic is that in 1990 the number of bias related attacks on Asians . . . almost doubled from the number reported in 1989."[66] A footnote provides the detail: "there were 11 bias crimes reported against Asians during the first four months of 1990, compared with 22 reports *in all* of 1989."[67] But, Abramovsky apparently extrapolated from 11 in four months to predict 33 for 1990— "almost double" the 22 in 1989. But as it turned out, the final 1990 total was *the same* as the 1989 total—22 anti-Asian attacks for 1989 and 22 for 1990. So much for alarming statistics! In any event, are 11, 22, or even 33 bias incidents against Asian Americans truly "alarming" in a city that has a 1990 Asian-American population of over one half million[68] and that generates over 700,000 index crimes (felonies) annually?[69]

The 11 bias crimes reported in the first four months of 1990 might have reflected a random crime fluctuation, the prolific criminality of a single offender or of a clique of teenagers, one police officer's dedicated investigations or enhanced data collection efficiency. Abramovsky acknowledges the latter possibility, but cites an NIAPV study that reports a "steady increase in hate crimes in the last two years from the majority of agencies who collect such data."[70] Citing the NIAPV study begs the question. As efficiency in bias data collection increases, whether by police or by nongovernmental organizations (and often in conjunction with each other), and more public attention is focused on the issue, the number of recorded bias-incidents will necessarily increase.

Student law review authors have also enthusiastically endorsed the existence of a hate crime epidemic. One writer in the *Harvard Law Review* states, "[i]n recent years, violence, threats, and vandalism committed because of the race, religion, sexual orientation, or other such characteristics of the victim have increased at an alarming rate."[71] This author explains that Congress passed a hate crime bill in 1990 and that the FBI reported 4,558 hate crimes in 1991. Since data available to the author are only for one year, it is remarkable that the author can discern an "increase." Another *Harvard Law Review* writer informs us that "the Howard Beach incident highlights an alarming trend of increasing racial violence against minorities in the United States."[72] The author's support for this "trend" was testimony at a 1983 House Judiciary Committee Hearing[73]—*three years prior* to the racial attack on three blacks in Howard Beach, Brooklyn.[74] If "racial minorities" is meant to refer to African Americans, as seems to be the author's intent, the hypothesis that there is increasing violence against racial minorities is clearly wrong.

Constructing the FBI Annual Reports

The Hate Crime Statistics Act of 1990 mandated a federal hate crime accounting system and required the attorney general to issue an annual public report on hate crimes in America. The reports have been compiled using "Hate Crime Incident Report" forms filled out by local police officers and then submitted to the FBI. One section of the form has boxes for the eleven predicate offenses. Another section provides codes for twenty-five different locations, such as "Bar/Night Club," "Construction Site," or "Lake/Waterway." A third section asks the officer to choose the type of bias motivation displayed by the offender, for example, "anti-black," "anti-Hispanic," "anti-Catholic," "anti-female," anti-homosexual," "anti-multiracial group," and so forth. A fourth section includes questions on type of victim (individual, business, society, etc.). Although one of the stated goals of the HCSA is to gather information that will allow law enforcement personnel and policy makers to gauge the nature and extent of the problem, the reporting system does not ask for information on the age or gender of the victim. The only offender-based questions are: (1) number of offenders; and (2) race. Information regarding sex, age, or other information is conspicuously absent.

The Annual Reports

In December 1992, prior to the release of its first official hate crimes report, the FBI issued a preliminary report, entitled *Hate Crime Statistics, 1990: A Resource Book*. This report, which compiled data from states that had their own reporting statutes, was a dismal failure. Only eleven states submitted any data. The FBI commented:

> Each state responded to its own needs and statutory requirements; therefore, a data collection instrument in one state is not necessarily comparable to that of another state. The groups covered by hate crime statutes often differed. In 1990, crimes motivated by hatred for an individual's sexual orientation were not covered by statute in Florida, Maryland, Pennsylvania, Rhode Island, and Virginia, but were covered in Connecticut, Massachusetts, Minnesota, New Jersey, New York, and Oregon. Moreover, Oregon's hate crime statute covered crimes committed against individuals based on marital status, political affiliation, and membership in a labor union. . . . Varied reporting procedures also restrict data comparability.[75]

In January 1993, the FBI released its first *official report* in the form of a one-page press release, presenting nationwide hate crime statistics for 1991.[76] The FBI accompanied this report, like its predecessor, with a disclaimer as to the usefulness of the data.[77] The report contained data from 32 states; only 2,771 law enforcement agencies (of the 12,805 agencies nationwide reporting to the FBI's Uniform Crime Reporting System) participated in the data collection effort.[78] Seventy-three percent of the reporting agencies reported *no hate crime incidents* for the entire year. Only 4,558 hate crime incidents were reported *for the entire United States*.[79] "Intimidation" was the most frequently reported offense, accounting for one-third of all hate crimes. Crimes against property accounted for 27.4 percent of reported hate crimes. The most frequently reported bias was racial (anti-black, anti-white, anti-American Indian, anti-Asian/Pacific Islander, and anti-multiracial group).[80]

A number of states that submitted data for the 1990 preliminary report documented fewer hate crimes for the next year. For example, in

1990, New York reported 1,130 hate crimes, whereas in 1991 it reported 943 hate crimes. Maryland reported 792 hate crimes for 1990 and 431 for 1991. Despite the drop in reported hate crime by some states and despite the 1991 report's finding of only 4,558 hate crimes nationwide (out of a total of *14 million* reported crimes), many newspapers cited this report as confirming a hate crime epidemic. A *Houston Chronicle* editorial stated: "[t]he specter of hate is unfortunately alive and well in the United States. . . . The national report reveals a grim picture."[81] The *Philadelphia Inquirer* announced that the "FBI and anti-bigotry groups report an alarming rise in hate crimes."[82] (Since this was the first report, how could the newspaper have discerned "a rise"?) *USA Today* bluntly stated that "no one needs a government report to know such [hate crime] offenses are rising."[83]

Ironically, the low incidence of hate crimes reported by the FBI led some of the groups that campaigned most vigorously for the passage of the Hate Crime Statistics Act to denounce the whole federal data collection project. Klanwatch dismissed the first FBI statistics as "inadequate and nearly worthless."[84]

The FBI report for 1992 showed only a marginal improvement in the number of states submitting data. Six thousand two hundred law enforcement agencies (about half of all law enforcement agencies) in 41 states and the District of Columbia reported only 6,623 hate crimes. Nevertheless, the media generally interpreted this report as confirming what "everyone already knew": the nation was experiencing a hate crime epidemic. *The National Law Journal* opined that the 1990s may be remembered as "the decade of hate crime."[85]

The 1992 report again found that the most frequently reported hate crime was intimidation (2,318 incidents), accounting for 35 percent of reported hate crimes. Vandalism (1,762 incidents) accounted for 27 percent, followed by simple assault (1,258 incidents), 19 percent; and aggravated assault (984 incidents), 15 percent.[86] Rape and murder, the most serious violent hate crimes and the ones that provoke the greatest amount of public outrage were rare—6 bias-motivated rapes and 15 murders. Table 3 lists the five most frequent hate crime biases for 1992 through 1994; Table 4 shows the most common hate crimes by offense.

The 1993 FBI report reflects increased participation by states and law enforcement agencies—46 states and 6,900 agencies submitted data showing a total of 7,587 hate crimes. As with the 1991 and 1992 reports, intimidation was the most frequently reported hate crime (2,451 incidents), followed by vandalism (2,222 incidents). There were 11 reported bias-motivated murders; the number of bias-motivated rapes

Table 3   Total Incidents by Bias Motivation*

	1992	1993	1994
Number of states reporting	41	46	43
Number of police departments reporting	6,200	6,900	7,200
Anti-black	2,296	3,559	2,476
Anti-white	1,342	1,853	1,299
Anti-Semitic	1,017	1,252	1,054
Anti-gay	750	1,015	777
Anti-ethnic	592	895	583

*Information based on FBI annual Hate Crime Reports.

doubled to 13. These increases are likely due to participation by more law enforcement agencies and states.

In 1994, 5,852 hate crimes were reported by 43 participating states and 7,200 law enforcement agencies. As Table 4 shows, intimidation and vandalism again accounted for a majority of all reported hate crimes.

What conclusions can we draw from these reports? First, most reported hate crimes are low-level offenses, not brutal or murderous

Table 4   Reported Hate Crimes by Offense Type*

	1992	1993	1994
Total incidents	6,623	7,587**	5,852***
Intimidation	2,318	2,451	2,792
Vandalism	1,762	2,222	1,734
Simple assault	1,258	1,462	1,305
Aggravated assault	984	1,044	998
Robbery	150	157	126
Burglary	63	84	58
Arson	37	53	63
Larceny-theft	26	55	40
Murder	15	11	13
Rape	6	13	7
Auto theft	4	9	2

•Information based on FBI annual Hate Crime Reports.

**The total of all offense types does not equal the total number of reported incidents. The total for offense types is 7,561. This is not a typo or authors' computing error; these are the totals provided by the FBI report.

***The total of all offense types does not equal the total number of reported incidents. The total for offense types is 7,138. The reason for the numerical discrepancy is that a single hate crime incident may involve more than one offense (e.g., a burglary plus vandalism; simple assault plus intimidation).

attacks. There does not seem to be a trend of escalating violence. Second, the absolute number of hate crimes of all types identified by the federal reporting system is very small. Third, the data do not reveal any significant fluctuation in reported hate crimes between 1992 and 1994. But, fourth, the HCSA data are all but useless for discerning trends, because of the variation in the number of states and police departments reporting.

Historical Perspective

It requires ignorance of history to state that "[n]ot since the days when the [Ku Klux] Klan regularly lynched people at the turn of the century . . . have we had anything like we have today,"[87] or to state that "black students today face a level of hatred, prejudice and ignorance comparable to that of the days of Bull Connor, Lester Maddox and Orval Faubus."[88] It is far beyond the scope of this chapter or this book to provide a comprehensive history of racial and ethnic violence, much less anti-religious violence, anti-homosexual violence, and anti-gender violence in the United States; that would require nothing less than a multivolume treatise. However, it is preposterous to claim that the country is now experiencing *unprecedented levels* of violence in all these categories.

Native Americans

Almost from the moment European settlers arrived in this country, Native Americans were the target of bigotry and hatred.[89] Viewed as savages, they were routinely removed from their land by force. The nineteenth century was punctuated with atrocities against Native Americans. During the 1820s, in North Carolina, Georgia, and other southern states, the Cherokees were rounded up by the U.S. military and force marched to Oklahoma. During this 3,000 mile "Trail of Tears," hundreds of Cherokees died either at the hands of their military escorts, or from starvation and exposure.[90]

In Arizona and New Mexico, settlers and officials of the Catholic Church attacked Navajo camps, kidnapping women and children to use as slaves. During the 1850s and 1860s, the U.S. military hunted down and killed Navajos in a carefully orchestrated campaign. The Navajos surrendered after their peach orchards and crops were burned. They too were subjected to a forced march, known as "The Long Walk," to Boscque Redondo, a remote military outpost in southeastern New Mexico. Those unable to keep up were shot. During the four years of imprisonment at Boscque Redondo, nearly half the Navajo population died.[91] This was government sponsored genocide, not criminality committed by socially marginal individuals.

In the late 1800s, several counties in Arizona and New Mexico offered bounties for Indian scalps—$500 for male scalps and $250 for those of women and children. A *New York Times* article, entitled "Arizona and New Mexico Settlers Propose to Destroy the Savages," reported that citizens were organizing "in armed bodies for the purpose of going on a real old-fashioned Indian hunt."[92]

The U.S. military, as well as private citizens, also targeted the Plains tribes.[93] The campaign to confine the various Plains tribes to reservations and liberate land for white settlement involved violent attacks and the mutilation and murder of entire families. Perhaps the most infamous private citizens' campaign was the Sand Creek massacre. Settlers in Colorado, upon hearing that a group of Cheyenne were camped several hours ride from Denver, attacked the sleeping Cheyenne at dawn. The mob shot and killed men and women of all ages; they also ran bayonets through infants and children, and mutilated the dead bodies.[94]

Blacks, Lynchings, and the Klan

Lynching has a long history in the United States. After the Revolutionary War, vigilante patriots lynched loyalists and criminals. In the American West during the 1800s, cattle and horse thieves, murderers, claim jumpers, Hispanics, and Native Americans were common targets of lynch mobs.[95] Lynching was most prevalent, however, under the Klan's terrorism, from the post-Civil War era until well into the twentieth century.[96]

From 1882 to 1968, 4,743 people were lynched; the vast majority were black. During the peak lynching years, 1889–1918, the five most active states were Georgia (360), Mississippi (350), Louisiana (264), Texas (263), and Alabama (244). In 1892, 200 lynchings occurred in a single year. These numbers include only the recorded lynchings.[97]

Many hundreds more blacks were injured and killed during race riots in the late nineteenth and early twentieth century. In March 1871, a riot erupted in Meridian, Mississippi, during the trial of three blacks accused of making "incendiary speeches." An argument escalated into a shooting spree in which 25 to 30 blacks were killed by rioters.[98] Blacks who escaped the rioters unharmed fled to the woods; Klansmen took the three blacks on trial from the courthouse and hanged them.[99] The early part of the twentieth century saw anti-black riots, often led by the Klan, in Chicago, Tulsa, Memphis, and Washington, D.C.[100]

The Ku Klux Klan, formed in 1865, terrorized southern blacks during the post-Civil War period to such a degree that many blacks went into semipermanent hiding. According to David Chalmers, author of *Hooded Americanism: The History of the Ku Klux Klan,*

> Unless there were federal troops at hand, the safest thing for Negroes to do was to hide during periods of Klan activity or after outbreaks of violence. It was reported that in some regions of South Carolina, more than a majority of the Negroes slept in the woods during the Klan's active winter of 1870–71.[101]

In the 1920s, Klan membership soared to 4–5 million people nationally.[102] In addition to blacks, the Klan targeted recent immigrants, Catholics, Jews, and communists.[103] By contrast, today Klan membership is estimated at approximately 5,000 nationwide.[104]

During the 1950s and 1960s, after *Brown v. Board of Education* and the rise of the civil rights movement, violence against blacks and Jews flared all across the South. Hundreds of homes, churches, and synagogues were fire bombed. By the mid-1950s, the crude homemade bombs of segregationists were exploding on a biweekly basis.[105] In 1958, Atlanta's oldest synagogue was bombed.[106] At least 200 black churches in Mississippi alone were bombed or burned during the early 1960s.[107] Gangs of whites organized "Citizens' Councils" all over the South; some of these spawned campaigns of beatings, burnings, intimidations, and lynchings.[108] Black students, attending newly desegregated public schools and universities, needed National Guard escorts to ensure their safety from mobs of protesting whites. In 1963, Medgar Evers was assassinated; four years later, Martin Luther King, Jr. met the same fate. The violence was so rampant that civil rights workers for the Council of Federated Organizations (COFO) (an umbrella group formed by the NAACP, the Congress of Racial Equality, the Southern Christian Leadership Conference, and the Student Nonviolent Coordinating Committee) were required to call in at scheduled times during each day. If they failed to call within fifteen minutes of the appointed time, COFO's Jackson, Mississippi office would notify local police, the FBI, and the Justice Department. When COFO civil rights workers Andrew Goodman, Michael Schwerner, and James Chaney failed to call in, Philadelphia, Mississippi Sheriff Lawrence Rainey dismissed their disappearance as a publicity stunt. Later, a deputy sheriff was among those accused of murdering the three men, who were found buried in an earthen dam two months after their disappearance.[109]

Nativism: A Politics of Hatred

Beginning in the 1820s and extending into the twentieth century, a mainstream political movement developed that was based on hatred of

Catholics, Jews, and recent immigrants, primarily Irish, Italians, and Germans. Nativist leaders were not merely a fringe element on the American scene. They were elected to political office and published widely read anti-Catholic and anti-immigrant newspapers. During the 1820s–30s, the movement was called "nativism." Eventually, it organized the "Know-Nothing Party." Later in the century, it went by the name of the American Protective Association. In the twentieth century, its formal organization dissolved. Today's nativism takes the form of lobbying for immigration controls and restrictions on benefits to illegal immigrants. There is very little organized violence against immigrants.[110]

The rhetoric of the nativists encouraged hatred. For decades, Catholic churches were burned. Gangs and mobs attacked priests and immigrants in Massachusetts, New Jersey, Maine, New York, Maryland, and Pennsylvania.[111] In the 1840s, Philadelphia was the scene of sporadic rioting.

> Natives and Irishmen, Protestants and Catholics clashed in fistfights and knifefights. They exchanged gunfire. They menaced each other with cannons, ready to be loaded with stacks of shot, powder, nails, chains, "anything" as one observer put it, that could be used "to kill and maim the foe." . . . [S]ome thirty people were killed, hundreds wounded, dozens of homes burned out.[112]

Anti-immigrant and anti-Catholic violence flourished into the twentieth century. In the early decades of the century, anti-Semitism was rampant in all areas of American life. Newspaper classified advertisements for employment, housing, and vacation rentals openly declared "no Jews."[113] Ironically, one of the most virulent American anti-Semites of the first half of the twentieth century was a Catholic priest, Charles Coughlin. Father Coughlin's church had been the target of many Klan-orchestrated cross burnings. During the late 1920s, Coughlin began broadcasting his sermons on radio. After the Great Depression hit, Coughlin focused on economic and social issues. An avowed enemy of the New Deal, Coughlin founded the National Union for Social Justice (NUSJ). By 1936, NUSJ had over 5 million members. Coughlin's radio broadcasts, to an audience of at least 10 million listeners, were peppered with anti-Semitic attacks and praise for Nazi Germany and the Third Reich. His anti-Semitic message appealed to nativism's past victims, Irish and German Catholics. Young followers of Father Coughlin bragged about attacking Jews in Boston and New York.[114]

Anti-Semitism also reached the highest levels of the federal government. President Roosevelt's assistant secretary of state in the early 1940s, Breckenridge Long, a nativist and an anti-Semite, wrote that large numbers of Jews from Russia and Poland "are entirely unfit to become citizens of this country . . . they are lawless, scheming, defiant . . . just the same as the criminal Jews who crowd our police court dockets in New York."[115]

Others

Admittedly, *reported* violence against women may be at historic highs. But if so, this fact may not be as ominous as it appears. Earlier in this century, society was far less attuned and sympathetic to victimized women; women, therefore, were often too embarrassed to report their victimization, and often had no one to whom they could report it. In the past, women had a less influential role in society. It may be, then, that violence against women is not on the rise, even if *reported* violence is.

As for homosexuals, it may be that the number of incidents of victimization (not just number of reports) is at a historic high. Until recently, gays and lesbians feared to openly affirm or demonstrate their sexual orientation. The visible *population* of homosexuals was smaller, so the number of potential victims was smaller. As the number of openly homosexual individuals has increased, the number (though not necessarily the rate) of crimes committed against them may also have increased.[116] However, on this issue, there are no trend data whatsoever.

Conclusion

Advocacy groups for gays and lesbians, Jews, blacks, women, Asian Americans, and disabled persons have all claimed that recent unprecedented violence against their members requires special hate crime legislation. These groups have sought to call attention to their members' victimization, subordinate status, and need for special governmental assistance. Journalists and academics have accepted the existence of a hate crime epidemic almost without question and, on occasion, even when statistics show just the opposite. The Hate Crime Statistics Act has failed to provide any reliable data on hate crime. But, for what they are worth, its reports show very small numbers of hate crimes, the majority of which are low-level offenses.

Minority groups have good reasons for claiming that we are in the throes of an epidemic. An "epidemic" demands attention, remedial actions, resources, and reparations. The electronic and print media also have an incentive to support the existence of a rampant hate crime epidemic. Crime sells; so does racism, sexism, and homophobia. Garden variety crime has become mundane. The law-and-order drama has to be revitalized if it is to command attention.

In contemporary American society there is less prejudice-motivated violence against minority groups than in many earlier periods of American history. Clearly, violence motivated by racism, xenophobia, anti-Semitism, and other biases is not new and is not "on the rise." Professor Abramovsky asserts that, "no one is seriously questioning the severity of the problem [of bias crime]."[117] We are. The uncritical acceptance of a hate crime epidemic may well have negative sociopolitical ramifications. This pessimistic and alarmist portrayal of a fractured warring community is likely to exacerbate societal divisions and contribute to a self-fulfilling prophesy. It distorts the discourse about crime in America, turning a social problem that used to unite Americans into one that divides us.

5

The Politics of Hate
Crime Laws

This legislation [ethnic intimidation law]
does more than punish. . . . It says something
about who we are, and about the ideals to
which this state is committed.

New Jersey Governor Jim Florio,
August 1990

Identity Politics

The proliferation of hate crime laws in the 1980s and 1990s should not
be attributed to insufficiently severe criminal sanctions. There is no reason to believe that prejudice-motivated offenders, particularly those who
commit violent crimes, were not or could not be punished severely
enough under generic criminal laws.

In this chapter, we argue that the passage of hate crime laws enacted
in the 1980s and 1990s is best explained by the growing influence of
identity politics. Fundamentally, the hate crime laws are symbolic statements requested by advocacy groups for material and symbolic reasons
and provided by politicians for political reasons.

The past thirty years have seen a shift from emphasis on nondiscrimination to emphasis on race and group consciousness. The very success
of the civil rights movement spawned a new "identity politics" that led
Americans to define themselves and others in terms of race, religion,
gender, and sexual-orientation.[1] According to political journalist Jim
Sleeper:

> Identity politics makes race, ethnicity, gender, and sexual orientation
> into the primary lenses through which people view themselves and

65

society. It tends to encourage new and old minority groups to with-
draw from—or assault—a mistrusted "majority" culture in the pursuit of their separate communal destinies.[2]

From a commitment to excising race and other such indelible characteristics from official notice, the nation moved to a position of demanding that these characteristics be officially recognized and weighed in a
wide range of social contexts, especially public and private employment,
college and university admissions, public contracting, and the design of
voting districts.[3] Group consciousness became the politically and morally dominant ideology of late-twentieth-century American society, and
various nationality and ethnic groups, women, gays and lesbians, the
elderly, and the handicapped, in addition to racial and religious groups,
came to see advantage in stressing their victimization.[4]

Identity politics is fueled by a sense of resentment based upon victimization, discrimination, and disadvantage. What gives a group its
character, status, and identity is its perception of mistreatment by the
white, male, Christian, heterosexual "majority" as well as by other minority groups. Under the logic of identity politics, a victim group can
assert a moral claim to special entitlements and affirmative action.[5] Even
minority groups that have been very successful in contemporary American society frequently stress their victimized and disadvantaged status.[6]
According to Professor Shelby Steele, victimization can metamorphosize
into political and social power, but this formula

> binds the victim to his victimization by linking his power to his status
> as a victim. . . . It is primarily a victim's power grounded too deeply
> in the entitlement derived from past injustice and in the innocence
> that Western/Christian tradition has always associated with poverty.[7]

Hate Crime Law as Symbolic Politics

Studies of legal change highlight the importance of interest groups in
the legislative process.[8] Laws do not spring forth from a groundswell of
public opinion, but rather are the product of lobbying by interested
("interest") groups that must mobilize support among politicians. The
hate crime laws were passed because of the lobbying efforts of organizations that advocate on behalf of blacks, Jews, gays and lesbians, a few
other ethnic and nationality groups, and in some cases, women.[9] Many
advocacy organizations set an annual legislative agenda, with the passage of federal and state laws becoming an end in itself and a main measure of their success. Regardless of what it accomplishes, the passage of
legislation boosts the morale and the status of the organizations and their
constituencies.[10]

The Appeal of Hate Crime Law For Politicians

The job of lobbyists is to convince politicians to support the proposals they favor. In exchange for the legislator's vote, the lobbyists can offer campaign contributions, election endorsements, or more diffuse expressions of gratitude and support. In deciding whether to support or oppose proposals put forward by lobbyists, politicians look to the costs and benefits. In the case of hate crime laws, except for the inclusion of sexual orientation, politicians faced a no lose proposition. By supporting hate crime legislation, they could please the advocacy groups without antagonizing any lobbyists on the other side (there were none) and without making hard budgetary choices. The hate crime laws provided an opportunity to denounce two evils—crime and bigotry—without offending any constituencies or spending any money.

There is today a social and political consensus that racial, religious, and gender prejudice is wrong. While more controversial, a majority of Americans believes that discrimination against homosexuals is also wrong. (For example, a 1993 Gallup Poll asked "[i]n general, do you think homosexuals should or should not have equal rights in terms of job opportunities?" Eighty percent of respondents replied that they should.[11])

Politicians specialize in symbolic pronouncements. They enthusiastically support laws that reaffirm widely revered values such as "the flag," "patriotism," "freedom," and "tolerance." Supporting hate crime legislation provides them an excellent opportunity to put themselves *on record* as opposed to criminals and prejudice and in favor of law and order, decency, and tolerance. Therefore, it is not surprising that most legislators responded enthusiastically when asked to denounce, recriminalize, and/or enhance maximum penalties for criminal conduct motivated by prejudice.

In the campaigns that lead up to passage of federal and state hate crime laws, there was invariably much talk of "message sending." Proponents demand that a message be sent to biased offenders that crimes of bigotry will not be tolerated. But a close look at the legislative politics suggests that the hate crime laws send messages to at least three different audiences of which offenders is probably the least important.

The most obvious audience is the lobbyists who desire hate crime legislation. Supporting, voting for, and passing hate crime laws "sends a message" to these groups: "we are on your side; we recognize your victimization and the abhorrent prejudice aimed against your group. In condemning those who commit heinous crimes against you, we express and exhibit solidarity with you and, in return, expect your support."

The second audience with which politicians seek to communicate via hate crime legislation is the general voting population. Hate crime legislation provides politicians the opportunity to say to this mass audience: "we condemn prejudice and bigotry in the strongest and most solemn way. Moreover, in condemning prejudice, we affirm our own prejudice-free character and assert a moral claim to your support." It may be hard to get this message heard because, unlike the lobbying groups, the general citizenry is not tuned in to the hate crime channel. The message can get lost among hundreds of commercial and noncommercial messages that continuously bombard the citizenry.

The third audience is comprised of hate crime offenders and potential offenders—racists, homophobes, sexists, anti-Semites, and other bigots. The message that hate crime legislation sends to them might be interpreted as: "don't even think about preying upon people because of their race, religion, gender, sexual orientation, etc. We regard this type of victimization as worse than victimizing a member of your own group. If you cannot hold your biases in check, you will be severely punished." Unlike the first two audiences, members of this third audience will not be enthused or inspired by the legislators' hate crime message. Undoubtedly, potential hate crime offenders are already well aware that the majority in our society, especially its elites, strongly opposes racial, religious, and gender prejudices. Indeed, the potential hate crime offender, feeling alienated and defining himself as an outcast or a rebel, may hold his prejudice in spite of or in protest against the values of mainstream society.

The message that hate crime laws communicate to this group is just one of a constant barrage of condemnations and threats beamed at criminals. It would take some heroic assumptions to believe that bigoted and anti-social criminals and potential criminals, if they are listening at all, will be any more responsive to this message than they have been to all the other threats and condemnations contained in criminal laws that they regularly ignore.

Passage of Federal Hate Crime Law

Since 1990 Congress has passed three different laws directed at hate crime—the Hate Crime Statistics Act of 1990 (HCSA), the Violence Against Women Act of 1994 (VAWA), and the Hate Crimes Sentencing Enhancement Act of 1994 (HCSEA). The legislative history of each of these laws demonstrates both the importance of symbolic politics and the dominance of identity politics.

The Hate Crime Statistics Act of 1990

In the mid-1980s, a number of civil rights groups made passage of federal hate crime legislation a priority. In 1985, the ADL, the Anti-Klan Network, the Institute for the Prevention and Control of Violence and Extremism, and the International Network for Jewish Holocaust Survivors began lobbying Congress for a federal hate crime reporting statute.[12] Not surprisingly, these groups lobbied for the collection of data on, and therefore special recognition of, crimes motivated by race, religion, and ethnicity. Other nationality groups trying to establish themselves as bona fide members of the civil rights coalition joined the lobbying effort. Congress held hearings on violence against Arab Americans,[13] Asian Americans,[14] anti-religious violence,[15] and racially motivated violence.[16] The House of Representatives passed the HCSA bill in 1985, but Congress adjourned before the Senate could vote on the bill.[17]

In the meantime, the National Gay and Lesbian Task Force (NGLTF) requested assistance from Representative Barney Frank (D-Mass.), an openly gay congressman, to have anti-gay and anti-lesbian-motivated crime included in the definition of hate crime. Although the HCSA conferred no substantive rights (it simply required the collection of data), gays and lesbians viewed "their inclusion" in the bill as an important first step toward official recognition of gay rights.[18] The Criminal Justice Subcommittee of the House Judiciary Committee conducted oversight hearings on anti-homosexual violence in October 1986.[19] According to Representative John Conyers (D-Mich.), the purpose of the hearings was to sensitize the public to the existence and prevalence of anti-gay violence.[20]

Following these hearings, gay and lesbian groups joined a coalition of advocacy groups lobbying for passage of the HCSA. The revised bill, which now included sexual orientation, was reintroduced in the 100th Congress.[21] Spokespersons for the ADL, the American Arab Anti-Discrimination Committee, Klanwatch, the National Institute Against Prejudice and Violence, the Japanese American Citizens League, the National Gay and Lesbian Task Force, the NAACP, and the Organization of Chinese Americans all testified in support of the bill.[22] Each spokesperson claimed that the number of hate crimes against his or her group was rising and that passage of the HCSA would (1) help communities, legislatures, and law enforcement personnel respond effectively by providing information on the frequency, location, extent, and patterns of hate crime; (2) improve law enforcement's response by increasing awareness of and sensitivity to hate crimes; (3) *raise public aware-*

ness of the existence of hate crimes, and (4) *send a message that the federal government is concerned about hate crime.*

The logic underlying justification 1 and 2 was never clearly explained and hate crime data have not proved useful in achieving these ends. From our perspective, the third and fourth reasons best explain the goal of the law's proponents. The HCSA would provide an official statement that hate crime, defined in terms of a handful of officially designated prejudices, is a serious problem deserving special attention and condemnation. Joan Weiss of the National Institute Against Prejudice and Violence testified that "one of the most significant reasons for passing this act is that finally . . . it would send a message to the citizens of this country that the Congress of the United States does not condone these acts."[23] Alan M. Schwartz of the ADL testified that "these acts must be clearly and firmly rejected as unacceptable by all levels of the community." One of the bill's sponsors, John Conyers,[24] stated that "[d]evoting federal resources to the collection of more information about this problem will demonstrate a national commitment to the eradication of hate crimes."[25]

The Senate Judiciary Committee's report on the bill emphasized the importance of sending a message to the advocacy groups and their constituents.

> The enactment of a Federal law requiring the systematic collection of hate crime data is a significant step. The very effort by the legislative branch to require the Justice Department to collect this information would send an additional important signal to victimized groups everywhere that the U.S. Government is concerned about this kind of crime.[26]

While there was near unanimous political enthusiasm in Congress for sending an anti-prejudice message by means of a law requiring collection of hate crime statistics, there was some controversy about whether the message should apply to anti-gay and anti-lesbian prejudice. Some senators and representatives opposed including sexual orientation prejudice within the hate crime bill because they did not want to send a message equating anti-gay and lesbian bias with racial and religious bias. They were not prepared to denounce the former type of prejudice, and they feared that if homosexuals were, in effect, treated as a "protected" group for purposes of hate crime legislation, the next step might be their routine inclusion in civil rights legislation. Senator Jesse Helms (R-N.C.) stated, "it may be that some will try to use this data [on anti-gay hate crimes gathered pursuant to the Hate Crime Statistics Act] to call for gay rights legislation."[27] As Representative William Dannemeyer (D-Cal.) put it, inclusion of sexual orientation prejudice in the Hate Crime Statistics Act would "change the basic definition of the 1964 Civil Rights

Act to include a new status that would have the dignity of being within the proscription [*sic*] of that act";[28] in other words, gays and lesbians would be equated with officially approved victim groups. Five members of the House Judiciary Committee were even more explicit:

> There is no mention of homosexual rights in the Constitution. . . . [T]he question recurs as to why statistics are important. They are valuable not in themselves but rather to help discover the existence and extent of a problem and to support its solution. Statistics merely lay the foundation for a subsequent Federal response. . . . [I]t is all the more essential that targeted groups be within the scope of Federal responsibility in the first place. It is a Federal responsibility to ensure equal protection of all citizens regardless of their race, religion or ethnic origin. It is not a Federal obligation to protect citizens in their sexual orientation.[29]

Senator Helms led the Senate opposition to the inclusion of sexual orientation. He authored a "Sense of the Senate" amendment that condemned homosexuality, rejected it as a lifestyle, condemned government support for extending civil rights to homosexuals, and called for strict enforcement of state sodomy laws.[30] In a compromise move, Senators Robert Dole (R-Kan.), Paul Simon (D-Ill.) and Orrin Hatch (R-Utah) offered a second section to the bill:

> Congress finds that:
> 1. American family life is the foundation of American society.
> 2. Federal policy should encourage the well-being, financial security, and health of the American family.
> 3. Schools should not deemphasize the critical value of American family life.
> "[*n*]*othing in this Act shall be construed . . . to promote or encourage homosexuality.*" (emphasis added)[31]

With that non sequitur in place, the Senate passed the HCSA by 92–4.[32] The House of Representatives amended the bill to include the Senate's "American family" provision and passed it by 368–47.[33] The symbolic importance of the Act was immediately apparent. The gay and lesbian advocacy groups felt that they had achieved a significant milestone, despite section 2. It was the first time that federal legislation included sexual orientation along with racial, religious, and ethnic groups.[34] Tim McFeeley, executive director of the Human Rights Campaign fund, a lesbian and gay advocacy organization, hailed the HCSA as "the first time in history that sexual orientation will be included in a federal civil rights law."[35] It also marked the first time that gay and lesbian leaders were invited to a public law-signing ceremony at the White House.[36]

Exclusion of Gender Prejudice

Passage of the Hate Crime Statistics Act was not a victory for women's advocacy groups. For more than a decade women had been treated as a disadvantaged group in federal and state civil rights laws and for purposes of affirmative action programs. "Blacks, women, and other minorities" had become a mantra for civil rights groups. Why would crimes motivated by gender prejudice not qualify as hate crime? The women's advocates argued that women are overwhelmingly victimized by men, and that many male offenders, especially rapists, serial murderers, batterers, and assaulters, are motivated by misogyny. They argued that treating gender-motivated violence, especially rape, as a hate crime would "constitute societal endorsement of a notion which has been repeatedly asserted by feminists and experts: rape is not simply a crime which happens to women, but an act of violence which is inflicted upon a person because she is a woman."[37] During congressional hearings on the HCSA, Molly Yard, president of the National Organization for Women, testified that:

> [w]hile national statistics are kept on the incidence of rape and domestic violence, categorization of such crimes as hate crimes is necessary in order for law enforcement personnel, legislators, educators, and the public at large to truly understand not just the full scope and complexity of the problem but the motivation behind these crimes.[38]

There is no clearer example of what we mean by the symbolic significance of hate crime laws.

The coalition lobbying for passage of the HCSA *rejected* gender prejudice as a hate crime trigger on the ground that the federal government already collected statistics on rape and domestic violence.[39] The coalition argued that violence against women was qualitatively different from true hate crime because many anti-female offenders are acquainted with their victims and are thus motivated by animosity against a particular woman, not against women in general.

> [A] substantial majority of women victims of violent crimes were previously acquainted with their attackers. While a hate crime against a black sends a message to all blacks, that same logic does not follow in many sexual assaults; *victims are not necessarily interchangeable in the same way*. (emphasis added)[40]

The coalition in effect added "victim interchangeability" to the definition of hate crime.[41] According to the coalition, a true hate crime involves an attack on a victim solely because of his membership in a group, not because of his individual identity. Because the crime is motivated by the victim's membership in a particular group, the crime terrorizes all members of that group; the victim could be interchanged with any other group member. Of course, that definition of hate crime would, for example, exclude the assassinations of Martin Luther King, Medgar Evers, and Rabbi Meyer Kahane, as well as all hate crimes where a victim and offender knew one another.

The women's advocates vigorously disputed these arguments and, not surprisingly, perceived them to be examples of gender bias.

> No one applies these [interchangeability] tests to violence against members of others groups. Burning a cross in the neighbor's yard, desecrating a classmate's place of worship or harassing a coworker with racial taunts are all understood as hate crimes despite the relationship between the offender and victim. In fact, the previous relationship makes the crime more heinous because the sense of connection and shared community implied in social familiarity is viciously shattered.[42]

The women's advocates also argued that many crimes against women, especially serial murders and serial rapes, do not involve acquaintances. Such crimes are often explicable only in terms of the offender's irrational fear and hatred of women and therefore would satisfy the victim interchangeability test. In addition, where a male aggressor and female victim are acquainted, it remains possible, and probably likely, that the aggressor's motivation is, at least in part, motivated by misogyny. The failure to include gender bias has been sharply criticized.

> The exclusion of sex-hate as a form of hate-violence is . . . a profound denial of the most pervasive form of violence in the United States. . . . It is an attempt to have it both ways: that is, to rage against such hate-violence when the victims are males (and occasionally females) and yet to protect male superiority over women. The denial of sexual violence as a hate crime is purposeful for the status quo, for it would be detrimental to the social order to define men's violence against women as a serious, hateful crime.[43]

Some analysts of the legislative politics leading up to the HCSA concluded that the coalition's opposition to the inclusion of gender bias as a hate crime trigger was based on a perception that, because misogynistic violence against women is so prevalent, its inclusion would overwhelm the other species of hate crime.[44] In other words, at this symbolic level, groups perceive themselves to be in competition with one another for attention. This again reinforces our thesis that the primary purpose of hate crime laws is to bolster the morale and strategic position of certain identity groups, not to impose heavier sanctions on prejudiced offenders.

The Violence Against Women Act of 1994

After failing to get gender bias included in the HCSA, the women's advocacy groups lobbied Congress for either an amendment to the HCSA or a separate law dealing with the criminal victimization of women. The politicians had every reason (including the fact that women constitute a majority of voters!) to support such a demand and hardly any reason to refuse. Consequently, Senate Judiciary Committee Chairman, Joe Biden (D-Del.), introduced the Violence Against Women Act (VAWA) as part of the Violent Crime Control and Law Enforcement Act of 1994.[45]

VAWA was introduced in Congress in 1990 and again in 1991.[46] It was favorably reported by the Senate Judiciary Committee in both the 101st and 102d Congresses, and finally passed in 1994.[47] Title IV[48] set out the following congressional findings:

> Crimes motivated by the victim's gender constitute bias crimes in violation of the victim's right to be free from discrimination on the basis of gender.
>
> . . .
>
> State and Federal criminal laws do not adequately protect against the bias element of gender crimes, which separates these crimes from acts of random violence, nor do they adequately provide victims the opportunity to vindicate their interests.[49]

The VAWA defined "crime of violence motivated by gender" as "a crime of violence committed because of gender or on the basis of gender, and due, at least in part, to an animus based on the victim's gender."[50] No prior criminal complaint, prosecution, or conviction is necessary before bringing suit under the so-called civil rights provision that permits female victims of gender-motivated assaults to sue their attackers in federal court for money damages and injunctive relief:

> A person (including a person who acts under color of any statute, ordinance, regulation, custom, or usage of any State) who commits a crime of violence motivated by gender . . . shall be liable to the party injured for the recovery of compensatory and punitive damages, injunctive and declaratory relief, and such other relief as a court may deem appropriate.[51]

Other provisions of the Act provide funding and grants for battered women's shelters and rape counseling, mandate interstate recognition and enforcement of restraining orders issued in other states, and make crossing state lines to commit a crime against a spouse a federal felony; these provisions generated little controversy. Our critique of the VAWA deals only with the symbolic nature of the civil rights provision.

NOW, NOW's Legal Defense and Education Fund, and the Fund for the Feminist Majority vigorously supported the civil rights provision.[52] Spokeswomen for these organizations emphasized the importance of the symbolic message that the VAWA's civil rights provision would convey. Sally Goldfarb of NOW's Legal Defense and Education Fund testified that "[e]nactment of [the civil rights provision] of the Violence Against Women Act would convey a very powerful message that violence motivated by gender is not just an individual crime or personal injury, but is a form of discrimination. It's an assault on our publicly shared idea of equality."[53] Eleanor Smeal, president of the Fund for the Feminist Majority, stressed the importance of sending a strong message, especially in light of the failure to include gender in the HCSA:

> We believe that with what has happened in the past, the leaving out of gender, for example, in the hate crimes statistics laws, that this could help correct that error, and say to the country once and for all that hate against women in the form of violence is something our country will not tolerate.[54]

Patricia Ireland, president of NOW, responding to the ACLU's concerns that the motive/intent requirement of the bill was so vague it would unduly confuse litigants, judges, and juries, stated, "I think that if there is concern that there will be confusion [about intent and motive], it is nothing compared to what we gain by giving a clear signal that this is recognized as a civil rights violation and a form of discrimination against women."[55]

The civil rights provision of the VAWA offers little, if anything, beyond a symbolic message opposing violence against women. Female victims of male batterers, like all crime victims, have always had a right to sue their assailants for compensatory and punitive damages in state courts.[56] Of course, this right is hollow because the vast majority of violent criminal offenders (gender biased or otherwise) are indigent. Elizabeth Symonds, the ACLU's legislative counsel, stated that the provision "creates many more questions than it actually answers . . . [and] does little to assist in determining which kinds of cases are in fact actionable. For example, the bill does not make clear whether all sexual assaults are considered to be per se 'motivated by gender.'"[57] She expressed doubts about the utility of the civil rights provision as a tool for fighting violence against women:

I think that's what all of us here want. I think we're in agreement that the goal of this bill is laudatory. We want to stop violent crime in America. But will this effectively do so? . . . Will this civil cause of action deter perpetrators? Will defendants, many or most of whom are indigent, have the financial resources to actually pay damages awards? Can the defendants be identified in most cases?[58]

More than two years after the Act's passage, only two lawsuits had been filed under the VAWA's civil rights provision.[59]

The Hate Crimes Sentencing Enhancement Act of 1994

The federal sentencing enhancement statute for hate crimes should also be understood as an act of symbolic politics. Representative Charles Schumer (D-N.Y.), introducing the Hate Crimes Sentencing Enhancement Act (HCSEA) in the 102d Congress, claimed that a federal sentence enhancement was important "not simply [as] a message of care about one another and live and let live, the great American tradition, but [as] a message that relates to the survival of this country as the leading country of this world."[60] At hearings held in 1992, those testifying in favor of the bill again and again stressed the importance of "sending a message." Robert K. Lifton of the American Jewish Congress testified that:

> The criminal law marks off those behaviors society is not prepared to tolerate, and indicates what seriousness society attaches to a violation of those norms. The criminal law is an expression of the nation's basic moral standards. Viewed in this way, enactment of a statute such as [the HCSEA] serves a valuable purpose even if no one is ever sentenced to an enhanced penalty as a result of its enactment.[61]

Elizabeth R. OuYang of the Asian American Legal Defense and Education Fund testified that "[t]he law must send a clear message that hate crime offenses are serious offenses and will not be tolerated."[62]

The HCSEA died in the 102d Congress, but Schumer reintroduced the bill the next year as part of the Violent Crime Control and Law Enforcement Act of 1994. The comprehensive crime package included: a "three strikes" law mandating life imprisonment for three-time violent offenders, funding to put 100,000 more police officers on the street, and midnight basketball for at-risk juveniles. The HCSEA passed almost unnoticed, despite its inclusion of sexual orientation prejudice as a hate crime trigger.

The HCSEA, Title XXVII of the Violent Crime Control and Law Enforcement Act of 1994, mandated a revision of the U.S. Sentencing Guidelines "to provide sentencing enhancements of not less than three offense levels for offenses that are hate crimes."[63] It defined hate crime as a crime in which the defendant is motivated by race, color, religion, national origin, ethnicity, gender, disability, or sexual orientation. The Sentencing Commission's implementing guidelines, effective November 1995, provide for an enhancement of three offense levels if "the defendant intentionally selected any victim or property as the object of the offense because of the actual or perceived race, color, religion, national origin, ethnicity, gender, disability, or sexual orientation of any person."[64] While the guidelines list gender as a hate crime category, the application notes which accompany the guidelines state that the enhancement does not apply to sexual offenses motivated by gender bias. In other words, the sentence for rape or sexual abuse is not increased because of gender bias. Perhaps the commissioners concluded that rape already takes gender bias into account.

Congress mandated that in formulating the enhancements, the U.S. Sentencing Commission "shall assure reasonable consistency with other guidelines, [and] avoid duplicative punishments for substantially the same offense."[65] The Commission explained that, in implementing the HCSEA, its goal was to "harmonize the existing guidelines with each other, reflect the additional [hate crime] enhancement now contained in [the guidelines], and better reflect the seriousness of the underlying conduct."[66] In effect, the Commission consolidated the sentencing guidelines for all the federal criminal civil rights offenses. This explains the inclusion of disability and gender in the HCSEA; if those two categories had not been included, offenders convicted of violating federal criminal civil rights laws would receive a lower sentence for targeting individuals based on disability or gender than if they targeted individuals based on race, religion, or ethnicity. This would certainly be offensive to the disabled. Of course, offenders who violate individual rights, unlinked to a recognized group prejudice, will not have their sentences enhanced.

Conclusion

The hate crime laws of the 1980s and 1990s demonstrate the impact of identity politics on criminal law. The new wave of hate crime laws follows in a long line of civil rights legislation that extends special legal rights and affirmative action to groups that are officially recognized as disadvantaged and victimized. The advocacy groups that work on behalf of racial, religious, and ethnic groups, gays and lesbians, and women are judged and judge themselves on their ability to procure legislation that affirms the worth of their members. Such symbolic morale-building legislation often gets top priority.

Lawmakers produce legislation in response to "consumer" demand. The politics of symbolic legislation differ from the politics of legislation that involves allocation of scarce resources. Symbolic legislation normally does not entail budgetary consequences. Although sometimes groups must compete for the political affirmation of rival symbols, practically all politicians pay lip service to "nondiscrimination," "fairness," and "tolerance," as long as they are not asked to be too specific.

While the HCSA of 1990 ostensibly involved only data collection, the subtext recognized a certain type of crime as especially abhorrent and a certain type of crime victim as especially vulnerable. The HCSA has historic significance because it treated prejudice against homosexuals for the first time as an officially condemnable prejudice.

The resistance of the civil rights coalition to inclusion of crimes motivated by gender prejudice in the hate crime laws illustrates the symbolic nature of this legislation. Hate crime legislation is valued to the extent that it calls special attention to a small class of crime. If a significant percentage of crimes by men against women were to count as hate crimes, then victims of other hate crimes would get less attention, and the significance of their victimization and the force of their moral claim would be diminished. If all crime victims are hate crime victims, then hate crime loses its special symbolic power.

6

Justification for Hate Crime Laws

> A hate crime resembles no other crime. The
> effects of hate crime reach beyond the
> immediate victim or institution and can
> damage society and fragment communities.
> Paul M. Sanderson, commander of NYC's
> Bias Crime Unit

*T*HE NEW HATE CRIME laws have been enacted for essentially symbolic reasons. However, once enacted, they must be defended against charges that they are unnecessary, unfair, and unconstitutional. Sophisticated jurisprudential rationales, frequently dependent on and bolstered by social science studies, emerge in the course of litigation and are elaborated, honed, and polished in the hands of appellate lawyers, judges, and professors. In this chapter, we examine and critique the most frequently offered justifications for hate crime laws. In chapter 8, we will take up the question of constitutionality.

Are Hate Criminals More Culpable?

The principle that, holding conduct constant, punishment should be calibrated to the offender's culpability and blameworthiness is axiomatic in the criminal law. This principle is illustrated by the differing punishments for homicides. Offenders who cause death are punished along a continuum depending upon whether they acted negligently, recklessly, knowingly, or intentionally. Criminals who kill intentionally are the most culpable and are punished the most severely. Not surprisingly, defenders of hate crime legislation argue that more severe penalties for crimi-

79

nals motivated by prejudice are justified because such offenders are morally worse—more culpable—than criminals who engage in the same conduct, but for reasons other than prejudice.

We do not object *in principle* to calibrating punishment to motive. In certain situations, the defendant's motive may justify more severe punishment. For example, a defendant who kills his wife to collect her life insurance ought to be punished more severely than a defendant who kills his wife to end her suffering from a terminal illness. Likewise, it seems appropriate to punish arson for profit more severely than arson motivated by mental delusions because the former shows a cold-blooded and calculating criminal mind.

Is prejudice more morally reprehensible than other criminal motivations like greed, power, lust, spite, desire to dominate, and pure sadism? A business person may dump toxic waste into the street rather than pay the cost for having it disposed of properly. A con artist may defraud widows out of their life savings in order to lead a life of luxury. An ideologue may assassinate a political leader in order to dramatize his cause or to coerce decision makers into changing national policy. Are these criminals less morally reprehensible than a gay basher or a black rioter who beats an Asian store owner? Of course not. As the legal philosopher Jeffrie Murphy, has commented: "perhaps all assaults, whether racial or not, involve motives of humiliation and are thus evil to the same degree."[1]

Legal philosopher, Lawrence Crocker writes that: "One who commits a racist assault with some awareness of the history of racism is not merely of worse character than the ordinary assailant. The worse character is crystallized into an act that is itself morally worse."[2] The basis for this conclusion is not obvious. First, taken on its own terms, this explanation would not justify treating anti-white prejudice as a hate crime motivation because of the absence of a history of racism against whites. Second, why should the *history* of a condemnable motivation be the basis for more punishment, and why should other criminal motivations—like greed, lust, politics, etc.—not be regarded as historically based?

Crocker explains that an offender acting on the basis of racial animus is morally worse because "to act from a racist motive is in part to ratify that history, to make it one's own through a concrete act."[3] Nevertheless, he acknowledges the problematic nature of hate crime laws, and asks "whether this particular sort of moral worseness is one that the criminal law may justly take cognisance."[4] Ultimately, Crocker concludes that it is, though for constitutional reasons, he approves only those hate crime laws drafted to require "racial animus," and rejects the more common "manifesting prejudice" and "selection of the victim based on race, religion, etc." models. Even in cases where racial animus is clear, he condemns sentence enhancement laws, such as the Wisconsin statute upheld by the Supreme Court in *Wisconsin v. Mitchell*,[5] that tripled the sentence for an assault motivated by prejudice.

Should offenders be held fully responsible for their prejudices? A prejudiced offender might plea that he is *less culpable* than a "cold-blooded" profit-motivated criminal, because he was indoctrinated by his parents and youthful peers. He might argue that he was brought up to believe that homosexuals, women, Jews, blacks, and/or others are inferior, evil, immoral, hostile, etc. He might even argue that his prejudice, for example, against homosexuals, was the result of religious training. According to this account, his prejudice was imposed, not chosen, and should make him a candidate for a lesser punishment, not a greater one.

Disproportionately Severe Impacts on the Individual

Physical Injury

The criminal law customarily proscribes more severe punishment for more serious injury (holding culpability constant); that is why, for example, there is greater punishment for aggravated assault than for simple assault. Thus, another frequently cited justification for punishing hate crimes more severely than nonhate crimes is that they cause more severe physical injury. Of course, if this were true, the normal rule—the infliction of more serious injuries is punished more severely—would mete out more serious punishments to hate crime offenders. In other words, when hate crimes result in severe injury, they would under generic criminal laws be punished as aggravated assault or attempted murder, not as simple assault. Therefore, when hate crime proponents assert that hate crimes are more brutal, they must mean more brutal than other crimes *in the same category*. In other words, they must mean that hate crime assaults are consistently more brutal than "ordinary" assaults, yet not brutal enough to be aggravated assaults. Even if this were true (and there is no logical reason or empirical evidence showing that it is), generic sentencing laws provide for a range of sentences within the same offense category (e.g., a fine up to $5000 and/or imprisonment up to 3 years); such ranges ought to be able to accommodate the difference.

Despite the lack of empirical evidence, the belief that bias crimes cause more physical harm than other crimes in the same offense category has practically become dogma.[6] Sociologists Jack Levin and Jack McDevitt claim that as compared to other crimes, "hate crimes tend to be *excessively brutal*."[7] To support this assertion, they point to the 452 hate crimes recorded by Boston police from 1983 to 1987; half of these were as-saults. They state, "Thus, one of every two hate crimes reported to the Boston police was a personal attack."[8] Simply reporting that assaults comprised half of all hate crime over a four-year period does not indi-cate whether the bias-motivated assaults caused more injury than nonbias-motivated assaults during the same period.

Levin and McDevitt's next claim is no more convincing:

> [a]lmost three-quarters of all assaultive hate crimes—unlawful per-sonal attacks, even if only with threatening words—result in at least some physical injury to the victim. The relative viciousness of these attacks can be seen by comparing them to the national figures for all crimes, in which only 29 percent of assault victims generally receive some physical injury.[9]

Stating that bias-motivated assaults usually result "in at least some physi-cal injury," does not support the conclusion that they are "excessively brutal." In order to support such a claim, empirical studies need to be conducted, comparing the seriousness of physical injuries inflicted in bias-motivated assaults and nonbias-motivated assaults. The authors don't explain how *threatening words* cause *physical injury*.

Psychological Injury

Some courts and commentators argue that hate crime victims suffer greater psychological and emotional injury than other victims. The U.S. Supreme Court in *Wisconsin v. Mitchell*, stated, without citing any authority, that hate crimes are "more likely to . . . inflict distinct emo-tional harm on their victims."[10] Professors Bennett Weisburd and Brian Levin claim that hate crime victims suffer greater emotional and psycho-logical injury than other crime victims. "[B]ecause the violence is so brutal, the degradation so complete and the vulnerability so omnipres-ent, bias crime victims exhibit greater psychological trauma than nonbias victims."[11] To support this claim, they cite a 1989 National Institute Against Prejudice and Violence (NIAPV) survey of hate crime victims.[12] The survey questioned *only hate crime victims;* it did not compare their mental and physical injuries with those of nonhate crime victims. Thus, this "study" provides no basis for concluding that hate crime victims suffer greater harm.

In 1986, the NIAPV conducted a "pilot study" of 72 hate crime victims in seven states. (The NIAPV uses the term "ethnoviolence" rather than hate crime.) This study, like the 1989 study cited by Weisburd and Levin, also failed to compare the victimization experience of hate crime victims with other crime victims. It created "a profile of an average hate crime victim and their [sic] reactions."[13] Despite the lack of comparative data, former NIAPV director Joan Weiss stated:

> One of the most striking findings was the impact of these incidents of ethnoviolence on victims compared to personal crimes. How does one know, for example, whether being the victim of an act . . . motivated by racial or religious prejudice, was any worse than being the victim of a random act . . . ? From working with victims, it is apparent that they were not comparable, *but there is no proof in terms of data.*[14] (our emphasis)

Despite the absence of data, Weiss concluded that:

> The comparison of symptoms of the victims of personal crimes with victims of ethnoviolence was very graphic in this study. There were more symptoms, a greater effect on the individual, when the motivation was prejudice.[15]

The NIAPV pilot study, in fact, did not compare the emotional damage to hate crime victims with the emotional damage to nonhate crime victims. The study drew on reports of 72 hate crime victims from seven states using "focus groups" and individual interviews. The focus groups, in which victims "shared [and perhaps influenced? amplified?] feelings, reactions, and thoughts," met ten times. There was no comparative research on nonhate crime victims.

It should come as no surprise that hate crime victims report psychological and emotional effects. *All victims do.* The American Psychological Association Task Force on the Victims of Crime and Violence found that victims of such different crimes as assault, rape, burglary, and robbery exhibit similar[16] immediate, short-term, and long-term reactions.[17] During the immediate reaction stage, which can last from hours to days, victims feel anger, shock, disbelief, fear, anxiety, and helplessness, often accompanied by sleep disturbances, nightmares, diarrhea, headaches, an increase in psychosomatic symptoms, and aggravation of previous medical problems.[18] During the short-term reaction stage, which can last up to a year, victims continue to experience anger, anxiety, and nightmares, as well as depression and loss of self-esteem. Personal relationships may deteriorate. Frequently, victims change their behavior and lifestyles to cope with fear of future crimes. They move, change phone numbers, leave home less often, install security devices, or purchase firearms.[19] Long-term reactions can include depression, distrustfulness, fear, and difficulty establishing personal relationships.[20] Clearly, if the NIAPV researchers had brought nonhate crime victims together in focus groups to share feelings, they would also have heard a great deal of anguish and pain.

In a 1994 follow-up study to the NIAPV's pilot study, sociologists Arnold Barnes and Paul Ephross used personal interviews, questionnaires, and focus group meetings to assess the reactions of 72 hate crime victims, and compared the findings with previously reported research on crime victims. They found that hate crime victims suffered in the same manner and degree as other crime victims.[21] Barnes and Ephross found only one significant difference in hate crime victims' emotional reactions, and this difference pointed to hate victims experiencing *less severe* injury.

> A major difference in the emotional response of hate violence victims appears to be the *absence of lowered self-esteem*. The ability of some hate violence victims to maintain their self-esteem may be associated with their attribution of responsibility for their attacks to the prejudice and racism of others.[22] (emphasis added)

Low-Level Offenses

The greater harm hypothesis is most plausible at the margin of the criminal law where free speech blends into criminal conduct. It is useful to make some distinctions between different types of low-level crimes that involve bias-motivations. Graffiti and vandalism may involve racist, anti-Semitic, misogynistic, or homophobic words, drawings, or symbols. Likewise, these crimes may be carried out with nonprejudiced words, drawings, and symbols, but against targets that are solely, primarily, or completely identified with a particular religious, racial, ethnic, sexual orientation, gender, or other group. Consider Table 5:

Table 5   Types of Low-level (Graffiti) Hate Crime

	Symbolic Property	Nonsymbolic Property
Symbolic Graffiti	1 swastika on Jewish tomb	2 swastika on car
Nonsymbolic Graffiti	paint splashed on Jewish tomb	paint splashed on car

We could treat all four types of graffiti and vandalism via a generic law with standard punishments. Or, we could decide that, for the purpose of punishment, graffiti and vandalism should be divided into two classes, cell 4 (which involves vandalism without prejudice), and cells 1, 2, and 3 (which involve vandalism with prejudice). Alternatively, we could decide that graffiti and vandalism should be treated by different laws or enhancement statutes that, in effect, recognize a hierarchy of seriousness based upon type of bias expressed. Thus, cell 1 might qualify for maximum punishment since it, in effect, involves a double insult—the swastika + the defacement of the Jewish property. Cells 2 and 3 might qualify for less-enhanced punishment because only one insult is involved. Cell 4, involving no prejudice, would receive the typically deserved punishment for that offense.

Which symbolic expressions deserve special punishment and which buildings and property deserve "special protection"? Coming up with a list of words and symbols that should trigger more severe punishments is especially troubling. Is scribbling "bitch" or "KKK" or "Hitler was right" or "I hate fags" on a subway car to be punished more severely than "fuck the draft," "down with the Pope," or "send the Republicans to hell"? Creating a blacklist of dirty ("hate-ist") words, expressions, and symbols that warrant enhanced punishment would be a very subjective, politically loaded and nonviewpoint-neutral task. Ultimately, it would amount to picking and choosing words, expressions, and symbols that the lawmaker finds offensive. This might violate the First Amendment under *Texas v. Johnson*, the flag burning case.[23] In *Johnson*, the defendant was convicted for burning a flag at a political rally in violation of a Texas statute prohibiting burning of the American flag. The Supreme Court held the law to be unconstitutional under the First Amendment.

A harder question is whether certain properties can and ought to be given "special protection." Many states have enacted "institutional vandalism," or venerated objects laws, which essentially enhance punishment for acts of vandalism when directed at a place of worship or burial center.[24] Frequently, secular property (like schools and public monuments), important to the community, is joined to the religious property in this specially protected category in an obvious attempt to avoid First Amendment problems. These laws do not require proof of biased motivation, only that the offender committed the act knowing that the object was a church, cemetery, government building, or other designated structure.[25] Proponents of such laws could argue that they do not amount to singling out certain religious property for special protection, since the category is made up of a gamut of properties that have particular importance to the community. This explanation has a hollow ring, and fails to disguise the attempt to punish certain conduct more severely because it is highly offensive.

In reality, will vandalism of a school or a public monument in a park actually be punished as severely as vandalism of a church or burial ground? Ultimately, going down this path requires us to identify certain properties that embody values and ideas that are more highly respected and cherished than other properties. Increasing punishments for vandalism of a designated set of buildings or monuments ought to raise First Amendment warnings.

Nothing prohibits a state from prosecuting an individual who steals or burns another person's flag for theft, arson, or disorderly conduct.[26] A question not raised in *Johnson* is whether a state could prosecute the flag thief or arsonist and enhance the punishment because the item stolen or burned—like a church, burial ground, public monument, or school—has significant public value. Given the Supreme Court's decision in *R.A.V. v. St. Paul* the answer is probably "no"; but *Wisconsin v. Mitchell* perhaps leads to the opposite answer (as we shall see in chapter 8). As a matter of policy, we oppose such enhancements. We believe that the generic criminal laws provide for adequate punishment.

The Impact of Hate Crimes on Innocent Third Parties

Another common justification for meting out more severe punishment for bias-motivated crimes is that they harm innocent third parties. According to Columbia University Law School professor Kent Greenawalt, "[s]uch crimes can frighten and humiliate other members of the community; they can also reinforce social divisions and hatred."[27] William Marovitz, chairman of the Illinois Senate Judiciary Committee, has written that "crimes motivated by race, religion, or national origin have a more profound potential impact on the community than other crimes."[28] Similarly, law professor James Weinstein states that hate-motivated violence "can inflict damage above and beyond the physical injury caused by a garden-variety assault, both to the immediate victim and to other members of the group to which the victim belongs."[29] The Oregon Supreme Court has emphasized the same point in an opinion upholding a hate crime statute.[30]

> [Hate crime] creates a harm to society distinct from and greater than the harm caused by the assault alone. Such crimes—because they are directed not only toward the victim but, in essence, toward an entire group of which the victim is perceived to be a member—invite imitation, retaliation, and insecurity on the part of persons in the group to which the victim was perceived by the assailants to belong.[31]

While *some* hate crimes have impacts beyond their immediate victims, hate crimes are by no means unique in this respect. Many crimes, whatever their motivation, have repercussions beyond the immediate victim and his or her family and friends. Child abductions and murders, like those of Polly Klaas in California and Megan Kanka in New Jersey, strike terror in the hearts of parents throughout the community, state, and country.[32] Carjackings and subway crimes frighten countless people.[33]

It would be an understatement to say that violent crime in the United States has impact beyond its immediate victims. Public opinion polls show that Americans consistently rank crime as one of the top three problems facing the country;[34] often they rank crime first.[35] Many residents of American cities fear random street violence, carjackings, and gangs. In the inner cities, black-on-black and gang-related violent crimes have devastated neighborhoods.

Crime often has repercussions beyond the immediate victim in specific contexts as well. For example, a vicious murder or rape in a park deters many people from using the park for months, some forever. In June 1996, the near fatal beating of a woman jogging in Central Park attracted a great deal of attention, especially because it occurred during the afternoon and in an area of the park where violent crime is rare.[36] One student told a reporter that, since the attack, she walks all the way around the park even during daylight hours. "Look at me. I'm so small, there's no way I could protect myself against someone bigger. There's [*sic*] tons of psychos in New York City, and anything could happen."[37] A killing or rape in a university or school has profound social and psychological ramifications. Studies have shown that learning about the victimization of friends, relatives, coworkers, or neighbors, "is likely to enhance feelings of vulnerability and fear."[38]

Given that hate crime is frequently defined broadly to include low level offenses like vandalism, harassment, and assault, to assert that hate crimes invariably spread *terror* through the victim's community seems exaggerated. According to the FBI's 1994 report, intimidation accounted for 35 percent of all hate crimes, followed by vandalism (25 percent), simple assault (19 percent), and aggravated assault (16 percent).[39] John Cook, commander of the Intelligence Unit for the Maryland State Police, reports similar statistics in Maryland: "A quick analysis of Maryland's five-year perspective [on hate crimes], which included 2,009 incidents, reveals that most incidents were vandalism, and 30 percent were assaults."[40]

Suppose that bias-motivated crimes do frighten, upset, anguish, and anger third parties more than nonbias-motivated crimes. Is third-party anguish a permissible basis for increasing an offender's sentence?[41] Suppose a judge were to enhance the punishment of a black defendant who robbed a white victim on the ground that fear of black robbers was creating deep anxiety and terror in the white community, leading to white flight from the city, and to the deterioration of the city's tax base? Civil libertarians would quite properly excoriate the judge and attack the sentence as unconstitutional. They would argue that third parties' (even the community's) fear and anxiety should not be legitimated and encouraged by judicial sentencing practices. Should the moral and constitutional result be different if the race of offender and victim is reversed and the offense is called a hate crime?

The Conflict-Generating Potential of Hate Crimes

Some proponents of hate crime legislation argue that hate crimes should be punished more severely because of their potential to trigger retaliation and group conflict. This proposed justification reminds us that hate crime is a broad category that lumps together a number of different social and psychological pathologies. Retaliation arises mostly in the context of race and ethnic conflicts and rarely in the context of gay-bashing, anti-Semitic incidents, anti-Asian violence, and violence against women.

Imposing a more severe sentence on an offender because his criminal conduct caused, or had the *potential* to cause, retaliatory violence would be difficult to justify. Should a person be punished more severely because third parties use the offender's conduct as an "excuse" or "justification" to randomly attack citizens who share the same racial, ethnic, or other characteristic as that offender? Should an offender who victimizes able-bodied, violent men be punished more severely than an offender who preys on elderly, wheelchair-bound individuals because the former are more likely to retaliate?[42] The disturbing logic of such a suggestion could lead a judge to punish offenders who commit crimes against members of retaliation-prone groups more severely than those who commit crimes against members of nonretaliation-prone groups or against individuals who are of the same race or ethnicity as the offender. Such a policy would detach criminal responsibility and blameworthiness from its roots in the defendant's culpability. Perversely, it would punish an offender more severely because he chose to victimize a member of a group whose members are more likely to engage in illegal random violence.

A more sophisticated version of the retaliation rationale, and one that does not appear in the literature, focuses on intergroup conflict short of retaliation. Hate crimes should be punished more severely not because they may provoke immediate retaliation, but because they may promote intergroup friction, suspicion, and distrust. Perhaps this is so. But does calibrating sentence severity to biased motivation mitigate this effect? It seems more plausible (as we argue in chapter 9) that hate crime laws and their enforcement exacerbate intergroup tension. To the extent that hate crimes promote intergroup mistrust, it may be that the law best mitigates this effect by treating intergroup crime like any other crime.

Greater Deterrent Threat Required

Another justification for punishing hate crimes more severely than non-hate crimes is that greater punishment is necessary to deter hate crimes. "A strong prison sentence sends a signal to would-be hatemongers everywhere that should they illegally express their bigotry, they can expect to receive more than a mere slap on the wrist."[43] The question is how many additional crimes will be deterred by threatening potential hate crime offenders with higher maximum or minimum penalties. The conduct that hate crime laws aim to suppress is already subject to long-standing generic criminal sanctions. The most serious crimes like murder, rape, and kidnapping are already punishable by imprisonment up to life and, in some cases, by capital punishment, so there is little, if any, room to increase the threat.

Another question is whether hate crimes are more amenable to deterrence than nonhate crimes. If not, there is no deterrence-based reason to increase sentences for hate crimes, but not other crimes. It is not clear why greater threat is necessary to deter potential bias-crime offenders than other potential offenders. On the one hand, perhaps proponents believe that because bias-crime offenders are more determined to commit their crimes than other offenders, a more severe threat is needed to make them desist. On the other hand, perhaps proponents believe that because bias-crime offenders are more impulsive than other offenders, a greater threat is necessary to get their attention and to reinforce their personal controls.

The fact that the majority of reported hate crimes is committed by teenagers is relevant to assessing the deterrence rationale. In New York City between 1981 and 1990, 70 percent of individuals arrested for hate crimes were under the age of nineteen; 40 percent under age sixteen.[44] When juveniles commit crimes, often they are not charged with the specific criminal law offense but with being *delinquent*. Thus, hate crime laws may not actually apply unless juveniles are transferred to adult criminal court. For adults, whose biases may be fully formed and incorporated into their personality, it is not clear that the threat of a penalty enhancement will have any marginal deterrent effect. In any event, a calculating hate criminal (perhaps the most prejudiced) could avoid the enhancement by committing his crime without the epithets that are usually necessary to trigger the hate crime laws.[45]

Moral Education

Some supporters of hate crime legislation insist that hate crime laws should be supported simply because they send a political and symbolic message that bias crime, and implicitly bias itself, is wrong. According to Weisburd and Levin:

> More important, however, is the powerful signaling effect inherent in bias crime legislation. The very existence of bias crime statutes sends out a clear message to society that a discriminatory motivation for a crime is a prescribable evil in and of itself; one that we as a society will not tolerate.[46]

This justification would be more persuasive if hate crime had previously been lawful, or if it had been a species of crime that had previously been criminalized in a minor way. But the opposite is true. Serious hate crimes—murders, arsons, rapes, assaults—have always been criminalized and punishable by harsh sanctions under generic criminal and sentencing law. Furthermore, prejudice is already denounced by a huge body of constitutional law, employment law, civil rights law, and administrative law. Private lawyers and government agencies are constantly bringing, and courts hearing, unlawful discrimination claims. To the extent that law should be a tool of moral education, it is already sending the right messages in a very strong manner.

Conclusion

The appearance of the new wave of hate crime laws is being tested in courts and in the crucible of academic journals. The basic question is whether it is justifiable to impose enhanced sentences on criminals because they are motivated by prejudice.

Many courts and commentators have attempted to justify enhanced sanctions on the grounds that hate crimes are morally worse than other crimes, cause more physical and psychic injury to victims, and cause more psychic injury to third parties. These assertions depend upon empirical assumptions that seem dubious and have not been substantiated.

The argument that hate crimes warrant harsher punishment because they carry the potential for retaliation and social conflict is also not persuasive. The logic of this argument would lead to harsher punishments for crimes against retaliation-prone groups than for crimes against victims who are members of law-abiding groups that do not retaliate. What kind of a message would that send?

The proposition that bias-criminals are morally worse and therefore more blameworthy than others who commit crimes of the same type is also hard to sustain. Many other motivations for criminal conduct seem at least equally reprehensible. Moreover, the claim of some bias-offenders that they are not fully to blame for their learned prejudice is not easy to refute. Just as with other criminal acts, hate crime offenders may fall along a continuum of blameworthiness.

For the most serious predicate crimes, maximum sentences are already very severe, usually life imprisonment or the death penalty. Obviously, in these cases the maximum cannot be enhanced. Of course, it would be possible to provide for a severe mandatory minimum penalty in the case of a serious predicate offense motivated by prejudice. However, mandatory minimum punishments are already increasing across the board. Thus, the greatest potential for punishing hate crimes significantly more severely than other crimes of the same type is in the domain of low-level offenses like graffiti, harassment, and simple assault.

Some supporters of hate crime laws may ask, "Well, so what if none of the above justifications for hate crime laws have any empirical basis? Even if hate crime laws are not really necessary and do not have any measurable effect, what harm do they do? Hate crime laws are passed by politicians primarily for reasons that are best understood in the context of symbolic politics. Don't they send the right message and thereby teach society a lesson and provide moral education?" This argument is difficult to refute. However, we think it unlikely that hate crime laws add much moral education to the huge body of denunciation of crime and prejudice that already exists. One potential unintended result is that people will take symbolism too seriously and assume that denouncing the problem through hate crime laws effectively addresses the problem. In other words, hate crime laws may substitute for true "institution building" in the area of community relations. Effectively, politicians may be getting off the hook too easily. Throwing laws at a problem costs no money and requires no real political energy. Finally, in chapter 9 we will argue that hate crime laws may have negative sociopolitical consequences, in effect exacerbating social divisions rather than contributing to social solidarity.

7

Enforcing Hate Crime Laws

I hate these cases because they become real
mysteries. . . . [E]verybody jumps on the
bandwagon but nobody has the facts.
  Detective John Leslie, New York City Police
                                      Department

Without doubt, most members of the
community have an opinion of whether "bias-
motivated" conduct should be criminalized
or even prosecuted. It is the search for this
opinion that presents the greatest challenge
to the prosecutor.
        Migdalia Maldonado, former assistant
     district attorney and hate crime prosecutor,
                          Brooklyn, New York

*F*EDERAL, STATE, AND LOCAL hate crime laws were passed to satisfy
political and symbolic needs, not to fill gaps in criminal law, sentencing law, or criminal procedure. Nevertheless, once these laws are on
the books, police and prosecutors must decide how to enforce them. This
chapter examines the challenges and enforcement dilemmas of hate crime
laws for police, prosecutors, criminal courts, trial judges, juries, and sentencing judges. It also examines what little is known about how these
laws are used, how often, and with what consequences.

The Police

Creation of Specialized Anti-Bias Units

In 1988, Abt Associates and the National Organization of Black Law
Enforcement Executives (NOBLE) released a joint report recommend-

ing that large police departments devote more resources to bias crime investigation, establish bias units, assign liaison officers to the "affected community," and create "activities designed to encourage victims to report bias crimes."[1] The majority of local police departments are small (52 percent of all police departments employ fewer than ten officers)[2] and lack resources and personnel to establish specialized units to focus on bias crimes. For small police departments, the Abt Report recommended creation of specific reporting procedures for hate crimes.

Several of the nation's largest police departments, like those in New York City, Boston, Baltimore, Chicago, and San Francisco, have established specialized bias units. But even in these very large police departments the bias crime units are quite small, typically between four and eighteen officers. What difference can such small units make?

What specialized strategies could a police bias unit aim exclusively or primarily at hate crimes? This is a particularly difficult challenge if, as is almost always true, the number of hate crimes (especially serious hate crimes) in any given jurisdiction is very small. For example, if there are only one or two hate crimes per week or per month, it makes little sense to talk in terms of prevention strategies. Preventing hate crimes with or without a bias unit is easier said than done. Police devote most of their time to patrolling and answering 911 calls, not to preventing or investigating specific crimes. Rank-and-file officers patrol a beat (typically by car) advertising their presence in the hope that would-be criminals, whether rapists, burglars, robbers, or thieves, will be deterred. Patrolling is a general crime prevention strategy and not "crime-specific."

In addition to prevention, hate crime units will necessarily be concerned with solving hate crimes. Of course, big city police forces already devote significant resources to investigating crimes, especially serious crimes. What will a hate crime unit be able to do that general investigative units are not already doing? Murder, for example, is intensely investigated whether or not a prejudice motivation is suspected. In fact, the NYPD Bias Incident Investigation Unit's mission statement explicitly *excludes* investigation of homicides and other crimes of extreme violence; homicides, for example, are handled by the highly expert and specialized homicide unit. This division of labor suggests that the creation of specialized bias units or other structural changes designed to focus greater police attention will have the most impact when directed at "low-level" crimes, like vandalism and graffiti. Perhaps such a reallocation of resources is appropriate, but it probably would mean shifting resources away from crimes traditionally considered to be more serious.

Sometimes police forces carry out proactive "crackdowns" on crimes like prostitution, drugs, and drunk driving. Cracking down on prostitutes and street-level drug sellers is relatively easy because such offenders are highly visible and plentiful; thus, the number of arrests can be increased at will. Hate crimes, however, are not usually addressable by crackdowns. Hate crime offenders are not involved in market transactions, do not engage in continuous criminality, and are usually not easily identifiable. Occasionally, cities or suburbs may experience a rash of hate crimes, for instance, swastikas or gay bashing. In such cases, some kind of crackdown might help.

A few cities have well-known gay neighborhoods, with highly visible bars, clubs, and street life. Perhaps assigning more officers to these neighborhoods could deter street crimes against gays and lesbians. The NYPD once instituted such an initiative in Greenwich Village, "disguising" some officers as gay men and sending them out as "decoys," but over three months, not a single decoy was attacked.[3] Ironically, the decoy program came under fire from gay and lesbian groups who perceived the decoys' portrayal of gay people to be derogatory. They urged the NYPD simply to put more *uniformed* officers on the streets to protect everyone, rather than decoys specifically focused on luring out gay bashers.[4] In other words, a special crackdown was not perceived as necessary or necessarily desirable.

Boston Police Department's Community Disorders Unit

Working directly out of the Police Commissioner's office, the Community Disorders Unit (CDU) assumed responsibility for supervising investigations of all bias-motivated crimes.

> It is the policy of this department to ensure that all citizens can be free of violence, threats or harassment due to their race, color, creed, or desire to live or travel in any neighborhood. . . . [I]t is the policy to make immediate arrests of those individuals who have committed such acts. Members of the police force responding to these incidents will be expected to take immediate and forceful action to identify the perpetrators, arrest them and bring them before the court.[5]

Although the CDU's policy made the investigation of low-level bias crimes, such as vandalism, as high a departmental priority as the investigation of murder, rape, and robbery, initially the policy was largely ignored.[6] Police supervisors, who were required by CDU procedures, often did not respond to vandalism or harassment crime scenes, oversee investigations, or notify the CDU. In the summer of 1978, however, harassment of blacks living in predominantly white neighborhoods and housing projects—through vandalism of homes and cars, verbal harassment, physical attack, and arson—was widely covered by the local and national media.[7] The police commissioner vowed that failure to comply with the CDU policy would be dealt with severely. He expanded the CDU from four to ten full-time officers, and promoted each officer to the rank of detective or above. He established a management information system to track incidents and determine patterns of racial violence. Each incident was supposed to be investigated intensively.

The CDU, although a very small unit, in some cases employed proactive strategies, such as covert surveillance and victim decoys, in the newly integrated public housing projects where the majority of incidents occurred. The number of reported incidents declined steadily, from a high of 533 in 1979 to 181 incidents in 1984.[8] However, no one can say whether the reduction was due to the CDU's efforts or to other factors that led to a decline of tensions over integration. The Boston Police Department's situation was atypical. The police were not responding to rare, scattered, and random bias crimes, but to concentrated, continuous anger directly related to court-ordered busing and the integration of public buildings, in particular schools and housing.

NYPD's Bias Incident Investigation Unit

In 1980, NYPD Commissioner Robert McGuire established a police task force to determine what could be done about a spate of synagogue vandalism. The task force's report led to the creation of a Bias Investigation Unit—consisting of one captain, one sergeant, and ten investigators—that would report directly to the department's highest ranking uniformed officer. Later, the unit, renamed the Bias Incident Investigation Unit (BIIU), expanded to eighteen persons (in a force numbering over 35,000). On January 1, 1995, the BIIU was moved out of the department chief's office, and placed under the aegis of the Chief of Detectives, a lower ranking officer. Advocacy groups angrily opposed this administrative reorganization for sending the wrong signals.[9]

The NYPD's Bias Unit's original mission was "to monitor and investigate acts committed against a person, group, or place because of race, religion or ethnicity." In 1985, its jurisdiction was expanded to include crimes motivated by anti-gay and lesbian prejudice, and in 1993 to crimes motivated by prejudice against a victim's real or perceived disability. In addition to after-the-fact investigation, the BIIU's duties include (1) providing support and assistance to victims; (2) preparing statistical reports on bias crimes; (3) analyzing incidents and determining bias trends; (4) maintaining liaisons with prosecutors' offices, and city, state, and federal law enforcement and support agencies; (5) maintaining contact with community and civic organizations, and addressing community groups; (6) conducting follow-up interviews with victims two months after closing cases; and (7) providing assistance for precinct level training.[10]

The BIIU's members are usually not the first officers called to the crime scene. "Ordinary" police officers are the first to respond; if there is evidence of a bias motive, they are supposed to report a possible bias crime to their precinct commander or duty captain who, in turn, is supposed to interview the victim. If the precinct commander finds any indication of bias, he or she must report a "possible bias crime" to the BIIU. Depending on the victim's perception of the offender's motivation, the responding officers' perceptions, and the responding officers' and precinct commander's response, the BIIU officers will typically not be called in until several days after the incident. In practice, the Bias Unit is often not called in at all. Though precinct commanders are required to report to the BIIU any and all crimes *possibly* motivated by bias, responding officers and precinct superiors routinely "weed" out those cases they do not believe merit further attention. If a possible bias crime report is filed, police at the precinct level sometimes take a "hands off" attitude; routine police responses—collecting evidence, locating witnesses, and making arrests—may be postponed until the BIIU arrives, by which time those tasks may have become more difficult or impossible.

When the BIIU does receive a report, it assigns an investigator to reinterview the victim and any witnesses. Within ten days of that interview, the BIIU is supposed to decide whether or not to label the incident bias motivated. The labeling decision may be the BIIU's most important function.

The Labeling Decision

The BIIU shares responsibility with the NYPD as a whole for solving bias crimes, but it has a unique responsibility for deciding whether particular crimes ought to be labeled "bias related," a job fraught with sensitive, even potentially explosive, social and political ramifications. To say the least, this role complicates and contributes to the politicization of police operations. While some critics argue that such politicization promotes greater police accountability, others argue that political pressure and considerations invariably distort the truth-finding process. Whatever one's position on the effects of politicization, it is clear that the bias-labeling process contributes to those effects. The BIIU is under constant pressure from advocacy groups to label particular crimes bias related. In some cases, there is counterpressure from members of the perpetrator's group (or from worried political officials) not to deploy the bias label.[11] According to Migdalia Maldonado, a former prosecutor in the Brooklyn District Attorney's Office, the labeling decision is a political mine field.

> Many victims believe that the mere utterance of a racial, ethnic, or other slur will suffice to sustain a charge. Regrettably, this mistaken interpretation of the law is often shared by the media. . . . This activity creates the misconception that some bias crimes are tolerated more than others. Some complainants who legitimately believe that they have been victimized because of their status cannot understand why the perpetrator was not arrested and prosecuted for the offense. They often conclude that they are simply not members of the "right" group.[12]

The NYPD Bias Unit has developed criteria for identifying bias crimes, based on questions an officer should ask himself or herself when investigating a possible bias crime. The guidelines define a bias crime as any crime "that is motivated *in whole or in part* by a person's, a group's, or a place's identification with a particular race, religion, ethnicity, sexual orientation or disability."[13] When investigating a possible bias crime the officer should consider the following criteria and questions:

Criteria
1. The motivation of the perpetrator.
2. The absence of any motive.
3. The perception of the victim.
4. The display of offensive symbols, words, or acts.
5. The date and time of occurrence (corresponding to a holiday of significance, i.e., Hanukkah, Martin Luther King Day, Chinese New Year, etc.).
6. A common-sense review of the circumstances surrounding the incident (considering the totality of circumstances).
   A. The group involved in the attack.
   B. The manner and means of the attack.
   C. Any similar incidents in the same area or against the same victim.
7. What statements, if any, were made by the perpetrator.

Questions to be Asked
1. Is the victim the only member or one of a few members of the targeted group in the neighborhood?
2. Are the victim and perpetrator from different racial, religious, ethnic, or sexual orientation groups?
3. Has the victim recently moved to the area?
4. If multiple incidents have occurred in a short time period, are all the victims of the same group?

5. Has the victim been involved in a recent public activity that would make him/her a target?
6. What was the modus operandi? Is it similar to other documented incidents?
7. Has the victim been the subject of past incidents of a similar nature?
8. Has there been recent news coverage of events of a similar nature?
9. Is there an on-going neighborhood problem that may have spurred the event?
10. Could the act be related to some neighborhood conflict involving area juveniles?
11. Was any hate literature distributed by or found in the possession of the perpetrator?
12. Did the incident occur, in whole or in part, because of a racial, religious, ethnic, or sexual orientation difference between the victim and the perpetrator, or did it occur for other reasons?
13. Are the perpetrators juveniles or adults, and if juveniles, do they understand the meaning (to the community at large and to the victim) of the symbols used?
14. Were the real intentions of the responsible person motivated in whole or in part by bias against the victim's race, religion, ethnicity, or sexual orientation, or was the motivation based on other than bias, ex: a childish prank, unrelated vandalism, etc?

Note: If after applying the criteria listed and asking the appropriate questions, substantial doubt exists as to whether or not the incident is bias motivated or not, the incident should be classified as bias motivated for investigative and statistical purposes.

Remember: The mere mention of a bias remark does not necessarily make an incident bias motivated, just as the absence of a bias remark does not make an incident non-bias. A common sense approach should be applied and the totality of the circumstances should be reviewed before any decision is made.[14]

These criteria are so broad and loose that practically any intergroup offense could plausibly be labeled a bias crime. In short, the criteria, rather than answering questions, create more questions. For example: Why should the "absence of any motive"—a criterion that, on its face, has virtually no meaning—support an inference of bias motivation? How much weight should be afforded the perception of the victim, who might be especially sensitive to any negative encounter with a member of another group, or himself be a racist, homophobe, or holder of another bias? In some neighborhoods of New York City, isn't there always "an ongoing neighborhood problem" that would suggest the possibility of a bias motivation? Indeed, criteria numbers 12 and 14 simply beg the question of whether the incident was bias motivated.

The labeling decision is so politically sensitive that, in 1987, the NYPD established a Bias Review Panel to determine whether a case initially labeled "bias motivated" should be reclassified. Prior to 1987, a case could be reclassified only after review of the facts by a BIIU investigator, his or her supervisor, the BIIU's commanding officer, and the precinct commander where the crime occurred. Community pressures and controversies made a bias review panel a political necessity. According to BIIU documents,

> [a]lthough the old review procedure was thought to be objective and administered in a manner that erred on the side of retaining a bias classification, the perception of those on the outside looking in may be QUITE different. The perception of those looking in may be that the procedure is subjective, self-serving and weighted in favor of reclassifying to non-bias.[15]

The Bias Review Panel, which consists of the Deputy Commissioner of Community Affairs, the Director of the Police Department's Advocate's Office, the Chief of Detectives, the Chief of Patrol, and the Deputy Commissioner of the Office of Equal Employment Opportunity, meets regularly. A case may be reclassified as nonbias only if *all* panel members agree.

Solving Bias Crimes

The majority of reported and confirmed bias crimes do not result in an arrest or prosecution. In 1994, the BIIU made arrests in only 26 percent of all reported bias crimes.[16] Where the bias crime is a crime against property, such as vandalism or criminal mischief, the arrest rate is much lower.[17] In New York, the vast majority of anti-Semitic crimes are against property; in 1994, of the 202 reported anti-Semitic bias crimes, 81 percent were property crimes, essentially vandalism.[18] Only 9 percent of those resulted in arrests.

Other types of bias crime also have persistently low clearance rates. For example, a 1995 comprehensive national study of anti-gay crime conducted by the National Coalition of Anti-Violence Programs and the New York City Gay and Lesbian Anti-Violence Project found that nationwide only 16 percent of anti-gay violent crimes reported to police resulted in an arrest, compared to a national average clearance rate of 45 percent for violent crime in general.[19] The study's authors attributed this discrepancy to a greater propensity for hate offenders to be strangers to their victims, and to the propensity of hate offenders to act in groups. However, the authors did not compare the clearance rate of stranger bias crimes committed by multiple perpetrators with that of stranger nonbias crimes committed by multiple perpetrators. The same study also attributes the low clearance rate to police hostility to hate crime victims. For example, 37 percent of victims who reported anti-gay crimes against them described the police response as "indifferent," and 9 percent described the response as "abusive."[20] The numbers were slightly different in New York City—43 percent indifferent and 4 percent abusive.[21] Again, it is impossible to draw conclusions from such statistics without comparison data for nonhate crime victims, many of whom are disappointed with the police response, especially when no arrest is made.

Given the difficulties of apprehending offenders, what are the BIIU's measures of success? Identifying hate crimes? Making hate crime arrests? Reducing the number of hate crimes? Obtaining more convictions and longer sentences? Expressing concern to victims? Satisfying advocacy groups? Giving the NYPD "cover" in high publicity intergroup incidents? All of the above are important, but the BIIU's most significant function is to let people know that bias crimes will be vigorously investigated, essentially, a public relations function. This function could be as easily, and more appropriately, served by a community relations unit.

The BIIU claims to have investigated synagogue vandalism, verbal harassment, and instances of criminal mischief that would have gone unattended had the unit not existed. This is apparently considered an accomplishment, even when no arrests are made. According to former Bias Unit Commander Paul Sanderson, "Many of these are minor crimes, but we treat them as if they were homicides."[22] The police, of course, hope that the victim and the victim's group will appreciate the effort. Even if they don't, the police department can cite those efforts in shielding itself from charges of insensitivity and discrimination toward certain categories of victims.

Intelligence Operations

One final function that the police could play in attempting to stymie hate crimes is gathering intelligence on extremist hate groups. Today one often reads alarming accounts of the rise of "extremist" groups, including militias, skinheads, neo-Nazis, and all sorts of separatist compounds and communes. The police could monitor the telephone conversations of members of such groups, pay members to act as informers on their comrades, and even infiltrate the groups with undercover agents and agents provocateurs. History suggest caution in launching such operations. The history of the FBI is blemished with undercover operations against the Communist Party, NAACP, anti-war groups, and others (COINTELPRO), violative of constitutional rights and civil liberties.[23] Indeed, the FBI's campaign against the Ku Klux Klan in the early 1960s involved violence and assassinations.[24] The New York City Police Department has an unhappy history of operations against leftist political groups.[25] And, only recently, the Bureau of Alcohol Tobacco and Firearms operation against David Koresh and followers in Waco, Texas, ended in disaster.

If police are to again employ such aggressive tactics, they will again be confronted with the question of which groups should count as hate groups. Are we certain that the FBI will not target ACT-UP, the Jewish Defense League, or Black Muslims, as groups worthy of surveillance?

Prosecution

Data on Hate Crime Prosecutions

As far as we have been able to determine, no agency or jurisdiction has reported prosecution and disposition data on hate crimes; there is no published research on the subject. Some jurisdictions have begun to address this information gap. For example, the head of the civil rights division of the Minnesota Attorney General's Office has initiated a survey of all county attorneys, asking them to report on bias prosecutions, dispositions, demographics of both victims and perpetrators, and perceptions of whether the state's hate crimes laws are useful.[26] Similarly, the California Attorney General requested that district attorneys and city attorneys collect statistics on bias charges filed and convictions entered during calendar year 1995.[27] However, as of spring 1997, no data have appeared.

Our research suggests that the number of hate crime prosecutions is very low. According to Migdalia Maldonado, a former Brooklyn assistant district attorney, "For the most part the hate crime laws aren't enforced. Once passed, these laws are forgotten about. Most perpetrators are not caught, so there aren't many prosecutions."[28] Data we have obtained from several jurisdictions illustrate this point. In Brooklyn, for example, the Civil Rights Bureau of the District Attorney's office received 169 bias crime complaints in 1992 and 69 complaints during the first six months of 1993. Of these complaints, only 29 cases, or 12 percent, resulted in prosecution. According to a California report, there were 1,754 bias-related incidents reported by police departments in California in 1995.[29] However, during that year, only 187 hate crime prosecutions were filed.[30] The San Francisco police department reported 290 bias incidents, 21 prosecutions, and 4 convictions.[31] According to San Francisco Assistant District Attorney Chuck Haines, former Hate Crime Unit head, even fewer cases—3 felonies and 7 misdemeanors—were prosecuted in 1994.[32]

Admittedly, the usefulness of the data is quite limited. The DOJ Division of Criminal Justice Information Services explicitly warns against "linking" the police and prosecution data, since it tracks information by year and not by case, and because many crimes reported as bias motivated may be prosecuted under nonbias statutes.[33]

From 1981 to 1987, in Suffolk County, Massachusetts (which includes Boston and Revere), prosecutors brought 123 charges (averaging 6 or 7 cases per year) involving 81 defendants under a statute criminalizing interference with a victim's "secured" civil rights by force or threat of force.[34] Ninety-one of those charges were resolved by guilty verdicts.[35] Similarly, from 1983 to 1989, 145 such cases were "investigated" and 71 "successfully prosecuted" in Middlesex County (covering Cambridge, Framingham, Lowell, and Somerville).[36]

From 1982 to 1989, the Attorney General obtained 84 injunctions prohibiting 233 defendants from harassing or approaching their victims; at least 8 of those injunctions later resulted in criminal contempt charges for violations.[37] These statistics seem to show much more activity and success than those reported by Jack McDevitt, a Northeastern University criminologist. He found that from 1983 to 1987, Boston police reported 452 hate crimes; 60 (15.4 percent) resulted in arrests; charges were filed in 38 cases; 30 convictions resulted.[38]

Problems in Prosecuting Bias Crimes

Most prosecutors have had little experience prosecuting hate crimes. However, a few large, urban prosecutors' offices, for example, Brooklyn, San Diego, San Francisco, and Sacramento, have specialized bureaus or prosecutors that handle hate crime prosecutions. The Chicago District Attorney's office established a Hate Crimes Prosecution Council comprised of representatives from business, government, law enforcement, religious, and community organizations. The Council was ceded a great deal of authority over enforcement policy, and in 1995, the Council published *A Prosecutor's Guide to Hate Crime*, which addresses such topics as supervising bias cases, deciding whether to charge, involving the victim in the case, conducting voir dire, and plea bargaining.[39] The Chicago District Attorney's office also employs liaisons to the gay and lesbian, African-American, and disabled communities, as well as a hate crime victim/witness specialist.[40]

Prosecuting a bias crime requires proving the defendant's bias motivation beyond a reasonable doubt. Even in seemingly clear-cut cases of bias motivation, prosecutors have failed to obtain convictions. San Diego prosecutor Luis Aragon stated, "When I went into this, I thought this was going to be easy."[41] In one of Aragon's cases, the judge dismissed hate crime charges brought against two white men, who bound and gagged a Mexican farm worker, taped a sign to his head which read "No more here," and dumped him in a field.[42] The judge cited insufficient evidence of a bias motivation as the reason for dismissal.

There are, of course, some easy cases. According to San Francisco's Haines, many of the cases he charged were so clearly motivated by bias that proving motivation was no problem. He points out that some perpetrators clearly broadcast their motivations. He cites a case in which the defendant, a black man, attacked an interracial couple after saying, "The black woman should not be with the white man." A bias conviction was obtained easily.[43] (Even in this "clear case," what if the defendant had argued that he was not prejudiced against white men, but highly concerned that the black race and culture not be diluted? Would his conduct obviously qualify as a bias crime?)

It is also difficult to prove that the bias motivation caused the criminal conduct.[44] Consider what it would have entailed for the prosecution to prove that the defendants were racists in the Rodney King or Reginald Denny cases.[45] In cases like these, prosecutors invariably strive to keep the jury focused on "the facts." ("Ladies and gentlemen of the jury, this is a simple case of assailants, who for no good reason, beat up, and even tried to kill, the victim.") It is typically the defense attorneys who see an advantage to playing "the race card" in order to divert the jurors from facts that are rarely in the defendant's favor.

Although prosecutors may find hate crime cases more difficult to prosecute than "ordinary" cases, there are undoubtedly times when prosecutors welcome the opportunity to "up the ante" by prosecuting certain defendants as hate criminals. Some prosecutions could be motivated by factors external to the merits of the case. A prosecutor could use such a trial to cement her support with an advocacy organization or a particular group. Under certain circumstances, for some prosecutors, demonstrating solidarity with the victim's group might be more important politically than obtaining a conviction. An acquittal could be blamed on juror racism, which happened when an all-white jury acquitted the white police officers charged with assaulting Rodney King. Thus, the whole criminal justice process could become even more politicized.

Juries

Hate crime charges have significant implications for jury selection and trials. Many jurors are likely to interpret a hate crime charge to mean that "this is a race [or other identities] trial," which in effect it is.[46] Jurors who are members of the same group as the defendant or victim might perceive the trial as an intergroup conflict that demands their racial, religious, gender, or other loyalty.

The challenge in selecting a jury for a hate crime trial, or any trial where issues of bigotry are prominent, is finding out whether a potential juror harbors prejudices that would interfere with a good faith determination of guilt or innocence.[47] Many persons hold conscious or subconscious racial, religious, ethnic, gender, and sexual orientation biases. The defense lawyer will want to ensure that a potential juror is not prejudiced against the defendant. The prosecutor will want to ensure that the prospective juror is not prejudiced against the victim, and is sensitive enough to the nature of prejudice to be able and willing to recognize the defendant's bias-motivation.

Ironically, both lawyers will have a harder time because of the Supreme Court's famous *Batson* decision, which held that prosecutors and defense attorneys may not use peremptory challenges to strike potential jurors from the panel on the basis of race;[48] this decision was extended to gender in *J.E.B. v. Alabama*.[49] Lower federal courts, as well as state courts have applied *Batson* to American Indians,[50] Italian Americans,[51] and Hispanics.[52] These decisions are all predicated on the belief that it is wrong to treat jurors according to racial, ethnic, gender, and other stereotypes. It is almost as though, in *Batson*, the Supreme Court was saying that there has to be a limit to the extent to which our legal institutions may be manipulated to conform to identity politics. Jurors must be treated as individuals, not as members of identity groups.

Hate crime laws represent a triumph for identity politics and promise trials that will make prejudice the central issue. *Batson* leaves the defense and prosecution with the task of ferreting out juror prejudices through voir dire questioning that might persuade the judge that a potential juror's prejudice is so strong, that he or she must be dismissed "for cause." Where racial, ethnic, religious, or other prejudices are at issue, the Supreme Court has held that refusal to permit questions about prejudice would threaten the fair trial guaranteed by due process.[53] Probing and clever questions about prejudices are necessary because few prospective jurors will admit to harboring any prejudice. One treatise on jury selection warns that, "one out of three potential jurors does not tell the truth during jury selection out of fear of being considered biased."[54]

Thus, it is not sufficient to ask jurors if they are prejudiced against blacks, Jews, etc.; a negative answer will be semi-automatic.[55] Jury consultants recommend open-ended questions.

Trial practice manuals recommend to trial lawyers attempting to ferret out prejudice, questions such as the following:

- What is your contact with [name of group] people?

- Do you have any [name of group] employees?

- Would you know anything about [name of group] rhetoric, culture, or speech?

- Do you believe that [name of group] have a greater propensity for criminal behavior than [name of another group]?

- Have you noticed an increased number of [name of group] coming into your neighborhood?

- Have you been disturbed by the changes in your neighborhood?

- Have you thought of moving out?

- Do you object to the number of [name of group] on the welfare rolls in the city?

- Do you think they are entitled to welfare?[56]

- Have you ever had an unfortunate experience with [name of group] in the community you live in or at any other place?[57]

- Do your children attend school with [name of group]?

- Do you approve of your children having [name of group] friends?[58]

Perhaps questions of this sort will expose conscious and unconscious prejudices, but jurors may also resent them and conclude that the trial is about racial or other intergroup conflict, and not really about the guilt or innocence of a particular person. Migdalia Maldonado has written that "there is no way to protect against a juror who believes, at least at some level, that one is entitled to 'protect' his or her neighborhood from being 'taken over' by another group."[59] She reports that, in her experience, many prospective jurors see bias crime laws as

an example of how public officials cave in to special interest groups. Also, some jurors believe that certain groups are more inclined to report the attacks against them than are other victimized persons, and thus receive more attention and services from law enforcement. These groups are charged with improperly reporting "regular" crimes as bias-motivated crimes in order to promote a political agenda.[60]

Trials

Since the existence and causal role of the defendant's bias is a key issue in bias crime prosecutions, the trial judge will have to deal with tough questions about the admissibility of evidence relevant to the defendant's prejudice. In order to prove that the defendant's criminal conduct was motivated by prejudice, prosecutors may seek to admit evidence of the defendant's membership in racist groups, subscription to racist publications, attendance at racist rallies, utterance of racist jokes, and wearing of racist insignias or tattoos. For example, in *People v. Aishman*,[61] the court admitted evidence that one of the defendants had two tattoos, one a swastika and the other "Thank God I'm White," because they were relevant to determining whether the defendant selected his Mexican-American victim based on ethnicity. The court explained that while the views expressed by the defendant's tattoos were clearly protected by the First Amendment, the tattoos were relevant to his criminal act and "support[ed] the proposition [that] he selected his victims because he was a racist."[62]

Judges will likely find in some situations that the admission of speech-related evidence of prejudiced motivation should be rejected because its prejudicial effect on the defendant outweighs its relevance; but, it is hard to see any way that a trial judge could keep the defendant from submitting evidence to show that he is not a racist, homophobe, anti-Semite, or holder of another bias. This may lead to the kind of distasteful cross-examination that occurred in *State v. Wyant*, a case involving an interracial dispute at an Ohio campground. The defendant took the stand to proclaim that he was not racist. On cross examination, the prosecutor sought to rebut that claim:[63]

> Q And you lived next door to [a 65-year-old black neighbor of the defendant's] for nine years and you don't even know her first name?
>
> A No.
>
> Q Never had dinner with her?
>
> A No.
>
> Q Never gone out and had a beer with her?
>
> A No.
>
> Q Never went to a movie?
>
> A No.
>
> Q Never invited her to a picnic at your house?
>
> A No.

Q Never invited her to Alum Creek?

A No. She never invited me nowhere.

Q You don't associate with her, do you?

A I talk with her when I can, whenever I see her out.

Q All these black people that you have described that are your friends, I want you to give me one person, just one who was really a good friend of yours.

Witnesses may be called on to testify about how the defendant told (or laughed at) racist or homophobic jokes, or whether he used racial slurs. In *Grimm v. Churchill*,[64] the arresting officer was permitted to testify that the defendant had a history of making racist remarks. Similarly, in *People v. Lampkin*,[65] the prosecution presented as evidence racist statements that the defendant had uttered six years before the crime for which he was on trial. In effect, a hate crime trial may become a wide-ranging inquiry into the defendant's character, values, and beliefs.

Sentencing

Many states have hate crime laws that provide for evidence of biased motivation to be proved at the sentencing phase as an aggravating factor that will increase the punishment. If hate crime motivation is to be determined at the sentencing stage, the judge, not the jury, decides whether the crime was motivated by prejudice. There is no voir dire problem and the challenge of getting a multiracial jury to agree on the defendant's prejudice does not arise.[66] However, the relevance of speech and association-related evidence still ought to be questioned. Such evidence has historically been admitted, but that doesn't make it right. The debate over the propriety and constitutionality of hate crime statutes ought to draw attention to the propriety and constitutionality of judges using such evidence in an ad hoc way to enhance the defendant's sentence.

Probation and Imprisonment

Implementation of hate crime laws also raises questions regarding sanctions. Many people who favor hate crime laws also advocate rehabilitation programs that will teach or persuade hate crime offenders to be more tolerant. A range of programs has sprung up. In New York City, the ADL offers an "anti-bias" course for anti-Semitic hate crime offenders with no prior criminal record. The course consists of thirty hours of instruction, counseling, and sensitivity training over ten weeks. The course is designed to be followed by community service for a Jewish organization.[67] A similar program, called Tolerance Rehabilitation for Youth (TRY), exists in Nassau County, New York. In 1994, 15 juvenile bias offenders (along with at least one parent) completed the program. Such courses are mandated for juveniles convicted of bias crimes.[68] According to Rabbi David F. Nesenoff, a TRY instructor, the majority of TRY participants are anti-Semitic offenders. He stated that the program consists of four sessions, involving lectures, conversations, psychodramas, and audiovisual presentations (one TRY instructor begins the course with a showing of the movie *Schindler's List*).[69] Rabbi Steven Moss, another TRY instructor, stated, "There is no formal way to measure the success of the program, but it has been positive in sensitizing young people about bias."[70]

Some anti-bias advocates have criticized these programs on the ground that they deprecate the seriousness of the crime, and may even put victims in further danger. In one 1993 New York City case, for example, a young man was convicted of third-degree assault for attacking a woman, calling her a "dyke," attempting to knife her, and punching her in the face. The victim suffered serious injuries to her mouth. Citing the assailant's "disadvantaged background," the judge—who moments before had praised the victim for her courage in coming forward—rejected jail time and sentenced him to a brief term of community service with the Mayor's Office for the Lesbian and Gay Community. Outraged community members who had packed the courtroom marched to the Mayor's office to protest. As it turned out, that office had not been consulted about the placement of a convicted anti-gay bias offender in its care, and the staff told the court that it would not accept the placement. Clearly, the implications of placing convicted hate criminals in agencies serving members of the victim's group must be carefully thought through.

Whether reeducation and sensitivity programs for bias offenders will have a positive effect remains to be seen, but imprisonment is unlikely to assist in transforming the offender into a more tolerant person. Sending low-level bias crime offenders to jail may satisfy some message-sending impulse about what "we as a society will tolerate," but it will probably enhance the offender's bias. First, the offender is likely to resent the antiprejudice ideology that has increased his punishment. Second, there is no institutional context in American society that spawns more virulent racism and other prejudices than jails and prisons. At times, in some jails and prisons, race relations have degenerated to the point of racial warfare.[71] Indeed, some of the hard core racist movements in the United States (like the Aryan Brotherhood) originated in prison. In addition to virulent racism, prisons have also been notable for their violence toward gay inmates.[72]

Conclusion

It is one thing to enact hate crime laws and another thing to implement and enforce them. Because bias crimes are relatively rare, they are difficult to deter through patrol. And low-level bias crimes like vandalism and graffiti are notoriously difficult to solve. With respect to the most serious crimes of violence, it is unlikely that a bias crime label will lead to any more investigative effort than would be made absent the label. In the investigation of serious violent felonies, like bias-related murder, the existence of a bias unit would not seem to add any significant resources to the investigation. Bias-related or not, the police department gives such crimes top priority by experienced homicide detectives and other specialized forensic units. The bias unit could make the most difference in police response to low-level offenses, like harassment, vandalism, and graffiti. But it is not clear whether society really wants to divert significant investigative resources to these offenses or to punish them as serious crimes. In the final analysis, the labeling decision may be the most important function the police perform in enforcing the bias crime laws.

Some large city police departments have formed specialized bias crime units. These units clearly have symbolic importance for some advocacy groups and, at a minimum, play a public relations role that may be quite important in the politicized crime and justice environment. However, research has yet to determine whether such bias units make a difference in preventing or solving bias crimes.

Prosecutors face a difficult task in trying hate crime cases. Proving bias-motivation poses a serious challenge, one that may distract and politicize the jury. Some jurors and judges may be so offended by and hostile to the hate crime charge that they will refuse to convict at all. If so, hate crime trials may reinforce and exacerbate the social divisions that already threaten the functioning of the jury system.

Some hate crime trials raise questions about the admissibility of evidence concerning the defendant's values, beliefs, and character. There is no escaping the danger that the trial will seem, to some observers, like an inquisition into the correctness of the defendant's statements, friendships, organizational affiliations, humor, and so forth.

Where hate crime laws come into play, not as substantive offenses, but as sentencing enhancements, the jury problems are sometimes avoided because the judge makes key findings on motivation, but the same evidentiary and constitutional questions ought to be faced. More-over, denying the defendant a jury trial on what is really the key charge against him—that his conduct was motivated by prejudice—threatens to unhinge our criminal procedure.

Finally, inventing a range of new sanctions for hate crime offenders launches us into uncharted waters. Most prison officials are very uncomfortable about suggestions that they should try to indoctrinate or propagandize prison inmates. Yet, when it comes to hate crime offenders, moral reeducation is a growth industry.

8

Hate Speech, Hate Crime, and the Constitution

[T]olerance of hate speech risks becoming a
species of endorsement of such speech. It
encourages the view that "it can't be all that
bad if it is not prohibited." Those who see
efforts to regulate group libel as taking us
down a "slippery slope" to censorship pay too
little attention to a second "slippery slope"—
one which can produce a swift slide into a
"marketplace of ideas" in which bad ideas
flourish and good ones die."
                Professor Abraham S. Goldstein,
                              Yale Law School

*I*MAGINE THAT JOHN DOE, a white man screaming anti-Asian epithets,
beats an Asian man with a baseball bat. Doe confesses that he dislikes Asian people, because he thinks they are responsible for his unem-
ployment. Imagine further that Richard Roe, also a white man, beats an
Asian man with a baseball bat, while screaming nonracist curses and
obscenities. Roe explains that he was appalled and angered by the victim's
cheering for the Boston Red Sox and booing the New York Yankees.
Both Doe and Roe are convicted of aggravated battery. Roe is sentenced
to two years imprisonment, the usual sentence for aggravated battery.
Doe is sentenced to seven years imprisonment, the judge explaining that
his anti-Asian prejudice requires the severest possible sentence. Does
Doe's punishment violate the First Amendment? Civil libertarians, torn
between commitments to equality and free speech, are divided on this
question.[1] On the one hand, for example, the national American Civil
Liberties Union (ACLU), in its amicus brief to the U.S. Supreme Court

in *Wisconsin v. Mitchell*, defended the extra punishment imposed by the Wisconsin hate crime law. "The issue in this case has been framed by some as a choice between preventing discrimination or preserving free speech. We believe this misstates the issue. . . . Mitchell was not punished for his beliefs; he was punished for *acting* on those beliefs."[2] (Interestingly, Mitchell himself only used words: his culpability was based on his liability as an inciter.) On the other hand, the Ohio chapter of the ACLU and the Center for Individual Rights submitted amicus briefs opposing the statute.

> The Wisconsin statute is expressly aimed at "*beliefs and perceptions,*" not conduct or speech. It is beyond debate that the First Amendment would be applicable to a penalty enhancement statute that was triggered, for example, . . . whenever the defendant "intentionally selected the victim because of [the victim's] support for government economic policies," "opposition to the Vietnam war," or "involvement in protests concerning abortion." Like each of the foregoing hypothetical statutes, the Wisconsin statute . . . will impose punishment only if (and precisely *because*) that conduct is accompanied by a defined set of beliefs.[3]

The latter position is more persuasive. Surely, the heavy punishment Mitchell received is accounted for solely because of his racist belief or motive. Nevertheless, the U.S. Supreme Court upheld Mitchell's sentence and the Wisconsin hate crime enhancement statute. This chapter examines the constitutional case against hate *crime* laws. We present the divided reactions of state courts and critique the Supreme Court's two decisions on the constitutionality of hate crime laws.

Prohibiting Hate Speech

The first step in analyzing the constitutionality of hate crime laws is a review of the historic controversy over criminal prohibitions on hate *speech*. Hate speech laws, like hate crime laws, seek to punish and prevent various types of opinions and expressions that the majority deems odious and harmful. Until well into the twentieth century, there was a great deal of judicial uncertainty about whether such prohibitions could pass First Amendment scrutiny.

The impulse to ban "offensive" speech runs deep in every society. The prohibitionist always acts in the name of a higher goal—patriotism, national security, decency, family values, equality, social harmony. While the First Amendment provides unique tolerance for all forms of speech, especially political speech,[4] our history is punctuated with legislative initiatives to ban expression that the majority considers odious—radical ideas, communism, sexually explicit art, flag burning, and group libel, to name a just a few. History has not treated these efforts kindly. We now look back on them as irrational and hysterical, as serious affronts to civil rights, and as blights on our commitment to civil liberties.[5]

Fighting Words

Of the limited exceptions to the First Amendment protection of expression, "fighting words" is most relevant to our subject. For a short time in American constitutional history, it appeared that a fighting words exception to the First Amendment might provide justification for the suppression of certain forms of hate speech. A half century ago, Walter Chaplinksy, a Jehovah's Witness, called a police officer "a God-damned racketeer," and "a damned Fascist." He was convicted under a New Hampshire law that made it a crime to "address any offensive, derisive or annoying word to any person who is lawfully in any street or other public place, nor call him by any offensive or derisive name." The U.S. Supreme Court rejected Chaplinsky's appeal and carved out a "fighting words" exception to the First Amendment.[6] The Court held that words "which by their very utterance inflict injury or tend to incite an immediate breach of the peace"[7] are not constitutionally protected. The *Chaplinsky* opinion seemingly opened the door to laws prohibiting the utterance of racial, religious, or ethnic insults, because arguably they would "by their very utterance inflict injury." However, in the years after *Chaplinsky*, the Court narrowed the definition of fighting words to utterances *tending to incite an immediate breach of the peace*. Further, the Court stated that in order to constitute "fighting words," the words must "naturally tend to provoke violent resentment" or an "immediate breach of the peace" and must be directed at an individual, rather than at a general group.[8] The Court defined "immediate breach of the peace" to mean more than a mere offensive remark or a breach of decorum; to be legally punishable, the words had to tend to incite the addressee to violent action.[9]

Remarkably, since *Chaplinsky*, the Supreme Court has *never* sustained a conviction under the fighting words doctrine.[10] In other words, every time a state or local government has sought to use criminal law to punish someone for offensive speech that might provoke violent retaliation, the Court has ruled against the government and reversed the conviction. This pattern has led constitutional scholars to doubt the continuing validity of the fighting words exception. As the eminent constitutional scholar, Professor Gerald Gunther, has observed: "one must wonder about the strength of an exception which, while theoretically recognized, has ever since 1942 not been found to be apt in practice."[11]

Group Libel

There have been numerous efforts over the course of our history to make it illegal to vilify racial or religious groups; in other words, to engage in what might be called "group libel." Early efforts to ban hate speech emerged during the 1930s in response to perceived Nazi threats. Conflicts between pro- and anti-Nazi groups frequently erupted into violence. According to Professor Samuel Walker, these conflicts produced many anti-expression laws, prohibiting meetings, demonstrations, and distribution of literature.[12] Sometimes called "race hate" or "group libel" laws, they forbade the screening of pro-Fascist films and the distribution of Fascist literature. Other laws banned picketing, parades, demonstrations, and the wearing of uniforms.

In the late 1930s, speech restrictions targeted the distribution of literature and door-to-door solicitation by Jehovah's Witnesses, who were punished for aggressive proselytizing and condemning other religions as "imposters" and "racketeers."[13] Ultimately, however, these laws were struck down as unconstitutional under the First Amendment.[14]

In 1934, in the wake of riots between Nazi sympathizers and anti-Nazi groups, New Jersey passed a group libel law, which outlawed racial and religious "propaganda." The law, premised on the idea that the preservation of liberty and equality required and justified restrictions on those who threaten liberty and equality,[15] provided criminal penalties for dissemination of "propaganda or statements creating or tending to create prejudice, hostility, hatred, ridicule, disgrace or contempt of people . . . by reason of their race, color, creed or manner of worship." It also made it criminal for two or more people to meet and exhibit such propaganda in public or private. For six years, there was not a single prosecution. In 1940, Nazi sympathizers and members of the German-American Bund were convicted of possession of race hate propaganda under the state group libel law. In *State v. Klapprott*,[16] the New Jersey Supreme Court overturned these convictions and declared the group libel law unconstitutional. The court held that the terms "hatred," "prejudice," "hostility," and "abuse" were so vague as to be virtually meaningless. According to the New Jersey court, in the realms of religion and politics there are inevitably strong feelings and sharp differences, including exaggeration, vilification, and false statements. Such expressions, however offensive, are entitled to First Amendment protection, which "in the long view, [is] essential to enlightened opinion and right conduct on the part of the citizens of a democracy."[17]

The U.S. Supreme Court's modern First Amendment jurisprudence regarding group libel emerged after World War II.[18] The Court's first step was a false start, which for the last time condoned the prohibition of a kind of group libel. In 1952, the Supreme Court heard *Beauharnais v. Illinois*,[19] a challenge to a 1917 Illinois law that made it a crime for anyone "to manufacture, sell, or offer for sale, advertise or publish, present or exhibit in any public place . . . [anything that] portrays depravity, criminality, unchastity, or lack of virtue of a class of citizens, of any race, color, creed, or religion," when such expression would expose such citizens "to contempt, derision, or obloquy or which is productive of breach of the peace or riots."[20] The defendant, Joseph Beauharnais, was the president of the White Circle League of America, a group that had formed in response to the racial integration of some all-white Chicago neighborhoods. White resistance to integration included discrimination by realtors and financial institutions, as well as threats, vandalism, and violence. Beauharnais's literature claimed that whites were threatened by the "rapes, robberies, knives, guns and marijuana of the Negro," and exhorted local government to "halt further encroachment, harassment and invasion of white people, their property, neighborhoods and persons by the Negro." He urged people to petition the government to stop integration. For this bigoted expression, he was charged and convicted.

The U.S. Supreme Court, rather than treating the case as a test of the fighting words doctrine (arguably racially inflammatory literature could trigger immediate violence), took the opportunity to consider whether there was a group libel exception to the First Amendment. In a 5–4 decision, the Court held that the civil unrest and riots in Chicago justified criminal penalties for offensive hate literature that posed a threat to public order. "[T]he willful purveyors of falsehood concerning racial and religious groups promote strife and tend powerfully to obstruct the manifold adjustments required for free, ordered life in a metropolitan, polyglot community."[21] However, Justice William O. Douglas's dissent provided a defense of free expression that later came to prevail:

> Today a white man stands convicted for protesting in unseemly language against our decisions invalidating restrictive [housing] covenants. . . . Tomorrow a Negro [may] be hailed before a court for denouncing lynch law in heated terms.[22]

While the Supreme Court has never explicitly overruled *Beauharnais*, subsequent opinions cast a pall over that ruling, and recognize that the First Amendment protects even the expression of vile prejudices against groups.[23] The landmark case of the modern era is *New York Times v. Sullivan*,[24] which involved a libel claim by an Alabama sheriff against the *New York Times* for publishing a political advertisement placed by a civil rights group. The advertisement charged Alabama officials with terrorizing and assaulting civil rights demonstrators. The Court held that the statements made in the advertisement were protected by the First Amendment, and that in order to prevail in a libel suit against a particular public figure, a plaintiff has to prove that the statement was "knowingly false or made with reckless disregard for the truth." Indeed, *New York Times v. Sullivan*, effectively sapped the *Beauharnais* group libel rationale of its vitality, by requiring that an individual bringing a libel suit prove the libelous statement was directed *at the individual*, personally, *and not simply at a group to which the individual belongs.*

Even in the case of individual libel, the "knowingly false" test is extremely difficult to satisfy, especially when politics or ideology is involved, as in hate speech cases. For example, statements like "the mayor is a white supremacist, who enjoys oppressing minorities," "Republicans are women-hating Fascists," or "Louis Farrakhan is a racist" would be constitutionally protected regardless of their truth or falsity. Because the First Amendment does not permit the federal government or the states to enshrine certain ideas and beliefs at the expense of others, there can be no law prohibiting an offensive idea.

The Seventh Circuit's famous decision in *Collin v. Smith*[25] poignantly illustrates the First Amendment's protection of expressions of prejudice or hate against groups. Faced with a pending march by a group of Nazis through a predominantly Jewish suburb where approximately 5,000 Holocaust survivors lived, Skokie (Illinois) lawmakers sought to block the Nazis via an ordinance explicitly modeled after the Illinois law upheld in *Beauharnais.* Skokie's ordinance provided that a parade permit could be issued only if a town official determined that the parade

> would not portray criminality, depravity, or lack of virtue in, or incite violence, hatred, abuse or hostility toward a person or group of persons by reason of reference to religious, racial, ethnic, national or regional affiliation.[26]

The Seventh Circuit held the Skokie ordinance unconstitutional because it sought to regulate speech based on its content. The court also said that the ban on the Nazis could not be justified as a prohibition against fighting words. While acknowledging that the Nazi march would be offensive and painful to the town's Jewish residents, especially the Holocaust survivors, the court stated that such anguish is the price we pay for free speech.

[W]e think the words of the [Supreme] Court in *Street v. New York* [394 U.S. 576, 592 (1969)] are very much on point: "Any shock effect . . . must be attributed to the content of the ideas expressed. It is firmly settled that under our Constitution the public expression of ideas may not be prohibited merely because the ideas are themselves offensive to some of their hearers."[27]

Referring to *Beauharnais,* the court noted that the Skokie ordinance could not be upheld simply on the basis of "blind obeisance to uncertain implications from an opinion issued years before the Supreme Court itself rewrote the rules." The Supreme Court denied Skokie's petition for *certiorari*, letting the Seventh Circuit's opinion stand. Today, even if riots were threatened, the First Amendment would protect offensive racist, anti-Semitic, anti-ethnic literature and expression because "[i]f there is a bedrock principle underlying the First Amendment, it is that the government may not prohibit the expression of an idea simply because society finds it offensive or disagreeable."[28]

Campus Speech Codes

By the late 1950s, group libel laws had fallen out of favor. Professor Walker attributes this trend primarily to the lack of support for such laws from civil rights and religious groups who were their putative beneficiaries.

[I]t is the lack of an effective advocate that accounts for the failure of hate speech restrictions to gain any ground in the United States. . . . The major civil rights groups came to understand that any exception to the seamless fabric of individual rights, which group libel represented, threatened the entire structure. One critical element of the civil rights movement, which had direct ramifications for the hate speech issue, was that activity on behalf of racial equality often involved provocative and offensive tactics by civil rights groups themselves.[29]

In the late 1980s, efforts to restrict hate speech surfaced again, this time in the form of college and university disciplinary codes outlawing bigoted expressions.[30] Proponents of these university-sponsored codes claim that prejudiced and bigoted speech injures members of minority groups and undermines minority students' ability to fulfill their academic potential. According to the proponents, "from the victim's perspective racist hate messages cause real damage";[31] "we have not listened to the real victims—we have shown so little understanding of their injury."[32] They argue that racist, anti-Semitic, misogynistic, and homophobic expressions and epithets inflict emotional and psychological injury on the individual and on members of the group to which the individual belongs. Professor Mari Matsuda, a leading proponent of hate speech codes, asserts that,

> [r]acist speech is best treated as a *sui generis* category, presenting an idea so historically untenable, so dangerous, and so tied to perpetuation of violence and degradation of the very classes of human beings who are least equipped to respond that it is properly treated as outside the realm of protected discourse.[33]

Campus hate speech codes have not fared well in court. All three constitutional challenges have been successful.[34] *Doe v. University of Michigan*[35] involved the University of Michigan's "Policy on Discrimination and Discriminatory Harassment of Students" which prohibited and punished *any* behavior that had the effect of "stigmatizing and victimizing individuals on the basis of race, ethnicity, religion, sex, sexual orientation, creed, national origin, ancestry, age, marital status, handicap or Vietnam-era veteran status."[36] An interpretive guide illuminated the types of expression subject to sanctions. Some examples included:

- A male student makes remarks in class like "Women just aren't as good in this field as men," thus creating a hostile learning atmosphere for female classmates.

- Students in a residence hall have a floor party and invite everyone on their floor except one person because they think she is a lesbian.[37]

The second example is curious because it does not involve expression. The interpretive guide also cited examples of harassment such as "telling jokes about homosexuals," sponsoring "entertainment that includes a comedian who slurs Hispanics," displaying a confederate flag in a private dorm room, laughing at jokes "about someone in your class who stutters."[38]

The federal district court held that the university's policy was unconstitutionally vague because it "swept within its scope a significant amount of 'verbal conduct' or 'verbal behavior' which is unquestionably protected speech under the First Amendment."[39] As to the issue of vagueness, the court held that "[l]ooking at the plain language of the Policy, it was simply impossible to discern any limitation on its scope or any conceptual distinction between protected and unprotected conduct." Although the university insisted that it had not applied the policy to protected speech, the court pointed to several students against whom disciplinary charges had been brought, despite their having engaged only in constitutionally protected speech. In one case, a complaint was filed against a graduate student who, during a class discussion, said that homosexuality was a disease and that he intended to develop a counseling plan to return gays to heterosexuality. Other instances involved (1) during a class public speaking exercise, a student read "an allegedly homophobic limerick which ridiculed a well known athlete for his presumed sexual orientation"; and (2) a student complained that "he had heard that minorities had a difficult time in [a dentistry] course . . . and that they were not treated fairly" by the minority professor. Both students "plea bargained," agreeing to "counseling." The student who read the limerick attended an "educational gay rap session" and wrote a letter of apology, which was published in the university newspaper. After being "counseled," the student who complained about the dentistry class agreed to write a letter apologizing for making the comment without adequately verifying the allegation.[40] The court observed that:

> The Administrator generally failed to consider whether a comment was protected by the First Amendment before informing the accused student that a complaint had been filed. The Administrator instead attempted to persuade the accused student to accept "voluntary" sanctions. Behind this persuasion was, of course, the subtle threat that failure to accept such sanctions might result in a formal hearing. There is no evidence in the record that the Administrator ever declined to pursue a complaint . . . because the alleged harassing conduct was protected by the First Amendment.[41]

In *UWM Post, Inc. v. Board of Regents of the University of Wisconsin*,[42] a federal court heard a challenge to a university policy that provided sanctions for "racist or discriminatory comments, epithets or other expressive behavior . . . [that] demean[s] the race, sex, religion, color, creed, disability, sexual orientation, national origin, ancestry or age of the individual or individuals; and creates an intimidating, hostile, or demeaning environment."[43] The university had relied upon the policy to punish:

- A student who called another student "Shakazulu."
- A student who shouted "fucking bitch" and "fucking cunt" at a woman because of her negative statements in the university's paper about the athletic department.
- A student who told an Asian student that "it's people like you—that's the reason this country is screwed up. You don't belong here. Whites are always getting screwed by minorities and some day the Whites will take over."

- A student who, during an argument, called another student "a fat-ass nigger."
- A student who yelled at a female student "you've got nice tits."[44]

While acknowledging the offensiveness of these comments, the court found the policy unconstitutionally overbroad and vague. The court rejected the university's claim that the policy prohibited only fighting words. "Since the elements of the [policy] do not require that the regulated speech, by its very utterance, tend to incite violent reaction, the rule goes beyond the present scope of the fighting words doctrine."[45] Further, "[i]t is unlikely that all or nearly all demeaning, expressive behavior which creates an intimidating, hostile or demeaning environment tends to provoke a violent response."[46]

In striking down UWM's speech code, the court relied upon the Seventh Circuit's decision in *Hudnut v. American Booksellers Association, Inc.*[47] (summarily affirmed by the Supreme Court).[48] *Hudnut* involved a First Amendment challenge to an Indianapolis ordinance which (1) prohibited the production, distribution, exhibition, or sale of pornography and the display of pornography in any place of employment, school, public place, or private home; (2) created a civil cause of action for persons coerced, intimidated, or tricked into appearing in a pornographic work; and (3) provided victims of sexual violence a cause of action against sellers of the pornography. The ordinance was premised on the city council's finding that:

> Pornography is a systematic practice of exploitation and subordination based on sex which differentially harms women. The bigotry and contempt it promotes, with the acts of aggression it fosters, harms women's opportunities for equality of rights in employment, education, access to and use of public accommodations, and acquisition of real property; promotes rape, battery, child abuse, kidnapping and prostitution. . . . ; and contributes significantly to restricting women in particular from full exercise of citizenship and participation in public life.[49]

The Seventh Circuit held that Indianapolis's definition of pornography— "the graphic sexually explicit subordination of women"—was impermissibly vague and overbroad. The Court of Appeals rejected the city's argument that the ordinance banned only speech that had a socially "low value." According to Judge Frank Easterbrook, the ordinance created an impermissible "approved view of women, of how they may react to sexual encounters [and] of how the sexes may relate to each other."[50]

Commenting on the *Hudnut* case, Harvard Law School professor Laurence Tribe stated,

[T]he First Amendment similarly protects advocacy . . . of the opinion that women were meant to be dominated by men, or blacks to be dominated by whites, or Jews by Christians, and that those so subordinated not only deserve but subconsciously enjoy their humiliating treatment. . . . It is an inadequate response to argue, as do some scholars, that ordinances like that enacted by Indianapolis take aim at harms, not at expression. *All* viewpoint-based regulations are targeted at some supposed harm.[51]

In summary, under existing First Amendment jurisprudence, hate *speech* cannot be prohibited or made illegal. The question we now address is what implications that interpretation of the First Amendment has for attempts to specially punish hate *crime*.

Constitutionality of Hate Crime Laws

There has been a spate of litigation and a lively debate among constitutional lawyers and civil libertarians over whether hate *crime* laws, like hate *speech* laws, violate the First Amendment.[52] The case for unconstitutionality is as follows: Generic criminal laws already punish injurious conduct; so recriminalization or sentence enhancement for the same injurious conduct when it is motivated by prejudice amounts to extra punishment for values, beliefs, and opinions that the government deems abhorrent. The critics ask: If the purpose of hate crime laws is to punish more severely offenders who are motivated by prejudices, is that not equivalent to punishing hate speech or hate thought?[53] Professor Tribe put it this way: "[t]o be sure, one who incites arson against an NAACP headquarters in a racist speech is more reprehensible than one who incites the very same arson to collect insurance proceeds, but to punish the former more severely than the latter is, arguably, to penalize a reprehensible point of view *as such*."[54] Professor Tribe's hypothetical example mirrors the facts in *Wisconsin v. Mitchell*, where a black defendant, who incited an attack against a white passerby, received a sentence more than three times as harsh as would ordinarily apply. Ironically, Professor Tribe supports hate crime laws; in the above quote, he refers to hate speech laws.

In a real sense, hate crime laws are a second best option for proponents of hate speech laws who recognize that the First Amendment poses an insurmountable barrier to the latter. Supporters of hate crime laws argue that hate crime laws are clearly constitutional because they punish conduct, not speech.[55] In their view, hate crime laws do not prohibit an individual from holding or advocating ideas, beliefs, and opinions that the government finds offensive. The individual is simply prohibited from committing crimes based on those ideas. If he seeks to further his bigoted views, or succumbs to his bigoted impulses, through criminal conduct, he will be more severely punished than an "ordinary" offender; his crime is more serious in that it causes more injury, indicates greater culpability, and undermines social harmony. According to Steven Freeman, ADL's director of legal affairs:

> Not only is the penalty-enhancement approach [constitutionally] sound, in our best judgment it works. Certainly, anyone who has ever spoken to the victim of a hate crime understands that crossburning is different from ordinary trespass; that a swastika daubing is different from ordinary vandalism; and that a gay-bashing or racial assault is different from an ordinary mugging. For victims of such incidents, penalty enhancement is a punishment which fits the crime.[56]

To the advocates, providing enhanced punishments for hate criminals is no different than enhancing the sentence of a murderer whose motive was pecuniary gain, or one who murders a police officer. However, to us, these other sentence enhancements do not have the same free speech implications as hate crime enhancements because they are content or viewpoint neutral.

Until the Supreme Court's decision in *Wisconsin v. Mitchell*, state courts were divided on the constitutionality of hate crime laws. In *State v. Plowman*,[57] the Oregon Supreme Court upheld a statute that prohibited "two or more assailants, acting together, from causing physical injury to another because the assailants perceive the victim to belong to one of the specified groups." The court rejected defendants' arguments that the statute criminalized constitutionally protected opinions and beliefs. Drawing a distinction between speech and conduct, the court stated that "[r]ather than proscribing opinion, that law proscribes a forbidden effect: the effect of acting together to cause physical injury to a victim whom the assailants have targeted because of their perception that the victim belongs to a particular group."[58] We do not find this reasoning convincing; the only thing that distinguishes a crime in which two or more assailants cause physical injury based on greed, anger, or some unknown criminal impulse, and a crime in which two or more assailants cause physical injury based on their perception that the victim is black, Jewish, Chinese, or a member of another "protected" group is the assailants' wrong-headed bias. The court noted that the statute could be violated, even if the assailants did not utter any slurs and had no opinion "other than the perception of the victim's characteristics."[59] (E.g., presumably: "Let's get that handicapped guy over there. He's the one who was messing with my motorcycle.") That might make the statute less constitutionally suspect, but it would also render it incoherent.

In *State v. Wyant*,[60] the Ohio Supreme Court took the opposite position, striking down a hate crime statute, which provided enhanced penalties if the offender committed a particular crime "by reason of the race, color, religion, or national origin of another person or group of persons."[61] The defendant had been sentenced to one and one-half years' imprisonment for aggravated menacing. The court held that the enhancement statute created an unconstitutional "thought crime."

> Once the proscribed act is committed, the government criminalizes the underlying thought by enhancing the penalty based on viewpoint. This is dangerous. If the legislature can enhance a penalty for crimes committed "by reason of" racial bigotry, why not "by reason of" opposition to abortion, war, the elderly (or any other political viewpoint)?[62]

Eventually, *Wyant* made its way to the U.S. Supreme Court, which vacated and remanded the case to the Ohio Supreme Court for reconsideration in light of *Wisconsin v. Mitchell*. The state supreme court summarily reversed its earlier (and in our view, persuasive) decision and held the Ohio hate crime statute constitutional.[63]

In *People v. Aishman*,[64] a California appeals court upheld a hate crime enhancement statute. The defendant, Daniel Stout, along with four other white men, went to look for a group of Mexican men who allegedly raped Stout's wife. The five men went to the scene of the crime and attacked three Mexicans. The defendants claimed they assaulted the men in retaliation for the alleged rape, not because of anti-Mexican bigotry. The prosecution relied on statements made before the attack about "hitting home runs with Mexicans," and the fact that one defendant had a swastika and "Thank God I'm White" tattooed on his arm. The appeals court stated that the statute presented no constitutional problems because it punished conduct and not speech.[65]

Supreme Court Decisions

R.A.V. v. St. Paul

The U.S. Supreme Court first ruled on the constitutionality of hate crime statutes in *R.A.V. v. St. Paul*.[66] R.A.V., a white juvenile, and several other youths burned a makeshift wooden cross on a black family's lawn. R.A.V. was arrested, charged, and convicted under a St. Paul ordinance which provided:

> whoever places on public or private property a symbol, object, appellation, characterization or graffiti, including but not limited to a burn-

ing cross or Nazi swastika, which one knows or has reasonable grounds
to know arouses anger, alarm, or resentment in others on the basis of
race, color, religion, or gender, commits disorderly conduct and shall
be guilty of a misdemeanor.

R.A.V. attacked the ordinance on First Amendment grounds.
St. Paul argued that the statute was directed only at constitutionally
unprotected fighting words. The Minnesota Supreme Court upheld the
conviction on the ground that the phrase "arouses anger, alarm or
resentment in others," only reached fighting words, which under
Chaplinsky, did not enjoy First Amendment protection. It also held that
the ordinance did not impermissibly regulate speech on the basis of
viewpoint, but was narrowly tailored to serve the "compelling state
interest in protecting the community from bias-motivated threats to
public safety and order."

The nine U.S. Supreme Court justices were unanimous in striking
down the ordinance, but differed as to why.[67] Justice Scalia's majority
opinion acknowledged that the government could criminalize constitutionally unprotected fighting words, but insisted that the government
could not criminalize only those fighting words that express ideas that
the government disfavors. In other words, the government cannot regulate fighting words on the basis of viewpoint.

> St. Paul has not singled out an especially offensive mode of expres-
> sion. . . . Rather, it has proscribed fighting words of whatever man-
> ner that communicate messages of racial, gender or religious intoler-
> ance. Selectivity of this sort creates the possibility that the city is
> seeking to handicap the expression of particular ideas.[68]

Justice White's concurrence stated that the majority opinion need
not have addressed whether the ordinance involved content-based discrimination. In his view, the ordinance could have been struck down
simply by holding that the St. Paul ordinance is fatally overbroad because it criminalizes not only unprotected expression (i.e., fighting
words), but also expression protected by the First Amendment.

Justice Stevens's concurring opinion insisted that the St. Paul ordinance did not, as the majority asserted, regulate speech based on subject matter or viewpoint. Rather, according to Stevens, the ordinance
distinguished different verbal conduct "on the basis of the *harm* the
speech causes."[69] Thus, the St. Paul ordinance does not prevent only "one
side [as Justice Scalia charged] from hurling fighting words at the other
on the basis of conflicting ideas, but [bars] *both* sides from hurling such
words on the basis of the target's race, color, creed, religion or gender."[70]
Nevertheless, he voted to strike down the law because it was overbroad;

in other words, the ordinance prohibits both constitutionally unprotected *and* protected speech.

Wisconsin v. Mitchell

The U.S. Supreme Court next addressed hate crime laws in *Wisconsin v. Mitchell*.[71] Mitchell, a black juvenile, was convicted (as an adult) in a Wisconsin trial court of *racially motivated aggravated battery* and sentenced to seven years imprisonment under the state's hate crime statute. Ordinarily, aggravated battery carries a maximum sentence of two years imprisonment. The attack came just after Mitchell and several friends had left a movie theater where they had seen *Mississippi Burning*, a film about the murder of civil rights workers in the South during the 1960s. One particularly disturbing scene from the film, in which a white man beats a black youth who was praying, inspired the attack by Mitchell and his friends. Outside the theater, Mitchell asked his friends, "Do you all feel hyped up to move on some white people?" When the victim, a white youth, walked by, Mitchell said, "You all want to fuck somebody up? There goes a white boy; go get him." The group beat the boy unconscious and caused severe physical injury. Mitchell, however, did not physically participate in the beating.[72]

Wisconsin's enhancement-type hate crime statute provided for an increased sentence when a person:

> [i]ntentionally selects the person against whom the crime . . . is committed or selects the property which is damaged or otherwise affected . . . because of race, religion, color, disability, sexual orientation, national origin or ancestry of that person or the owner or occupant of that property.

Believing that it was following the Supreme Court's *R.A.V.* decision, the Wisconsin Supreme Court struck down the statute for creating an unconstitutional thought crime via a sentencing scheme that assigned more severe punishment to offenses motivated by disfavored viewpoints.[73] "The ideological content of the thought targeted by [this] hate crime statute is identical to that targeted by the St. Paul ordinance."[74] Relying on civil liberties attorney Susan Gellman's influential law review article,[75] the Wisconsin court characterized the conduct/speech distinction put forth by proponents of hate crime laws as entirely unconvincing.

> Merely because the statute refers in a literal sense to the intentional "conduct" of selecting, does not mean the court must turn a blind eye to the intent and practical effect of the law—punishment of offensive motive or thought.[76]

Because the underlying conduct was already proscribed by the state's criminal code, the only remaining element triggering an enhanced penalty was the expression of bigotry.[77] The conduct involved in "intentionally selecting" a victim, according to the court, is more closely akin to speech and thought, than to behavior and conduct; "[t]he conduct of 'selecting' is not akin to the conduct of assaulting, burglarizing, murdering and other criminal conduct."

The U.S. Supreme Court reversed in a unanimous opinion authored by Chief Justice Rehnquist. He distinguished Wisconsin's sentence enhancement law from St. Paul's ordinance on the ground that the latter aimed at politically incorrect *viewpoints*, whereas the former aimed at criminal *conduct*. (Ironically perhaps, Mitchell himself only used words, while R.A.V. engaged in trespass and arson.) According to the Court, the legislature may properly single out such criminal conduct for increased punishment based on the judgment that such conduct causes greater harm to victims, third parties, and society generally.[78]

We do not find the Supreme Court decision convincing. The Court does not explain the distinction between speech and conduct. Admittedly, the Wisconsin statute deals with criminal conduct, but the point remains that the sentence enhancement is triggered by some prejudices and not others. A similarly situated offender, who engaged in the same conduct, but for reasons of personal jealousy or spite, would have received one-third the sentence that Mitchell received.

The Court may have been concerned that striking down the Wisconsin law would have put in doubt the constitutionality of all judicial sentencing based on motive. The Chief Justice explained that judges have traditionally taken motives into account in determining sentences.[79] "Motives are most relevant when the trial judge sets the defendant's sentence, and it is not uncommon for a defendant to receive a minimum sentence because he was acting with good motives, or a rather higher sentence because of his bad motives."[80] In support of this proposition, the Chief Justice cited the Court's decision in *Dawson v. Delaware*.[81] In that case, the Court struck down a death sentence that was based in part on evidence that the defendant—convicted of a brutal felony murder—was a member of the Aryan Brotherhood, a white supremacist organization with "chapters" in many American prisons. The Court ruled that the admission of this evidence violated the First Amendment because there had been no showing that the defendant's membership had any relationship to the murder for which he was sentenced to death. Apparently, the Court meant that if there were a causal link, adherence to the tenets of a racist ideology could by itself constitute an appropriate aggravating factor supporting the death penalty.

Where it has no relevance to the offense charged, introduction of a defendant's associational and "abstract beliefs" violates the First Amendment. That is the easy question. The hard question is: What if the speech or belief *was* relevant to the crime? May the legislature calibrate one's sentence to the vileness of one's ideas or ideology? The *Mitchell* Court rejected the claim that sentencing cannot be based on associational and speech-related activity. The Court noted that such evidence has traditionally been admissible for sentencing purposes when it bears a direct relationship to the crime charged. Specifically, the Court held that the Constitution does not erect an impregnable barrier to the admission of evidence concerning one's beliefs and associations at sentencing, simply because those beliefs and associations are protected by the First Amendment."[82]

In support of this thesis, Chief Justice Rehnquist cited *Barclay v. Florida*[83] which upheld imposition of the death penalty, where the sentencing judge relied, in part, on the element of racial hatred in the defendant's crime, as well as on his "desire to start a race war."[84] Unlike Dawson's membership in the Aryan Brotherhood, Barclay's membership in the Black Liberation Army was directly related to his crime: the murder of a white hitchhiker. In other words, Barclay's sentence was not based on his "abstract beliefs," whereas Dawson's was. But this does not solve the problem. Just because an enhanced penalty based on motive does not *always* constitute punishment for an abstract belief does not mean that it *never* does. Sentence enhancements for other motives often do not have the same free speech implications. Unlike greed, jealousy, or simple cold-bloodedness, bigotry is often connected to a system of political beliefs and is never content neutral. The concepts of prejudice and bigotry are political to the core. Hate crime laws explicitly seek to punish people for having bigoted beliefs. The Supreme Court did not even begin to grapple with this issue.

In its *Mitchell* decision, the U.S. Supreme Court seemed to be criticizing the Wisconsin Supreme Court for condemning motive as a valid sentencing factor. However, the Wisconsin Supreme Court did not say that motive could never be considered during sentencing; rather, it condemned the use of a politically loaded category—bigotry—as a trigger to enhance punishment.

> The hate crimes statute enhances the punishment of bigoted criminals because they are bigoted. The statute is directed solely at the subjective motivation of the actor—his or her prejudice. Punishment of one's thought, however repugnant the thought, is unconstitutional.[85]

The Supreme Court also compared the Wisconsin statute to Title VII of the Civil Rights Act of 1964, reasoning that since Title VII is constitutional, so is Wisconsin's statute.[86] In effect, the Court stated that hate crime laws serve the same purpose as Title VII—each provides a remedy for discriminatory conduct, not a prohibition of speech. But the harms that hate crime laws are designed to remedy are not clearly identifiable. The harm to the victim is already punished by generic criminal law. It would appear that the only additional purpose in punishing more severely those who commit a bias crime is to provide extra punishment based on the offender's politically incorrect opinions and viewpoints.

Conclusion

There is a long history of attempts to suppress bigoted expression in the United States. In the first half of the twentieth century, some states prohibited Nazi and Communist "propaganda." Other states outlawed group libel based on race, nationality, and ethnicity. Unlike most other countries in the world, in the United States these laws have not withstood judicial scrutiny or political judgment. Tolerance for vile expression is the price we pay for the right to free speech. As Supreme Court Justice Oliver Wendell Holmes expressed it a half century ago: "If there is any principle of the Constitution that more imperatively calls for attachment than any other, it is the principle of free thought—not free thought for those who agree with us but freedom for the thought we hate."[87]

In recent years, bigotry and prejudice have become increasingly deplored in American society. Indeed, anti-prejudice itself has become a reigning ideology, one that the government heartily and rightly endorses. Despite the near universal condemnation of bigots, the First Amendment protects their offensive speech. If a bigot acts on those views, the criminal law is there to punish him. But, in our view, the First Amendment is implicated when extra punishment is meted out for bigoted beliefs and motives.

The campus hate speech codes have emerged as the contemporary successor to the old group libel laws. These codes attempt, in the name of multiculturalism, to regulate student expression, including personal discussions, jokes, and comments in class. Not surprisingly, they have failed to withstand legal challenge.

Passing hate crime laws is now the fallback position for those who wish to denounce prejudiced and bigoted thought and expression via criminal law. By linking hate speech prohibitions to generic criminal law, many well-meaning advocacy groups and politicians seek to shake a fist at the kind of ideas, opinions, and degenerate personalities that "right-thinking" people abhor. But we must consider whether punishing crimes motivated by politically unpopular beliefs more severely than crimes motivated by other factors itself violates our First Amendment traditions.

The Supreme Court's unanimous decision in *R.A.V.*, striking down the St. Paul ordinance, seemed to sound the death knell for hate crime laws. Indeed, the plurality opinion emphasized that lawmakers cannot make viewpoint-based distinctions in regulating even unprotected expression. For example, a law that punished the assassins of Democratic politicians twice as severely as assassins of Republican politicians could not stand. However, in *Wisconsin v. Mitchell*, the Supreme Court drew a sharp line between laws that punish expression per se and those that punish expression that manifests itself in, or is integrally connected to, criminal conduct. Laws that punish expression itself are constitutionally unacceptable, but laws that punish expression linked to criminal conduct are constitutionally acceptable. Thus, federal and state legislatures have a green light to target politically unpopular prejudices for more severe punishment, whenever these prejudices can be linked to a generic crime. The same impulse that propels a college administrator to haul a student before a disciplinary board for voicing an offensive opinion about blacks, whites, women, men, or others, might propel a prosecutor to slap a hate crime charge on a defendant who uttered politically and socially abhorrent opinions during the commission of a crime. It seems to us that what is constitutionally impermissible under *R.A.V.* and what is constitutionally permissible under *Mitchell* is a distinction without a difference. *Mitchell* has declared the hate crime laws constitutional for purposes of the federal constitution. But in our view, the Court's reasoning is not persuasive. The very facts of that case present a defendant who was punished more severely, based on his viewpoints.

9

Identity Politics
and Hate Crimes

> If any problem unites gay people with non-
> gay people, it is crime. If any issue does not
> call for special interest pleading, this is it.
> Minority advocates, including gay ones, have
> blundered insensitively by trying to carve out
> hate crime statutes and other special interest
> crime laws instead of focusing on tougher
> measures against violence of all kinds. In
> trying to sensitize people to crimes aimed
> specifically at minorities, they are inadvert-
> ently desensitizing them to the vastly greater
> threat of crimes against everyone.
>
> Jonathan Rauch, gay journalist and scholar

*I*T HARDLY NEEDS SAYING that we share with the proponents of hate
crime laws the goal of a tolerant society, in which people are judged
by "the content of their character," not by their race, religion, sexual
orientation, or gender.[1] We differ over the means for achieving that goal.
The proponents believe that the message-sending potential and the deterrent power of criminal law will deter or persuade criminals and would-
be criminals to desist from hate crimes and perhaps to hold fewer and
less virulent prejudices. We find this implausible. The conduct which hate
crime laws aim at is already criminal. Given that criminals ignore existing criminal laws and punishment threats, we doubt that the additional
threat promised by hate crime laws adds much, if any, marginal deterrence; this is especially true for the most serious offenses. In any event,
a highly bigoted offender can probably avoid the hate crime tariff by
committing his crime silently. It is possible that the mere promulgation

of hate crime laws will contribute to long-term social education and the production of fewer hate criminals, but this too seems implausible given the web of laws already on the books, and the plethora of "messages" and symbols that already denounce bigotry. The occasional hate crime trial or sentence enhancement might reinforce the sociopolitical message of tolerance, but only assuming that the trial is successful, and is widely interpreted as fair and not politically motivated.

Emile Durkheim, the great French sociologist, contributed the remarkable insight that the punishment of crime plays a positive role for society.[2] By denouncing crime and the criminal, the population reaffirms its commitment to the society's core values and norms. Our concern is that rewriting criminal law to take into account the racial, religious, sexual, and other identities of offenders and victims will undermine the criminal law's potential for bolstering social solidarity. By redefining crime as a facet of intergroup conflict, hate crime laws encourage citizens to think of themselves as members of identity groups and encourage identity groups to think of themselves as victimized and besieged, thereby hardening each group's sense of resentment. That in turn contributes to the balkanization of American society, not to its unification.[3]

The conflict-generating tendency of identity politics has been decried by writers of all political persuasions. The liberal historian, Arthur Schlesinger, Jr. has written a compelling essay about how a kind of "multicultural" ideology associated with identity politics promotes group chauvinism at the expense of a unifying American culture. David Frum, Todd Gitlin, and Michael Tomasky, writers associated with the "new left," have each written books sharply critical of identity politics for shattering the left-liberal political coalition. According to Tomasky,

> The personal is political. This catch-phrase of identity politics that originated with feminism implies that identity is all, that ideas and arguments are nullities, and that to think independently and perhaps reach unorthodox conclusions is therefore to put one's authenticity and group membership at risk. It also implies that the nonpersonal isn't; one need only mull that over for a few moments to understand the woeful implications for those (working-class whites, housewives, church-goers, Kurds) whose personal experiences are not those of the anointed group. Thus are many potential allies simply written off, and many concerns and causes that should preoccupy the left—concerns that would help build . . . coalitions [across racial, gender, ethnic, etc. lines]—ignored.[4]

Political journalist Jim Sleeper has put it with characteristic insight:

> America's civic culture remains one of the world's few great resources for both individual freedom and social justice. The best way to ad-

vance these values is to nourish and renew our common civic culture, not promote its balkanization in identity politics or its dissolution in a largely empty rhetoric of class warfare. . . . [This] means challenging activists, educators, and public officials who, ironically, in the name of combatting racism and sexism, are working to ensure that we classify each other by color and ethnicity.[5]

Conservatives have been even more critical, seeing identity politics as leading toward a breakdown of the world's greatest multiethnic society. According to political journalist Richard Bernstein:

The dangers that do lurk on the dark side of the multiculturalist revolution are . . . nonetheless serious enough. Some writers before me have dwelled on one particular consequence of the multiculturalist impulse, deriving from its tendency to make a religion of "difference" and to exalt race, ethnicity, and sex as the sole components of identity. This, as the essayist Charles Krauthammer has said, is shoving us toward a "new tribalism," a splintering of the national culture and an intensification of our conflicts. After all . . . we have arrayed before us . . . the tragedies being played out elsewhere among people who have stressed their differences, rather than their commonalities. There is the nightmare in the former Yugoslavia, for example.[6]

The new hate crime laws are both a cause and a consequence of identity politics and may in several ways contribute to splintering our society. First, picking and choosing which prejudices transform ordinary crime into hate crime inevitably generates political conflict; witness the controversies in many jurisdictions over defining hate crime laws to include or exclude misogynistic and homophobic motivations. These issues have to be fought out state by state and group by group (women, gays, disabled, elderly). Second, the collection, reporting, and interpretation of hate crime data produces an exaggerated perception of the incidence of hate crime and an unduly negative picture of the state of intergroup relations. Third, the decision to label and prosecute individual crimes as hate crimes creates recurrent occasions for intergroup conflict. This chapter illuminates each of these conflict-generating features of hate crime laws.

Conflicts over which Prejudices Hate Crime Laws Should Include

Hate crime laws are based on the belief that all crime is not created equal; rather, crimes motivated by certain prejudices are worse than crimes similar in every respect other than motivation. Not surprisingly, that assumption is likely to be controversial. Many will argue that all perpetrators of serious crimes are equally deserving of condemnation and all victims equally deserving of sympathy.

It might be tempting to conclude that jealousies and resentments over exclusions from the hate crime laws can be avoided by drafting these laws to include all salient prejudices. While that would solve the problem of disparaging some groups' victimizations in comparison to others', it would also negate the primary purpose of the hate crime laws: to specially condemn offenders with certain prejudices and specially recognize their victims. Hate crime laws only make sense if certain bigoted offenders are condemned more forcefully and punished more severely than offenders who commit the same crimes but for nonprejudiced reasons. It is the *exclusion* that gives these laws their symbolic power and meaning.

Even if more group prejudices were brought under the hate crime umbrella, some individuals whose victimization could not be attributed to an established *group* prejudice would resent the implied disparagement of their victimization. As an editorial in the conservative *National Review* argued:

> Hate crime categorization tells society that some murders and beatings, and therefore some victims, are more important than others. Indeed, Congress's passion over ideologically disapproved crime is inversely proportional to its concern about the wider crime problem that keeps a large fraction of the population in daily terror. By assuring selected victims of its concern, it is telling the rest of us that we must look out for ourselves.[7]

New Mexico Governor Gary E. Johnson vetoed a hate crime bill in April 1995, on the ground that the law was "unnecessary because hate exists in all crimes."[8]

The jurisdiction-by-jurisdiction politicking over which prejudices should be included in the definition of hate crime hardly contributes to a more tolerant and harmonious society. Some jurisdictions have not included homophobic prejudice as a hate crime trigger. Representative William Dannemeyer (R-Cal.) minced no words when he stated, "Sexual preference has no business being elevated to the same status as race, color, religion or national origin."[9] Gays and lesbians naturally fought back. According to Kevin Berrill, director of the National Gay and Lesbian Task Force, "If it [sexual orientation bias] does not stay in [the HCSA], it sends out a dangerous signal that this kind of crime is less reprehensible. It makes us second class citizens."[10]

The exclusion of gender prejudice from hate crime laws—on the ground that it would water down the special significance of racial, religious, and ethnic prejudice-related crime—is likely to cause a rift among historic civil rights movement allies. Following passage of the HCSA, there was a spate of angry protests by feminists.

> Currently, the Hate Crime Statistics Act discriminates against women; it says nothing of women's lives—and deaths. Only when the act is amended to include women will this nation have responded seriously and forthrightly to prejudice in all its various and deadly forms.[11]

The hate crime laws also focus attention on black racism because many intergroup crimes are committed by blacks against whites. Treated under generic criminal laws, these black on white crimes are mostly understood as "street crime," "violent crime," or crime generated by poverty. What will be the social consequences of scouring black on white crime for indications of racism?

The prevalence of crimes by minority perpetrators against white victims makes many liberals and hate crime law proponents uncomfortable. When the FBI's 1993 hate crime statistics reported that whites comprised 20 percent of all hate crime *victims*, some advocacy groups questioned whether the hate crime laws were being perverted.[12] Jill Tregor, executive director of the San Francisco-based Intergroup Clearinghouse, which provides legal and emotional counseling to hate crime victims, stated, "This is an abuse of what the hate crime laws were intended to cover."[13] Tregor accused white hate crime victims of using the laws to enhance penalties against minorities, who already experience prejudice within the criminal justice system.[14] Whites, generally sympathetic to the aspirations of minorities, may bristle at the suggestion that crimes motivated by blacks' racism against whites should be treated as a less virulent strain of hate crime, or not as hate crime at all. While no enacted hate crime law makes that distinction, a number of writers in prominent publications, likening hate crime laws to affirmative action for "protected groups," advocate the exclusion of racist crimes against whites from their coverage.[15] This issue alone seems fraught with potential for social conflict and constitutional concerns.

The Unduly Negative Picture of Intergroup Relations

What's counted counts. The very collection and reporting of hate crime statistics encourages Americans to think of the crime problem in terms of intergroup conflict. Even when statistics show only a minuscule number of hate crimes—and those mostly low-level offenses committed by juveniles and young offenders—the media, some advocacy groups, and academics see an epidemic and portray America as awash in "a wave of hate crime . . . that is getting worse."[16] In 1992, the Minnesota Department of Public Safety released statistics reporting 425 hate crimes statewide for 1991. District attorney, Tom Foley, saw this as proof of a "massive increase" in bigotry.[17] But as political journalist Richard Bernstein has pointed out, the 425 hate crimes represent a tiny percentage of crimes reported in Minnesota: "roughly 0.002 percent of the total 203,107 reported crimes, or about one in every 500."[18] Bernstein notes that this translates into about one bias crime per 8,800 Minnesota residents. Moreover, excluding the low-level crimes of simple assault (defined as an attack resulting in no wounds or broken bones) and verbal abuse, there is one bias crime per 16,000 residents.[19] Bernstein concludes that

> [T]he figures on bias crimes themselves do not seem to indicate a state that is rife with racism and bigotry. Four swastikas drawn on public buildings in a year is four swastikas too many, but, assuming that the four were drawn by four different people, that would be one swastika drawer per 1.2 million Minnesotans.[20]

Hate crime statistics become even more socially divisive when they are put forward as an indicator of the values and beliefs of all citizens, not just criminals. It would be possible, and indeed logical, to regard hate crimes, like other horrendous crimes, as reflecting nothing more than the distorted personalities of their authors; under that view, hate criminals, like all criminals, are anti-social deviants whom all decent people condemn. It is hard to understand why well-meaning people, striving for a more tolerant society, would cite hate crime statistics as evidence of widespread bigotry among law-abiding people who have the same gender, skin color, or sexual orientation as hate crime offenders. It is not sensible to infer the values and beliefs of our citizenry from the prejudices and conduct of a small number of vicious criminals. It would make far more sense to look at the attitudes, values, and conduct of our political, economic, and educational leaders, or to use survey research reports, as a basis for drawing conclusions about the prevalence and intensity of various prejudices.

Widespread claims that numerous black church fires from early 1995 to late 1996 indicate pervasive anti-black racism illustrate this current tendency to view American society in the most negative possible light. Some time in mid-1996, advocacy groups and the media began to see a connection among fires that had occurred at "predominantly black" churches over the previous two years. Without any investigations to determine the causes of the fires, much less the identities and motivations of the perpetrators, the Reverend Mac Charles Jones, associate general secretary for Racial Justice for the National Council of Churches

(NCC), proclaimed that racism was a factor in "99 percent" of the fires at black churches. He further asserted that (1) arsons are targeted disproportionately against black churches; (2) these arsons are perpetrated almost entirely by whites, as an expression of racial hostility, in a pattern of "domestic terrorism" verging on a race "war"; and (3) the church burnings can be blamed broadly upon political and religious conservatives, who are accused of creating a racist climate propitious to such acts.[21]

In the enthusiastic rush to proclaim the opening salvos in a race war,[22] facts that supported a different conclusion were ignored. Statistics that later came to light showed that from January 1995 to September 1996, suspicious fires had been reported at 230 churches. Of these, 122 were predominantly white churches, six were synagogues, and two were mosques; the remaining 100 churches had predominantly black congregations. Of course, some percentage of these fires were not arsons. Some that were arsons might have been the work of anti-religious zealots, or criminals with nonideological motives.

When questioned about whether too little attention was being paid to white church fires, Assistant U.S. Attorney General Deval Patrick stated, "The public shouldn't get the wrong impression that we aren't paying attention to attacks on other religious property. But in those cases, racial intolerance isn't behind them." Where did this conclusion come from? Why should it be assumed that the arson of a predominantly white church is not a bias crime, but that the arson of a predominantly black church almost invariably is?

The massive investigation, led by the National Church Arson Task Force (NCATF), involved 500 federal and state law enforcement officials. As the investigation progressed, doubt was cast on the existence of a white racist conspiracy, and on the assumption that most of the fires were racially motivated. Of the 100 suspects arrested from January 1995 to September 1996, one-third were black.[23] According to a NCATF report, white supremacist groups were involved in only "a handful of cases."[24] For the remaining apparent arsons, investigators identified as perpetrators devil worshipping vandals, teenage pranksters, insurance scam artists, volunteer firefighters, and "copycat arsonists."[25]

In one instance, a black ex-convict set fire to a black church after an inmate, with whom the arsonist served time, offered him $10,000 to burn the church. In a bizarre scam, the inmate planned to turn in the arsonist and collect the reward money.[26] The arsonists in three fires were church pastors who hoped to collect insurance money.[27] In Texas, a black teenager was arrested for burning a black church and a vacant house.[28] In South Carolina, three white teenagers were arrested for burning a black church. Investigators attributed their criminal conduct to a combination of drinking and shooting off fireworks.[29] In another case, a black man burned a predominantly black church after having an argument with his mother.[30] Two of the fires, one in Texas and one in Alabama, were set by volunteer firefighters, one white and one black.[31]

Conflict began to emerge along the usual racial fault lines. The Institute on Religion and Democracy (IRD), a conservative Protestant group, called for the resignation of Mac Charles Jones and Don Rojas, administrator of the NCC's Burned Churches Fund, a partnership of mainstream religious organizations. IRD president, Diane Knippers, accused Jones of being the "architect of the NCC campaign to spotlight arsons against black churches as evidence of a dangerous surge of white racism in America,"[32] and of exploiting the church burnings "for unworthy political and fundraising purposes."[33] The NCC raised nearly $9 million for the Burned Churches Fund, $3.5 million of which, according to Jones, was earmarked for "program advocacy to address economic justice and interlocking oppressions from gender to homophobia."[34] NCC general secretary, Joan Brown Campbell, claimed that only 15 percent of the money will go toward these programs. The IRD charged that

> [t]he [Burned Churches] Fund has been advertised to the public through newspaper ads placed around the nation as a "joint mission to restore the damaged churches and to challenge racism throughout the country." Potential donors are given no clue about the large sums of money that the Fund will devote to controversial political projects that many people of faith would find inappropriate and not related to the task of resisting racism.[35]

In June 1997, the NCATF issued a report summarizing its investigation and reporting its findings. Despite the initial fears of a racist conspiracy targeting black churches, the NCATF found that the fires were "motivated by a wide array of factors, including not only blatant racism or religious hatred, but also financial profit, burglary, and personal revenge. Of 110 convictions 14 involved federal criminal civil rights charges.[36]

Conflicts over Labeling Individual Hate Crimes

The existence of the hate crime category assures a steady stream of decisions on whether to label particular incidents as hate crimes. In New York City, there have been a series of disputes about whether particular crimes, which all rational people condemn, should be labeled as hate crimes. Various newspapers and other media greet the labeling decision with praise or criticism. Whichever way the labeling decision goes, some journalists, advocacy organizations, politicians, and individuals charge the police and rival commentators, with hypocrisy, bias, double standards, and pandering to one group or another.

In 1992, a small group of Orthodox Jews was arrested for assaulting a homeless black man. They claimed that they restrained the man after he was found attempting to commit a burglary. The victim claimed he was looking through garbage cans for clothes. When the police determined that racial slurs were uttered during the incident, they labeled it a bias crime.[37] Some Jewish leaders criticized Mayor David Dinkins (NYC's first black mayor) for endorsing the label, and accused him of favoring black Crown Heights residents in everything from police protection to social service contracts.[38] Jewish leaders from Brooklyn neighborhoods such as Crown Heights, Borough Park, and Williamsburg, and from Manhattan's Lower East Side, denounced the mayor's handling of the incident as "repugnant," and an example of the city administration's double standard for appraising conflicts between blacks and Jews. The Jewish leaders pointed to an incident two months earlier, when a Brooklyn jury acquitted Lemerick Nelson of murder in the stabbing death of a rabbinical student during the 1990 Crown Heights riots; the mayor had not criticized the jury in that case, as he had done in several cases in which whites had been exonerated of crimes against blacks.[39] City Council President Andrew Stein criticized the mayor for "prematurely" labeling the present incident a bias crime.[40] Ultimately, the victim disappeared and all charges were dropped.

Another controversy flared over the police department's decision not to apply the bias crime label to the killing of John Kelly, a young black man. Kelly was beaten to death with a baseball bat at 4:00 A.M. in Queens, after he and a friend got into a confrontation with a group of white youths. Initially, police labeled the homicide a bias crime, but after interviewing witnesses they reclassified it.[41] Witnesses told police that Kelly initiated the fatal assault by threatening the white youths with a metal pipe, and that the white assailants shouted the racial epithet *during* the attack. Police explained that if the racial remark occurred *before* the fatal attack, the killing would have been labeled a bias crime. Deputy Chief Raymond Abruzzi stated, "We think it is just a macho incident that got out of hand."[42] Many blacks denounced the police's labeling decision as racist. Journalist and author, Michelle Fuller, wrote:

> I cannot understand why the police (and media) are taking pains to
> say that Kelly's murder is not "bias-related" because the word "nigger"
> was used after the alleged confrontation began. This is nonsense. To
> hit a human being whose skin color is different over the head with a

baseball bat with the intent to hurt severely or kill is racial. You cannot convince me otherwise.[43]

She branded as racist newspaper reports that prior to the attack, Kelly had seen a violent film, drank beer, smoked marijuana, and snorted cocaine.[44] Ultimately, no charges were brought against the perpetrators.

In December 1993, Colin Ferguson, a black man, boarded an evening rush hour Long Island Railroad commuter train packed mostly with white commuters and opened fire, killing six people and injuring 19 others. Police recovered from Ferguson's pocket a handwritten note titled, "Reasons for This." It expressed hatred toward whites, Asians, and "Uncle Tom blacks," and stated that Nassau County, Long Island was chosen as "the venue" because of its predominantly white population.[45] Despite clear evidence that racial animosity motivated Ferguson's shooting spree, commentators who ordinarily are quick to employ the hate crime label in cases of anti-black crimes, "puzzled . . . about how to classify the slaying."[46] Bob Purvis of the Center for Applied Study of Ethnoviolence, said that "technically" the LIRR massacre could be considered a hate crime, but such a characterization "would distort the accepted definition of bias-motivated attacks. . . . Mass murder is mass murder, it's not a hate crime."[47] Similarly, the Reverend Joseph Lowery of the Southern Christian Leadership Conference, stated that the LIRR massacre was not the type of crime he considered a hate crime, but "I think that man [Ferguson] was insane."[48] Professor Ronald Holmes, a sociologist and professor at the University of Louisville, conceded that Ferguson picked his victims on the basis of race, but did not think this justified the hate crime label. "He picked his victims and they were deserving in his mind. This person was disgruntled with the way things were going in society."[49]

Jim Sleeper, political columnist for the *New York Daily News*, deplored the failure of the media and politicians to label Ferguson a racist and to acknowledge a link between Ferguson's hatred against whites and the racist and anti-Semitic rhetoric of some black leaders.

> So why not give . . . attention to Ferguson's apparent susceptibility to the delusions of white conspiracy that have come to characterize some strains of black protest politics? Why not consider the influence of rhetoric that vilifies members of other groups, elevates rage to a virtue and speaks simplistically of "fighting the power" by any means necessary.[50]

Politicians who usually jump at the chance to condemn anti-black racism did not condemn Ferguson's mass murders as bias motivated. Historian, Richard F. Welch, highlighted this double standard in a scathing op-ed piece. Welch lambasted President Bill Clinton and Representative Charles Schumer (D-Brooklyn), who responded to the LIRR massacre with pleas for stricter gun control laws.

> The knee-jerk gun-control response allowed politicians and pundits to avoid dealing with the messy issue that provoked the massacre—black racism. . . . While any form of white racism is instantaneously denounced by all mainstream politicians and excoriated by the educational establishment and the media, its black counterpart, despite its glaring visibility, seldom evokes similar apprehension [or] condemnation.[51]

Other commentators argued that whether Ferguson was motivated by racism or not was irrelevant. Professor Marc Fleisher noted that Ferguson was charged with twelve counts of murder, nineteen counts of attempted murder, thirty-four counts of assault, and numerous firearms charges.[52] Although these counts exposed Ferguson to several hundred years in prison, the prosecutor also charged Ferguson with misdemeanor aggravated harassment under the New York Penal Law, for "intent to harass, annoy, threaten and alarm any person because of their race, color, or national origin."[53] Fleisher stated,

> Accordingly, [during trial], much of the focus will be on race and proving that had the train been filled with black people whom the deranged defendant would not consider to be "Uncle Toms," he would never have engaged in this carnage. Who benefits from this?"[54]

One of the surviving LIRR shooting victims said that all the conflict over the question of racism "misses the point and trivializes the horror."[55]

In 1989, the near-fatal rape and beating of a white female jogger in New York City's Central Park by a group of black and Hispanic youths generated extreme racial tension in the city, not because of the race and gender of the victim and the perpetrators, but because of the way the crime was politicized in service of identity politics. The police ultimately declined to label the incident a hate crime,[56] on the ground that the group of youths had assaulted and robbed other people in Central Park that same evening, including two Hispanic men. Surprisingly, the racist accusations came not from members of the victim's group, white women, but from New York City's two black newspapers, the *City Sun* and the *Amsterdam News*. The *Amsterdam News*, contrary to standard journalistic practice, printed the jogger's name and referred to her as an "alleged" victim, questioning whether the rape and beating actually occurred.[57] Wilbert Tatum, editor-in-chief, claimed that by printing the jogger's name, he was taking a stand against the racist injustice of naming the black suspects and not the white victim. Tatum stated that "[t]hese liberals [the mainstream New York newspapers] . . . saw no problem at all with naming Black children who got themselves caught up in the form of terrorizing for which the Black community has apologized on bended knee."[58]

Black critics accused the media of racism for calling the defendants a "wolf pack," and for describing the jogger as an "investment banker"; they charged that black crime victims are not described in terms of occupation.[59] Rev. Al Sharpton, the attorneys for the defendants, and black media, such as the *Amsterdam News* and radio station WBLI, all called the "white" media, the police, and later the trial judge racists. In a radio broadcast on WBLI, Alton Maddox, a key player in the Tawana Brawley case, stated:

> I have not seen any evidence of this woman being assaulted or attacked at all. . . . What are we going to do, accept some white person's word that she's over there . . . at Metropolitan Hospital? . . . This whole thing could be an outright hoax.[60]

City Sun editor, Utrice Leid, compared this crime to the Tawana Brawley case.

> The same media that demanded that Brawley "prove" her sexual assault made no such demands in the Central Park case. The same media had no difficulty identifying the underage Wappinger-Falls teenager by name [and] invading the sanctity of her home to show her face . . . have been careful to avoid identifying the Central Park woman. . . .[61]

During the two trials of five defendants (the sixth plead guilty), demonstrators gathered outside the courthouse to protest racism in the judicial system: they charged that the judge, the prosecutor, the police, and the jogger were all part of a racist conspiracy to convict six innocent black youths. The evidence against the defendants was very strong. It included videotaped confessions, identification of the defendants by the other victims attacked that same evening, and grass, mud, and hair matching the jogger's on one defendant's underwear.

Protesters outside the courthouse called white passersby "white racists," and chanted "Why are they trying to lynch these boys?"[62] Wilbert Tatum of the *Amsterdam News* wrote, "[t]he truth of the matter is that there is a conspiracy of interest attendant in this case that dictates that someone Black must go to jail for this crime against the 'jogger': and any Black will do."[63] Each defendant was convicted of a variety of charges and sentenced to prison terms ranging from one and one-half to fifteen years.[64]

The Central Park jogger case stands as one of the most racially polarizing criminal trials of the 1980s. Instead of bringing New Yorkers together in condemnation of a horrendous crime, the case divided the city along racial lines. In addition, many women were outraged that a gang rape did not qualify as a hate crime. But would this polarization have been lessened by a hate crime designation? Or would the spectacle of the prosecution attempting to prove the defendants' bias—against whites, women, or white women—have exacerbated tensions in New York City?

Retaliation and False Reporting

As the Tawana Brawley case demonstrates,[65] false claims about interracial and other intergroup crimes can occur without special hate crime laws and an official hate crime labeling apparatus. But the hate crime laws heightened the visibility of such crimes, and may therefore encourage some individuals to claim falsely that they were the victim of prejudice-motivated violence in order to strike a blow against a group they dislike or fear, or simply because they crave attention and publicity.

According to Migdalia Maldonado, a former Brooklyn assistant district attorney in the civil rights bureau:

> Given the heightened social awareness of bias crime and the concomitant special attention that allegations of this sort receive from law enforcement officials and the media, the complainant is keenly aware that if the crime perpetrated against him or her is deemed a bias crime, he or she will be accorded special protections, and the perpetrator will be dealt with more harshly by the courts. A complainant, therefore, has an incentive to tailor his or her presentation of facts so as to obtain a bias crime designation. This motive . . . leads to a relatively high incidence of false reports.[66]

In one case of false reporting, three fifteen-year-old white girls told police that a dozen black teenagers assaulted and cut them with knives on the way to school on Staten Island. Ultimately, the girls admitted that they made up the story and cut themselves in order to get a day off from school.[67] Another false report involved an Iranian woman in Fargo, North Dakota. The woman, a restaurant owner, was found bound, with a knife wound, amid a fire set by an arsonist in the restaurant.[68] Reports of the attack set off a community uproar. The night after the incident approximately 1,000 people marched against bigotry. Another rally was held the next evening. After examining the woman's wounds, the police grew suspicious. The U.S. Attorney stated that the slash wounds were self-inflicted. After the hoax was exposed, a city commissioner said the rally and speeches against bigotry and hate were not "for naught." The people who marched did it for the right reason.[69] A similar rationale emerged in the wake of the Tawana Brawley hoax. Attorney William Kunstler dismissed the importance of whether Brawley had been raped. "It makes no difference whether the attack on Tawana really happened. It doesn't disguise the fact that a lot of black women are treated the way she said she was treated."[70] This view comes close to claiming that reports of hate crimes are healthy and therapeutic for the society.

Because of the raw nerve they irritate, it is politically difficult for the police and the mayor to announce that a claimed bias crime was a hoax. Consider the case involving charges by two black children that on January 6, 1992, white assailants had robbed them of their lunch money and sprayed them with white shoe polish.[71] For weeks, scores of detectives conducted hundreds of interviews and scoured the neighborhood where the crime occurred. A $20,000 reward for information leading to the arrest of the offenders was offered, and a telephone hotline was set up. Ultimately, no witnesses came forward, and police apparently concluded that the assault was a hoax. However, local politicians demanded that the investigation continue and excoriated any talk of the charges being unfounded. The case had spilled out of the criminal justice system into the city's racial politics.[72] Finally, Police Commissioner Lee Brown agreed to keep the case officially "open," but terminated the investigation.

The alleged shoe polish assault touched off numerous retaliatory bias crimes. Between January 6, 1992, when the attack was reported, and January 28th, 61 bias crimes were reported, 14 of which occurred in the Bronx neighborhood where the shoe polish attack had been reported. A group of black youths committed three separate retaliatory attacks; they robbed a Hispanic girl, punched and kicked an Indian girl on a city bus after demanding, "Is [sic] there any white people on the bus?", and beat up two Hispanic boys.[73] In another retaliatory attack, three black men on the subway slapped a white man in the face, telling him, "this is for what happened in the Bronx." In Brooklyn, a white homeless man was punched in the face by two black men who said, "How about we paint you white, whitey?"[74] In a predominantly Polish apartment house in Brooklyn, anti-white graffiti was spray painted in the hallway. Police explained that the apparent surge in bias crimes was a predictable phenomenon that often occurs in the aftermath of a widely publicized bias crime.[75]

Such a cluster often begins with an extraordinary single incident that strikes an emotional chord with the public and the media. . . . And it is followed by a spate of other episodes with a variety of motives: some are retaliatory, some copycat, some simply everyday discord drawn under the hot spotlight of public attention.[76]

Conclusion

The proponents of bias crime laws believe that their symbolic impact will be to teach Americans that prejudice is wrong and, in the long run, lead to less prejudice and less prejudice-motivated crime. We have argued in this chapter that this belief may be misguided. Breaking down generic criminal law into new crimes and punishment hierarchies depending on the prejudices of offenders and the demographic identities of victims may exacerbate rather than ameliorate social schisms and conflicts.

Crime ought to be a social problem that brings together and unites all Americans. All law-abiding citizens oppose criminality and sympathize with crime victims. By condemning and punishing criminals, Americans ought to be affirming the values and norms that they share. However, bias crime laws and their enforcement redefine crime as one more arena for intergroup conflict. The hate crime laws and their enforcement have the potential to undermine social solidarity by redefining crime as a subcategory of the intergroup struggles between races, ethnic groups, religious groups, genders, and people of different sexual orientations.

With the emergence of hate crime law, jurisprudence, and politics, we are no longer dealing with crime and garden variety criminals, but with racists and sexists and a society irrevocably divided among victims' groups. The politics involved in passing hate crime laws reinforces identity politics; so too does the collection and reporting of hate crime statistics, which are invariably cited to support the proposition that each group's victimization at the hands of other groups is worsening. Finally, the process of labeling intergroup crimes as bias-motivated or not generates constant, low-level, intergroup strife.

10

Policy Recommendations

*T*HIS BOOK OFFERS an extended argument against the formulation and enforcement of hate crime laws. These well-intentioned laws represent the importation of identity politics into criminal law by seeking to give special recognition to the victimization of members of historically discriminated against groups. But the fit is, at best, uneasy.

First, when it comes to hate crime we are not dealing with otherwise legal behavior (like hiring decisions) that ought to be illegal when carried out in a discriminatory manner; without laws like Title VII and others, discrimination would go unredressed. The underlying conduct covered by hate crime laws is already prohibited by criminal statutes; the state has an interest in punishing such conduct regardless of motivation. Second, the civil rights laws attempt to rectify gross power imbalances in the society by providing remedies against illegal discriminatory action by the government and by powerful private sector institutions. By contrast, it is almost bizarre to talk about encouraging criminals to choose their victims on a nondiscriminatory basis. Moreover, in comparison with the individuals who engage in employment, housing, and election discrimination, a significant percentage of prejudiced offenders are themselves members of minority groups. Third, enhancing the punishment of prejudiced criminals does not provide victims a "remedy" against criminals' discriminatory conduct. The enforcement of generic criminal law is adequate to vindicate the interests of "hate crime" victims as it is of other crime victims. Most important, hate crime laws may not promote social harmony but, to the contrary, may reinforce social divisions and exacerbate social conflict. Thus, our primary recommendation is clear: repeal the new wave of hate crime laws and enforce the generic criminal laws evenhandedly and without prejudice.

145

Define Hate Crime Narrowly

It a serious mistake for the government to pursue the goal of seeking to identify and highlight the maximum possible amount of prejudice in the crime problem by counting as a hate crime every offense motivated *in any degree* by the offender's prejudice. This definition sweeps under the hate crime umbrella crimes involving low-intensity prejudices that bubble to the surface during ad hoc conflicts. The majority of hate crimes turn out to be fights involving epithets rather than "hard core" ideologically driven violence by people identified with extremist groups or causes. Because the former are much more numerous than the latter, the numbers suggest a picture of American society as a conglomeration of clashing identity groups. Defining the prejudice-motivated criminal as a group representative rather than as a lone outlaw transforms the social understanding of crime from aberrant and deviant behavior into the kind of sociopolitical conflict among broad social groupings that marks the current situation in the former Yugoslavia.

If a hate crime category is required, we favor the narrowest possible definition, something like "those criminal acts primarily motivated by the actor's hatred for a particular group." Another alternative would be to define hate crime to require a showing, in addition to the narrow definition above, that the offender's conduct was linked, in some way, to furthering the ideology and goals of a recognized racist, anti-Semitic, or other such group. (Even then there will be great disagreement over what constitutes a recognized hate group.) Such a definition would conform to many peoples' impression of what is meant by the term "hate crime."

Repeal the Hate Crime Reporting Statutes

Hate crime cannot be accurately counted because, given the ambiguous, subjective, and contentious concept of prejudice, it cannot be accurately defined. Anything like an accurate accounting is also doomed by the difficulty of reliably determining the motivation of individual and group offenders.

The FBI's annual reports, produced pursuant to the Hate Crime Statistics Act of 1990, have been fragmentary, nonuniform, and distortive. They have shed much more heat than light. Clearly, they have not contributed to a more accurate understanding of crime, prejudice, or prejudice-motivated crime in American society; nor have these reports laid the basis for more effective law enforcement. If anything, some journalists, advocacy groups, and academics have used this government-sponsored hate crime accounting system to create the false impression that the nation is experiencing an epidemic of prejudice-motivated crime of every kind. Then pundits and commentators claim that the statistics only represent the tip of the iceberg, that is, they indicate massive prejudice among the vast majority of law-abiding citizens. Some writers find in the statistics evidence of an imminent race war. Ironically, all this stems from a well-meaning effort to make a symbolic gesture denouncing racist, sexist, anti-Semitic, and other prejudice-driven crimes. But the net effect is to exacerbate social and political tension. The long term consequence may be to reinforce a sense of group victimization and grievance like that which exists in the Balkans where one journalist has observed:

> The aggrieved innocence so commonly and unaffectedly displayed by individual [Serbian] fighters made it clear that they felt themselves and not those they were killing or displacing to be the real victims of the war. And like victims everywhere, they thirsted for what they usually called justice but were sometimes willing to categorize as revenge.[1]

Repeal the Hate Crime Sentence Enhancement Statutes

We do not believe that crimes motivated by hate invariably are morally worse or lead to more severe consequences for victims than the same criminal act prompted by other motivations. Of course, assassinations and firebombings rooted in prejudice and hate deserve the severest punishments, but so do all assassinations and firebombings. Generic criminal and sentencing laws provide draconian penalties, including the death penalty in some jurisdictions, for murder, terrorism, and bombings. There is no need for, and sometimes no possibility of, more severe penalties when such terrible crimes are motivated by anti-Semitism, misogyny, or other prejudices. It would certainly be ironic if the consequence of the importation of the civil rights paradigm into criminal law was the execution of prejudiced murderers, some percentage of whom would be blacks and members of other minority groups.

We do not believe that across-the-board sentence enhancement for hate crimes can be justified. The breadth of the definition of hate crime means that the typical hate crime will not be a neo-Nazi assassination of a civil rights worker but, more likely, a fight in a campground or on a basketball court involving the utterance of a racist, sexist, or other bigoted epithet. Further, most crimes labeled as hate crime are committed by young people, a high percentage of them juveniles.

To punish prejudiced offenders two or three times more severely than otherwise similarly situated offenders strains constitutional doctrine and violates principles of proportionality. We think that the Supreme Court had it right in *R.A.V.* and wrong in *Mitchell.* Enhancing the criminal sentence because of the offender's prejudiced motivation is essentially punishing the offender for his beliefs and opinions. While we have no doubt that holding and acting on negative stereotypes and prejudiced beliefs is wrong and ought to be condemned, punishing an offender whose crime traces to such views twice or three times more severely than his fellow otherwise-motivated colleague in crime seems to us disproportionate punishment and a violation of the First Amendment.

Judicially Imposed Enhancements Are Just as Offensive as Legislatively Imposed Enhancements

Traditionally, judges have had discretion, within a range (i.e., a maximum and a minimum), to set criminal sentences according to whatever criteria they thought appropriate. Under the discretionary sentencing regime, a judge can sentence an offender to the highest allowable sentence on such grounds as lack of remorse, likelihood of future dangerousness, or for no articulable reason whatsoever. For example, some judges might sentence young offenders to longer terms believing, perhaps, that they will be "scared straight"; other judges might sentence young offenders more leniently because they do not regard them as fully responsible for their conduct. Some judges might sentence prejudiced offenders more severely on the ground that prejudice is an evil that deserves punishment in its own right; other judges might believe that prejudice is a kind of disease or that it is the product of bad socialization and therefore deserves less punishment.

The regime of untrammeled judicial sentencing discretion came under a barrage of political and jurisprudential attacks in the 1970s and 1980s. One of the most potent criticisms was that sentencing discretion could be used in furtherance of the judge's conscious or unconscious prejudices. The attack on indeterminate sentencing led the federal government and a number of states to pass sentencing guidelines specifying factors (such as seriousness of the offense and prior criminal record) that should enhance a sentence above a presumptive level. Until the federal Hate Crime Sentencing Enhancement Act (HCSEA), no sentencing guidelines system defined prejudice as a sentence enhancing factor and, for the reasons stated in the previous paragraph, we think the HCSEA was a mistake.

The majority of states have retained the judicial discretion model that allows judges to impose higher sentences on the basis of aggravating factors, such as lack of remorse, cold-bloodedness, or because of the offender's biases, ideologies, and conspiratorial affiliations. If it is inappropriate and unconstitutional for a legislature to enhance punishment for graffiti and vandalism on the ground that it expresses offensive ideas and beliefs, it must be similarly inappropriate and unconstitutional for a sentencing judge to mete out extra punishment for those same reasons.

Sentence Enhancements for Low-Level Hate Crimes

Many readers may find that they readily agree with us that it makes no sense to call a prejudice-motivated murder or rape "worse" than an otherwise-motivated murder and rape. In any event, even if hate-motivated murder or rape is worse, there is not much room for extra punishment. But these readers may have the intuition that when it comes to low-level offenses, like vandalism and graffiti, the prejudice-motivated offense is morally worse and causes more pain. For example, it is a common and understandable to believe that defacing public or private property with a swastika or a "KKK" is more disturbing and upsetting, at least to Jews and blacks respectively, than graffiti that carries no additional symbolic message.

We agree; words and symbols hurt. But should the cross burner, swastika painter, or KKK drawer be punished more severely? If we go down that road, won't we have to sort out all crass symbols and expressions into two piles—those that are really offensive and merit extra punishment and those that are not and do not? Consider common graffiti words like "bitch," "cunt," "fag," "gook," "dyke," "prick," "fatso," and so on—do we really want a legislature to sort them all into one of two categories? Does anyone really think that such an exercise would be consistent with First Amendment values? We think the criminal law is on safer ground, focusing on the extent of damage and defacement rather than the offensiveness of the expressive message.

The Federal Criminal Civil Rights Statutes

The usefulness of the federal criminal statutes that punish government officials and ordinary citizens for violating the rights of their fellow citizens are not called into question by our critique. These statutes are important because they can be called into service when state and local law enforcement is nonexistent or ineffective because of the prejudices of state and local law enforcement officials themselves. They do not implement subjective sociopolitical distinctions about which ethnic, religious, racial, or sexual orientation groups are entitled to "more protection," in the odd sense that those who victimize their members for prejudice reasons are punished more severely. These laws simply say that the violation of *everybody's* constitutional and statutory rights is punishable by the sovereign that guarantees those rights; that is very different from the hate crime laws that define some biases as more abhorrent than others.

A Cautionary Note on the "Rehabilitation" of Hate Crime Offenders

The creation of hate crime offenses has led inexorably to the proliferation of proposals for novel sanctions. Thus, it has been suggested that hate crime offenders, in particular low-level offenders, should be rehabilitated, not punished, and a number of jurisdictions have begun meting out sanctions designed to correct wrongful prejudice. The key question in assessing such proposals is the meaning of "rehabilitated." We can imagine so-called rehabilitation programs that give cause for concern. Suppose that a highly politicized criminal justice system picked up juveniles and low-level offenders for all sorts of crimes that are usually not punished, or punished only lightly, and used the arrest as a hook to force the offender into programs to correct their thinking—that is, persuade them to adopt the "right position" on gay marriage, affirmative action, and multicultural history curricula. One need go no further than Richard Bernstein's description of politically correct college orientation programs, or Todd Gitlin's recitation of the school curriculum debates in California, to realize that there are serious dangers lurking here.[2] Suppose the offender, undergoing such "treatment," had to pass a test showing proper attitudes, values, and beliefs in order to be released?

Not all reeducation programs sponsored by the criminal justice system ought to be rejected as unacceptable forays into reprogramming for political correctness. In spring 1997, a fourteen-year-old youth arrested in Westchester County, New York for a series of swastika incidents that had greatly upset the community was sentenced to read *The Diary of Ann Frank*. To us, that seems to be reasonable, as long as the sanction does not require at the end that the juvenile adhere to a list of correct positions. Nevertheless, it is easy to imagine how such sanctions could lead us down the road to having to opine about the appropriateness of a vast number of books, articles, and curricula that involve literature, history, and sociology that would attract varying levels of consensus and support.

The line between education and indoctrination may be fuzzy, but it is important that we be alert to staying on the right side of the line. Rather than subjecting only hate crime offenders to thought reform programs focusing on the group targeted by a particular offender, we are more comfortable with "education" for all offenders regarding good citizenship. We can imagine "educational" programs whereby offenders are subjected, even involuntarily, to a course about America's history, its constitution, and its laws and to the contribution of minorities and women to American society. This would seem perfectly appropriate and desirable.

What's To Be Done?

In the second half of the twentieth century, the United States has made tremendous strides toward becoming a more tolerant multicultural society. Schools and other public institutions in the South were desegregated, job and educational discrimination has been significantly eradicated (although not completely), gays and lesbians are much better able to live openly, and misogyny is every day being confronted. Of course, we have a long way to go, but we can also take pride in having come a very long way. For our purposes, the point is that the progress that has been made over these five decades has very little to do with criminal law. We have not punished our way along the road to a more tolerant society. In fact, it is quite likely that the criminal justice system has been more of an impediment than a facilitator of positive social change in this area.

The criminal law and its enforcement have, at most, only a limited role to play in producing a more tolerant and harmonious society, but it has enormous potential, through the misuse of authority and power, to sew the seeds of dissension and conflict. There is no greater source of grievance for minority groups than not being treated fairly by the government, especially by the police and the courts. Chants of "no justice, no peace" only dramatize how salient issues of criminal justice are for minority communities. Practically every urban riot in the last several decades has been touched off by actual or perceived police misconduct. Blacks, Hispanics, and other minorities have long charged, and with much justification, that they are the victims of police harassment and abuse of force. Women, as well as gays and lesbians, have rightly been outraged when the police, because of their prejudices, have ignored or disregarded crimes against them. Thus, the most important contribution that the criminal justice system can make to social harmony is the avoidance of unfair treatment and discrimination against offenders as well as victims. Unfair treatment can range from brutality to hassling to disrespect to insensitivity.

Unfortunately, it is a historical fact that the police and other agencies of criminal justice, at least at some times and places, have discriminated against blacks, gays and lesbians, Hispanics, Asians, women, and the full range of white ethnic groups. Such discrimination has sometimes taken the form of more aggressive and harsher treatment of minority offenders and less serious punishments for those who victimize racial and ethnic minorities, gays and lesbians, and women. Fortunately, there is good reason to believe that the civil rights movement, the women's movement, the gay rights movement, and other movements of the last several decades have substantially reduced such discriminatory and prejudiced treatment by the agencies and officials of the state. Increasing the number of minorities who serve in police departments and in the other agencies of criminal justice is vital and has made a major difference. Nevertheless, the legacy of discrimination lingers and sometimes flares, as in the beating administered to Rodney King by members of the Los Angeles Police Department.

It is crucial to building a more harmonious society that the police and other criminal justice agencies enforce, and be seen as enforcing, the criminal law fairly, both in the treatment of offenders and in the regard for victims. However questionable affirmative action may be in other societal contexts, there could be nothing more damaging to American society than an all "white" criminal justice system vigorously enforcing the law against members of minority groups and against their communities.

It makes sense for large police departments and even some district attorneys' offices to maintain community relations units. The primary purpose of such units should not be to ensure more severe punishments for prejudice-motivated crimes, but to ensure that the complaints of historically discriminated against groups are listened to and evaluated and that their communities are assisted in dealing with crime problems, most of which, of course, are intragroup not intergroup. In a sense, the philosophy behind such units lays the basis for today's community policing movement: the police should be an arm of the community not a fist in the face of the community. The community relations unit must listen to and address the concerns of the "community," especially groups historically slighted by, discriminated against, and abused by the police and other criminal justice agencies. Police and prosecutors must make fairness and evenhandedness their top priority. We cannot have a successful democracy unless the institutions of criminal justice, which wield the heavy hand of state power, are widely judged as fair and legitimate. Purging the criminal justice system of prejudice and discrimination must continue to be the lodestar of those employed by, professionally committed to, and interested in the criminal justice system.

Certainly, crime is a problem in the United States today. But the crime problem is not synonymous with the prejudice problem; indeed, there is very little overlap between the two. With the important exception of crime against women, most crime is intraracial and intragroup. Hard core ideologically driven hate crimes are fortunately rare. Teasing out the bias that exists in a wider range of context-specific crimes that may occur between members of different groups serves no useful purpose. To the contrary, it is likely to be divisive, conflict-generating, and socially and politically counterproductive.

Notes

Chapter 1

1. Hate Crime Statistics Act of 1990, Public Law No. 100–275, 104 Stat. 140 (1990).

2. John Leo, "The Politics of Hate," U.S. News & World Report, Oct. 9, 1989, p. 24.

3. Lester Olmstead-Rose, Hate Violence: Symptom of Prejudice, 17 William Mitchell Law Review 439 (Spring 1991).

4. Olmstead-Rose, Hate Violence, p. 441.

5. See Charles L. Sykes, A Nation of Victims (New York: St. Martin's Press, 1992); Dinesh D'Souza, Illiberal Education: The Politics of Race and Sex on Campus (New York: Free Press, 1991); Joseph Epstein, "The Joys of Victimhood," N.Y. Times Magazine, July 2, 1988, p. 20; Democratic Leadership Council, "Getting Beyond Victimization," 5 The New Democrat 4 (November 1993). For a chilling discussion of ethnic conflict, victim politics, and genocide, see David Reiff, Slaughterhouse: Bosnia and the Failure of the West (New York: Simon & Schuster, 1995).

6. Samuel Walker, Hate Speech: The History of an American Controversy (Lincoln: University of Nebraska Press, 1994); Milton Heumann, Thomas Church, & David Redlawsk, Hate Speech on Campus: Cases, Case Studies, and Commentary (Boston: Northeastern University Press, 1997); Henry Louis Gates, Jr., Anthony P. Griffin, Donald E. Lively, Robert C. Post, William B. Rubenstein, & Nadine Strossen, Speaking of Race, Speaking of Sex (New York: NYU Press, 1994).

7. Heumann, et al., Hate Speech on Campus.

8. Gary Wills, "The Turner Diaries," New York Review of Books, August 10, 1995, p. 50 (book review); Chip Barlet & Matthew N. Lyons, "Militia Nation," The Progressive, June 1995, p. 22.

9. Jack Levin & Jack McDevitt, Hate Crimes: The Rising Tide of Bigotry and Bloodshed (New York: Plenum Press, 1993) pp. xi, 113–14.

10. Niel Gilbert, "Advocacy Research and Social Policy, p. 101, in Michael Tonry, ed., Crime and Justice: A Review of Research, Vol. 22 (Chicago: University of Chicago Press, 1997); Stanley Cohen, Folk Devils and Moral Panics (London: MacGibbon and Kee, 1972); Joel Best, Threatened Children: Rhetoric and Concern About Child Victims (Chicago: University of Chicago Press, 1990).

11. Joel Best, "Missing Children, Misleading Statistics," 92 The Public Interest 84 (Summer 1988).

12. James B. Jacobs, Drunk Driving: An American Dilemma (Chicago: University of Chicago Press, 1989).

13. Christopher Jencks, The Homeless (Cambridge: Harvard University Press, 1994).

Chapter 2

1. Robert M. Baird & Stuart E. Rosenbaum, eds., Bigotry, Prejudice & Hatred: Definitions, Causes & Solutions (Buffalo, NY: Prometheus Books, 1992), p. 13.

2. Abraham Kaplan, "Equality," in Baird & Rosenbaum, eds., Bigotry, Prejudice & Hatred, p. 21.

3. Gordon Allport, The Nature of Prejudice (New York: Addison-Wesley, 1954), p. 363.

4. Allport, The Nature of Prejudice, p. 363.

5. Ibid., p. 25.

6. Ibid., p. 26.

7. Charles Murray & Richard Herenstein, The Bell Curve (New York: Free Press, 1994).

8. Allport, The Nature of Prejudice, p. 372.

9. Ibid., p. 12.

10. International Encyclopedia of the Social Sciences (1968), p. 444.

11. Charles R. Lawrence III, "The Id, the Ego, and Equal Protection: Reckoning with Unconscious Racism," 39 Stanford Law Review 317, 335 (1987), citing Joel Kovel, White Racism: A Psychohistory (1970), pp. 54–55.

12. The Gallup Poll, Public Opinion 1993, p. 178.

13. Ibid., p. 179.

14. Lawrence, "The Id, the Ego & Equal Protection," p. 322.

15. Adam Jukes, Why Men Hate Women (London: Free Association Books, 1993), p. 1.

16. Jukes, Why Men Hate Women, p. xxix.

17. See Richard Bernstein, Dictatorship of Virtue (New York: Vintage Books, 1994), p. 189.

18. Dinesh D'Souza, Illiberal Education: The Politics of Race and Sex on Campus (New York: Free Press, 1991), p. 8.

19. Andrew M. Greeley, "Unpleasant Truth of Anti-Catholicism Seen in Survey," The Arizona Republic, April 16, 1994, p. C1.

20. Greeley, "Unpleasant Truth of Anti-Catholicism," p. C1.

21. For an extensive examination of this perception, see Jim Sleeper, The Closest of Strangers (New York: W.W. Norton, 1990).

22. Bureau of Justice Statistics, Highlights From 20 Years of Surveying Crime Victims: The National Crime Victimization Survey, 1972–92 (Oct. 1993), p. 23.

23. Bureau of Justice Statistics, Violent State Prisoners and Their Victims (July 1990), p. 5.

24. BJS, Violent State Prisoners, p. 5.

25. Ibid., p. 5.

26. Marc L. Fleischauer, "Teeth for a Paper Tiger: A Proposal to Add Enforceability to Florida's Hate Crimes Act," 17 Florida State University Law Review 697, 706 (1990).

27. Carey Goldberg, "Neighbors Play Down Race, Seeing Act of Crazy Man," New York Times, Dec. 10, 1995, at 50.

28. Pedro Ponce, "Some Question Use of Hate-Crime Laws by Victimized Whites," The San Diego Union-Tribune, May 5, 1994, p. A36.

29. Fleischauer, "Teeth for a Paper Tiger," p. 706; Paul Butler, "Racially Based Jury Nullification: Black Power in the Criminal Justice System," 105 Yale Law Journal 677 (1995); Note, "Combatting Racial Violence: A Legislative Proposal," 101 Harvard Law Review 1270 (1988).

30. "The Shame of Black Rage Defense," Chicago Tribune, Perspective, June 6, 1994; Jim Sleeper, "Racial Roots of the LIRR Massacre," The Daily News, December 23, 1993, p. 49.

31. Wendy Melillo & Hamil Harris, "Dissent Raised as Ex-Farrakhan Aide Returns to Howard U.," Washington Post, April 20, 1994, p. B1.

32. "Conviction in Jogger Case is for Attempted Murder; Minor Could Get Up to Ten Years in Prison," Washington Post, Dec. 12, 1990 at p. A6.

33. Sleeper, The Closest of Strangers, p. 19.

34. "Labels Mask 'Latino' Diversity," 22 The Ford Foundation Letter, 10–11 (1991); Peter Skerry, "The New Politics of Assimilation," 3 City Journal 6–7 (1993); Jim Sleeper, In Defense of Civic Culture (Washington, D.C.: Progressive Foundation, 1993).

35. Adrienne T. Washington, "Touchy Topic Fits in District," The Washington Times, Oct. 10, 1994, p. C6; "Fired Beauty School Employee Loses Bias Suit," Pennsylvania Law Weekly, April 17, 1995, p. 5.

36. Bureau of Justice Statistics, Violence Against Women: Estimates from the Redesigned Survey (August 1995), p. 2.

37. Nan D. Hunter, et al. The Rights of Lesbians and Gay Men (Carbondale: Southern Illinois University Press, 1992).

38. Jonathan Katz, Gay American History: Lesbians and Gay Men in the U.S.A. (New York: Crowell, 1976); Eric Marcus, Making History: The Struggle for Gay and Lesbian Equal Rights (New York: HarperCollins, 1992).

39. In 1967, Congress passed the Age Discrimination in Employment Act, which outlawed discrimination based on age. 29 U.S.C. §§ 621–634 (1988).

40. N. R. Kleinfeld, "Bias Crimes Hold Steady, But Leave Many Scars," New York Times, January 27, 1992, p. A1.

41. James Coates, Armed and Dangerous: The Rise of the Survivalist Right (New York: Hill & Wang, 1987), pp. 7–8, 66.

42. Francis X. Clines, "Gunman in a Train Aisle Passes Out Death," New York *Times*, Dec. 9, 1993, Sec. A, p. 3.

43. Clines, "Gunman in a Train Aisle," p. 10; Laurie Wilson, "Scholars Say NY Attack Hard to Assess," The Dallas Morning News, Dec. 9, 1993, p. A14.

44. Wilson, "Scholars Say NY Attack Hard to Assess," p. A14.

45. Torri Minton, "Quiet Marin Confronts Hate Crimes," San Francisco Chronicle, Nov. 29, 1995, p. A13.

46. Jacob Sullum, "How Perilous are Hate Crimes?" Sacramento Bee, Dec. 6, 1992, p. F1.

47. Pam Belluck, "Police Say Killer in Harlem Fire Was a Laborer and a Protester," New York Times, Dec. 11, 1995, p. A1.

48. Clyde Haberman, "Badly Needed: More Speakers Against Extremism," New York Times, Dec. 11, 1995, p. B3.

49. Sylvia Adcock, "Rifkin Jury Search Grinds On," Newsday, April 16, 1994, p. 12.

50. Shirley E. Perlman, "Talks with Joel, Psychiatrist: Rifkin Lived Out Fantasies of Sex, Violence," Newsday, May 4, 1994, p. 3.

51. Dawson v. Delaware, 112 S.Ct. 1093, 1098 (1992).

52. Jo Thomas, "Bank Robbery Trial Offers a Glimpse of a Right-Wing World," New York Times, January 9, 1997, p. A12.

53. Wiley A. Hall, "Color of Crime is Green, Not Black or White," The Baltimore Sun, Jan. 6, 1994, p. A2.

54. Elaine Silverstrini, "Man Jailed, Defaced Church, Temple," Asbury Park Press, Oct. 7, 1995, p. A4.

55. Rick Bragg, "Killings Jolt Fort Bragg Area Back to an Angry, Ugly Past," New York Times, Dec. 11, 1995, p. A1.

56. In re Joshua H., 17 Cal. Rptr. 291, 293–95 (1993).

57. Paul J. Toomey, "Prosecutor Calls Sign Theft a Bias Crime," The Bergen Record, December 31, 1993, p. B1.

Chapter 3

1. Mont. Code Ann. § 45-5-222. Montana also created a separate substantive hate crime offense modeled after the ADL intimidation statute. See Mont. Code Ann. § 45-4-221. The sentence enhancement provision applies to *all other crimes* where bias is the motive.

2. Code of Ala. §13A-5-13. For a Class B felony, the minimum sentence is 10 years, and for misdemeanors, the minimum sentence is three months.

3. Vt. Stat. Ann. tit. 13, §§ 1454 & 1455.

4. Fla. Stat. Ann. § 775.085.

5. 113 S.Ct. 2194 (1993).

6. Pub. L. No. 102–322.

7. 18 U.S.C. Appendix § 3A1.1.

8. Lu-in Wang, Hate Crimes Law (New York: Clark Boardman Callaghan, 1995), Appendix B.

9. Ibid.

10. Vt. Stat. Ann. tit. 13, § 1455.

11. Mont. Code Ann. §§ 45-5-221.

12. Pa. Cons. Stat. § 2710(a); Vt. Stat. Ann. tit. 13, § 1455; Code of Ala. § 13A-5-13.

13. Code of Ala. § 13A-5-13.

14. Ohio Rev. Code Ann. § 2927.12.

15. N.J. Stat. Ann. § 2C:12-1.

16. Ill. Juris. Crim. Law & Proc. § 61:02.

17. D.C. Code Ann. § 22-4001.

18. Ill. Comp. Stats. Ann. ch. 720, § 5/12-7.1; Ohio Rev. Code nn. 2927.12; Nev. Rev. Stats. Ann. § 207.185.

19. S.D. Cod. Laws § 22-19B-1; Ore. Rev. Stats. § 166.155; Okla. Stats. § 850; N.C. Gen. Stats. § 14-401-14.

20. Conn. Gen. Stats. § 53a-181b; Ann. Rev. Code Wash. § 9A.36.080.

21. D.C. Code § 22-4001. (Authors' emphasis.)

22. State v. Stalder, 630 So.2d 1072, 1076–77 (1994).

23. Wisc. Stats. § 939.645; Cal. Penal Code § 190.2(a) (16); Ore. Rev. Stats. § 166.165.

24. In re M.S., 42 Cal. Rptr. 2d 355 (1995); People v. Aishman, 22 Cal. Rptr. 2d 311, 319 (Ct. App.), review granted, 862 P.2d 663 (1993); State v. Plowman, 838 P.2d 558 (Ore. 1992).

25. Wang, Hate Crimes Law, p. 10–16 and 10–17.

26. Commonwealth v. Ferino, 640 A.2d 934, 938 (1994).

27. ADL, Hate Crime Statutes: A 1991 Status Report, p. 4.

28. State v. Wyant, 597 N.E.2d 450 (1992), *vacated & remanded*, 113 S.Ct. 2954 (1993), *reversed*, 624 N.E. 2d 722 (1994).

29. Larry Rohter, "Without Smiling, to Call Floridian a 'Cracker' May be a Crime," New York Times, August 25, 1991, at A1; "Hate Crime Charge Hinges on Term 'Cracker,'" United Press International, July 9, 1991; "Hate Crime Charge Dropped Against Black Man in Florida," New York Times, August 31, 1991, at A10.

30. State v. Stalder, 630 So.2d 1072 (1994).

31. ADL, Hate Crime Statutes: A 1991 Status Report, p. 4.

32. Ibid.

33. Conn. Penal Code § 53a-181b.

34. Mich. Comp. Laws Ann. § 750.147b; Alaska Stat. § 12.55.155 (c) (22).

35. N.Y. Penal Law § 240.30(3) (McKinney 1988).

36. 141 Misc.2d 6, 532 N.Y.S.2d 815 (N.Y. Crim. Ct. 1988).

37. Susan Gellman, "Sticks and Stones Can Put You in Jail, But Can Words Increase Your Sentence? Constitutional and Policy Dilemmas of Ethnic Intimidation Laws," 39 UCLA Law Review 333 (1991).

38. Richard O. Curry, ed., Radicalism, Racism and Party Realignment: The Border States During the Reconstruction (Baltimore, MD: Johns Hopkins

Press, 1969); Leon F. Litwack, Been in the Storm So Long: The Aftermath of Slavery (New York: Knopf, 1979); Eric Foner, Reconstruction: America's Unfinished Revolution (New York: Harper & Row, 1988).

39. For a history of the post-Civil War statutes, see Frederick M. Lawrence, "Civil Rights and Criminal Wrongs: The Mens Rea of Federal Civil Rights Crimes," 67 Tulane Law Review 2113 (1993).

40. Lawrence, "Civil Rights and Criminal Wrongs," p. 2229.

41. 18 U.S.C. 241.

42. If the offense results in bodily injury, or involves the use or threatened use of a dangerous weapon, explosives, or firearm, the offender faces up to ten years imprisonment. A life sentence or the death penalty may be imposed if the offense results in death or involves the predicate offenses listed in § 241.18 U.S.C. 242.

43. United States v. Classic, 313 U.S. 299 (1941).

44. United States v. Senak, 527 F.2d 129 (7th Cir. 1975), cert. denied, 425 U.S. 907 (1976) (holding that public defender violated § 242 by charging fees for legal services, which he was required to provide for free, and threatening inadequate representation unless the fees were paid).

45. United States v. Ehrlichman, 546 F.2d 910 (D.C. Cir. 1976).

46. United States v. Pacelli, 491 F.2d 1108 (2d Cir.), cert. denied, 419 U.S. 826 (1974).

47. United States v. Dise, 763 F.2d 586 (3d Cir.), cert. denied, 474 U.S. 982 (1985).

48. United States v. Price, 383 U.S. 787 (1966).

49. United States v. Koon, 34 F.3d 1416 (9th Cir. 1994), *reversed*, 116 S. Ct. 2035 (1996).

50. See U.S.C.A., p. 5937; Pub. L. 100–647 1990 U.S.C.A. 6472 and Pub. L. 103-322 1994 U.S.C.A. 1801; S. Rep. No. 721, 90th Cong., 2d Sess. (1967), reprinted in 1968 U.S.C.C.A.N. 1837, 1839–40; see also, Note, "Discretion to Prosecute Federal Civil Rights Crimes," 74 Yale Law Journal 1297, 1302 (1965); Gregory L. Padgett, "Racially-Motivated Violence and Intimidation: Inadequate State Enforcement and Federal Civil Rights Remedies," 75 Journal of Criminal Law & Criminology 103 (1984).

51. 18 U.S.C. § 245.

52. United States v. Bledsoe, 728 F.2d 1094 (8th Cir.), cert. denied, 469 U.S. 838 (1984).

53. 18 U.S.C. § 245 (b) (2). Subsection (b) (4) and (5), the "chilling effect" provisions, prohibit anyone from interfering with or intimidating anyone attempting to "participat[e], without discrimination on account of race, color, religion, or national origin," in any of the enumerated federal activities or the (b) (2) bias crime activities. Subsection (b) (5) extends these protections to anyone participating in speeches, parades, or assemblies, and anyone encouraging other persons to participate in the enumerated federal activities, the (b) (2) bias crime activities.

54. U.S. Department of Justice, Legal Activities, 1993–94, p. 42.

55. No prosecution may be brought under § 245 unless certified by the United States Attorney General, the Deputy Attorney General, the Associate

Attorney General, or "any Assistant Attorney General specially designated by the Attorney General." 18 U.S.C. § 245 (a) (1).

56. Wang, Hate Crimes Law, p. 5–13.

57. W.Va. Code § 61-6-21 (1995).

58. 28 C.F.R. § 0.85 (m) (1990).

59. Wang, Hate Crimes Law, Appendix B.

60. Ore. Rev. Stat. § 181.550(1) (1989).

61. Va. Code Ann. § 52-8.5C (1991).

62. Arizona, Arkansas, Georgia, Hawaii, Indiana, Kansas, Kentucky, Louisiana, Nebraska, New Mexico, South Carolina, Virginia, and Wyoming do not have hate crime laws.

Chapter 4

1. Lt. Gov. Leo McCarthy of California, quoted in "Bills Introduced to Combat Hate Crimes," United Press International, March 22, 1993.

2. Gina Holland, "Mississippi Ills Require Hate Crimes Bill, Backers Maintain," The Commercial Appeal, January 7, 1994, Metro, p. B1.

3. Richard Bernstein, Dictatorship of Virtue (New York: Vintage Books, 1995), p. 184, quoting Tom Foley.

4. Suzanne Espinosa, "Black-on-White Hate Crimes Rising," The San Francisco Chronicle, November 17, 1993, p. A10.

5. Maria Newman, "Officials Pledge Drive to Counter Bias Attack," New York Times, Jan. 8, 1992, p. B3.

6. Lynda Richardson, "61 Acts of Bias: One Fuse Lights Many Different Explosions," New York Times, Jan. 28, 1992, p. B1.

7. Anthony Flint, "Speech Codes On Campus Stir Debate Over Rights," Boston Globe, March 31, 1991, p. B1.

8. David E. Rovella, "Attack on Hate Crimes is Enhanced," National Law Journal, August 29, 1994, p. A1.

9. Walt Albro, "Report: Anti-Gay Violence Shows Dramatic Increase," United Press International, March 19, 1993.

10. Statement of David M. Smith, quoted in "Survey Finds Decrease in Anti-Gay Violence," New York Times, March 8, 1994, p. A13.

11. U.S. Departments of Commerce, Justice and State, the Judiciary, And Related Agencies, Appropriations for 1995: Hearings on the Community Relations Service (May 3, 1994) (Testimony of Tanya L. Domi, Legislative Director of the National Gay and Lesbian Task Force on Behalf of the American Jewish Committee, Anti-Defamation League, and the People for the American Way Action Fund).

12. Paul A. Winters, ed. Hate Crimes (San Diego: Greenhaven Press, 1996), p. 17.

13. Statement of Michael Petrelli, quoted in "Advocacy Group Urges Police to Consider Anti-Gay Motive," Gannett News Service, October 11, 1994.

14. Anti-Defamation League, "1992 Audit of Anti-Semitic Incidents," p. 24.

15. Hearings on H.R. 4797 Before the House Subcommittee on Crime and Criminal Justice of the House Committee on the Judiciary, 102d Cong., 2d sess. (July 29, 1992), p. 168 (prepared statement of ADL) [hereinafter House Hearings on H.R. 4797].

16. "ADL Audit of Anti-Semitic Incidents for 1993," U.S. Newswire, February 16, 1995.

17. Hearings Before the United States Commission on Civil Rights, Racial and Ethnic Tensions in American Communities: Poverty, Inequality, and Discrimination—A National Perspective, May 21–22, 1992, p. 75 (statement of Jesse Hordes, Washington director, ADL).

18. Michael Hedges, "Study Shows Racial Crimes by Blacks on Rise," Washington Times, Dec. 15, 1993, p. A4.

19. Klanwatch Intelligence Report, February 1993, no. 65, p. 1.

20. The National Institute Against Prejudice and Violence grew out of Maryland Governor Harry Hughes' 1981 Task Force on Violence and Extremism. The NIAPV conducts research on the causes and effects of hate incidents on individuals and communities, especially colleges and universities.

21. Klanwatch Intelligence Report, February 1993, p. 1.

22. Ibid.

23. "Table 7—Number of Offenses Known to the Police, Universities and College Campuses, 1990," Crime in the United States: 1990 (Uniform Crime Reports, Federal Bureau of Investigation, August 11, 1991), p. 122 [hereinafter Uniform Crime Reports: 1990]

24. Howard J. Ehrlich, Campus Ethnoviolence, Institute Report No. 4, NIAPV (March 1990), pp. 12–13.

25. Bernstein, Dictatorship of Virtue, p. 203.

26. John Leo, "Racism on American Campuses," U.S. News & World Report, Jan. 8, 1990, p. 53.

27. Hearings Before the U.S. Commission on Civil Rights, p. 70 (statement of Howard Ehrlich, director, NIAPV).

28. John Leo, "The Words of the Culture War," U.S. News & World Report, Oct. 28, 1991, p. 31.

29. Hearings Before the U.S. Commission on Civil Rights, p. 71 (statement of Howard Ehrlich, director, NIAPV).

30. Hate Crime Statistics Act of 1988: Hearings Before the Subcommittee on the Constitution of the Senate Committee on the Judiciary, 100th Cong., 2d sess. (1988) at p. 261 (Letter to Senator Paul Simon from Susan Lee) [hereinafter Senate Hearings 1988].

31. Senate Hearings 1988, p. 84 (Testimony of William Yoshimo).

32. Senate Hearings 1988, p. 246 (Letter to Senator Paul Simon from Karen Kwong).

33. "There are a lot of incidents of what we think is [sic] bias in the metropolitan area. That statistic, I just don't think it's very reliable." Bill Anderson, "State Reports First Drop in Bias Crime," Bergen Record, June 29, 1995, p. A3.

34. Spencer Rumsey, "A Cancer of Hatred Afflicts America," Newsday, May 27, 1993, Viewpoints, p. 129.

35. Benjamin J. Hubbard, "Commentary on Tolerance: Rise in Hate Crimes Signals Alarming Resurgence of Bigotry," L.A. Times, April 4, 1993, Op-Ed Desk, p. B9.

36. Suzanne Espinosa, "Black-on-White Hate Crimes Rising," San Francisco Chronicle, November 17, 1993, p. A10.

37. Sheryl Stolberg, "Decade Ended in Blaze of Hate," Los Angeles Times, Feb. 23, 1990, p. B3.

38. Denise Hamilton, "Combatting Hate: Crimes Against Minorities are Increasing Across the Board," Los Angeles Times, May 17, 1994, p. B1.

39. Claire Safran, "They Burn Churches, Don't They?" Women's Day, November 21, 1989, p. 68.

40. "Civil Rights Commission to Hold Forum on Hate Crimes in Detroit," U.S. Newswire, July 15, 1991.

41. William Douglas, "Bias Crimes Flare Up in City's Heat," Newsday, July 21, 1991, p. 19.

42. Douglas, "Bias Crimes Flare Up in City's Heat" (emphasis added).

43. Tom Scherberger, Sue Carlton, "A Quiet Life Suddenly Shattered by Hatred," St. Petersburg Times, January 16, 1993, p. 1A.

44. Admittedly, one can find stories downplaying the prevalence of hate crimes. For example, a headline in the *Atlanta Constitution* boasted of Atlanta (as it gears up to host the 1996 Olympics): "Hate Crimes Becoming More Rare, Police Say." This article quoted a Gwinnett County police sergeant who proudly proclaimed that "in 1992 we had almost no . . . [hate crimes and cult activity]." Gail Hagans, "King Week '93 Hate Crime Becoming More Rare, Police Say," The Atlanta Constitution, January 18, 1993, p. J1. Interestingly, Larry Pelligrini, president of the ACLU Georgia's Lesbian and Gay Rights Chapter, says the ACLU in 1991 received 93 reports of hate crimes in the Atlanta area alone. Kathy Scruggs, "Police Insensitive, Activists Say Handcuff Man Case, Crime Report Cited," Atlanta Constitution, March 1, 1992, p. D5.

45. Newman, "Officials Pledge Drive to Counter Bias Attack."

46. Ibid.

47. "Update: Leads Have Run Out in Youth Bias Attacks," New York Times, May 10, 1992, p. A42.

48. Ray Sanchez, "Bias-Attack Doubts Hit," Newsday, Feb. 7, 1992, p. 26.

49. Sanchez, "Bias-Attack Doubts Hit," p. A42.

50. Richard Bernstein, a journalist and author of *Dictatorship of Virtue*, has sharply criticized the media's uncritical acceptance and support of the epidemic claim.

> There is a sizeable industry of exaggeration that combines with fear of appearing complacent about racism to create a misleading impression of American life. It is misleading, not because it describes the existence of the ancient evils of bigotry and discrimination, but because it holds those evils to be

endemic and intensifying, not as disapproved and diminishing. And it is misleading because it confuses the genuine article, the actual bigotry and intolerance that exist, with almost anything that rubs against the moralistic grain. (p. 189)

51. "Education," Time Magazine, May 7, 1990, p. 104.

52. Torri Minton, "Quiet Marin Confronts Hate Crimes: National Study Sees Rise in Violence Against Asians," San Francisco Chronicle, Nov. 29, 1995, p. A13.

53. Joann Lee, "A Look at Asians as Portrayed in the News," Editor & Publisher Magazine, April 30, 1994, p. 56.

54. House Hearings on H.R. 4797, p. 4.

55. Senate Hearings 1988, p. 248.

56. Ibid., p. 253.

57. Hate Crime Statistics Act, Pub. L. 100–275, 104 Stat. 140 (1990).

58. H.Rep. 102-981, 102d Cong., 2d sess. (Oct. 2, 1992), p. 3. A federal hate crime sentence enhancement was passed as part of the Violent Crime Control and Law Enforcement Act of 1994, Pub. Law No. 102-322. The 1994 Hate Crimes Sentencing Enhancement Act mandated a revision of the federal Sentencing Guidelines to provide for a mandatory sentence enhancement for hate crimes.

59. Often called "triggering" events, these are incidents that "achieve enough publicity to incite public discussion and, occasionally, result in a public mandate that 'something be done.'" Valerie Jenness & Ryken Grattet, "The Criminalization of Hate: A Comparison of Structural and Policy Influences on the Passage of 'Bias-Crime' Legislation in the United States," 39 Sociological Perspectives 129, 148 (1996).

60. Joan C. Weiss, "Ethnoviolence: Impact and Response in Victims and the Community," in Robert J. Kelly, ed., Bias Crime: American Law Enforcement and Legal Responses (Chicago: Office of International Criminal Justice, 1991), p. 179 (emphasis added).

61. Allen D. Sapp, Richard N. Holden, & Michael E. Wiggins, "Value and Belief Systems of Right-Wing Extremists: Rationale and Motivation of Bias-Motivated Crimes," in Kelly, Bias Crime, p. 105.

62. Alphonso Pinkney, Lest We Forget: White Hate Crimes (Chicago: Third World Press, 1994), p. 20.

63. Pinkney, Lest We Forget, p. 27.

64. Abraham Abramovsky, "Bias Crime: A Call for Alternative Responses," 19 Fordham Urban Law Journal 875, 876 (1992).

65. Abramovsky, "Bias Crime," p. 882.

66. Ibid., p. 883.

67. Ibid., p. 883, fn. 56 (emphasis added).

68. "Table 5: General Characteristics of Asian or Pacific Islander Persons: 1990," 1990 Census of Population and Housing for Census Tracts and Block Numbering Areas, New York, NY PMSA, 1990 CPH-3-245H. This number represents the census count of all Asian and Pacific Islander persons in New York City's five boroughs.

69. "Table 6—Number of Offenses Known to the Police, Cities and Towns 10,000 and Over in Population, 1990," Uniform Crime Reports, 1990, p. 101. Crime Index Offenses include murder, nonnegligent manslaughter, forcible rape, robbery, aggravated assault, burglary, larceny-theft, motor vehicle theft, and arson.

70. Abramovsky, "Bias Crime," p. 885.

71. Note, "Hate is Not Speech: A Constitutional Defense of Penalty Enhancement for Hate Crimes," 106 Harvard Law Review 1314 (April 1993).

72. Note, "Combatting Racial Violence: A Legislative Proposal," 101 Harvard Law Review 1270 (1988).

73. Note, "Combatting Racial Violence" (citing, Racially Motivated Violence, Hearings Before the Subcommittee on Criminal Justice of the House Committee on the Judiciary, 97th Cong., 1st sess. 77 (1983)).

74. The Howard Beach incident occurred in 1986 when three black men, Michael Griffith, Timothy Grimes, and Cedric Sandiford, walked into the Howard Beach section of Queens, N.Y. looking for a pay phone after their car broke down. A group of white teenagers confronted the three men telling them, "Niggers, you don't belong here." The group then attacked and beat Sandiford. Griffith and Grimes fled with the youths in pursuit. Grimes escaped, but Griffith was struck and killed by a passing car. Howard Kurtz, "3 Convicted of Manslaughter in '86 Howard Beach Attack," Washington Post, Dec. 22, 1987, p. A1.

75. Hate Crime Statistics, 1990: A Resource Book (Uniform Crime Reports, Federal Bureau of Investigation, 1992), p. 3.

76. FBI Press Release 1993.

77. FBI Director William Sessions stated, "While these initial data are limited, they give us our first assessment of the nature of crimes motivated by bias in our society." FBI Press Release.

78. The 1990 FBI Resource Book compares 11 states' hate data collection methods (prehate crime bill). In some states, data collection was voluntary, in others it was mandated. Some states provided additional resources for data collection, while others hoped to stretch existing resources to encompass hate crime reporting. In addition, some states applied a much broader definition of what qualifies as a hate crime than others.

79. FBI Press Release 1993.

80. Ibid.

81. "First-Time FBI Report Reveals Prevalence of Malice," Houston Chronicle, January 11, 1993, p. 12.

82. Monica Rhor & Sabrina Walters, "'A Meanness Afoot' Gives Push to Update Hate Crimes Laws," Philadelphia Inquirer, January 25, 1993, p. S1.

83. Dan Lovely, Richard Vega, "A Death in Coral Springs: We Came Here For Freedom . . . We Live In Hell," USA Today, January 10, 1992, p. 4.

84. Klanwatch Director Dan Welch, Klanwatch Intelligence Report, February 1993, p. 5.

85. Rovella, "Attack on Hate Crimes is Enhanced," at A1.

86. Hate Crime Statistics: 1992 (Uniform Crime Reports, FBI, 1994), p. 7.

87. Racially Motivated Violence, Hearings Before the Subcommittee on Criminal Justice of the House Committee on the Judiciary, 100th Cong., 2d sess. 14 (1988) (statement of the Rev. C. T. Vivian, chairman of the board, Center for Democratic Renewal).

88. Bernstein, Dictatorship of Virtue, p. 190, quoting statement of John Slaughter, president of Occidental College, January 1990.

89. Angie Debo, History of the Indians of the United States (Norman, OK: University of Oklahoma Press, 1983).

90. John Ehle, Trail of Tears: The Rise and Fall of the Cherokee Nation (New York: Doubleday, 1988).

91. Clyde Kluckhohn & Dorothea Leighton, The Navaho (New York: Doubleday, 1962).

92. Lewis H. Carlson & George A. Colburn, In Their Place: White America Defines Her Minorities, 1850–1950 (New York: John Wiley & Sons, 1972), p. 24.

93. Debo, History of the Indians of the United States; Dee Brown, Bury My Heart at Wounded Knee (New York: Bantam, 1973).

94. Debo, History of the Indians of the United States, p. 194–95; Brown, Bury My Heart at Wounded Knee, p. 87–92.

95. Walter T. Howard, Lynchings: Extra-Legal Violence in Florida During the 1930s (London: Associated University Press, 1995), p. 17.

96. Claudine L. Ferrell, Nightmare and Dream: Anti-Lynching in Congress, 1917–1922 (New York: Garland Publishing, 1986), p. 92; see also, Ted Robert Gurr, Violence In America (Newbury Park, CA: Sage Publications, 1989).

97. Howard, Lynchings, p. 18; Ferrell, Nightmare and Dream, p. 91.

98. Everette Swinney, Suppressing the Ku Klux Klan: The Enforcement of the Reconstruction Amendments, 1870–1877 (New York: Garland Publishing, 1987), p. 145.

99. David M. Chalmers, Hooded Americanism: The History of the Ku Klux Klan (Durham, NC: Duke University Press, 1987), p. 14.

100. Ferrell, Nightmare and Dream, p. 92.

101. Chalmers, Hooded Americanism, p. 14.

102. ADL, Hate Groups in America: A Record of Bigotry and Violence (1988).

103. Chalmers, Hooded Americanism, p. 110–11; Jack Nelson, Terror in the Night: The Klan's Campaign Against the Jews (Jackson, MS: University of Mississippi Press, 1996).

104. ADL, Hate Groups in America.

105. Melissa Fay Greene, The Temple Bombing (New York: Addison-Wesley, 1996).

106. Greene, The Temple Bombing, p. 5.

107. Nelson, Terror in the Night, p. 124.

108. Juan Williams, Eyes on the Prize: America's Civil Rights Years (New York: Viking, 1987), p. 38.

109. Williams, Eyes on the Prize, p. 230–31.

110. Except by other immigrants who, in some cases, exploit and prey on their fellows.

111. David H. Bennett, The Party of Fear: The American Far Right from Nativism to the Militia Movement (New York: Vintage Books, 1995), p. 37–39.

112. Bennett, Party of Fear, p. 56.

113. Carlson & Colburn, In Their Place, p. 279–81; see also, Leonard Dinnerstein, Anti-Semitism in America (New York: Oxford University Press, 1994); Leonard Dinnerstein, Uneasy at Home: Anti-Semitism and the American Jewish Experience (New York: Columbia University Press, 1987).

114. Marcus Sheldon, Father Coughlin: The Tumultuous Life of the Priest of the Little Flower (Boston: Little, Brown, 1973); Charles J. Tull, Father Coughlin and the New Deal (Syracuse, NY: Syracuse University Press, 1965).

115. Carlson & Colburn, In Their Place, p. 269.

116. "Just as 'feminists have uncovered a vast amount of sexual abuse of women by men' since the 1970s, recent gay and lesbian activism has 'discovered' violence against gays and lesbians. Documenting antigay and lesbian violence is the most prevalent form of political action currently being undertaken by gay and lesbian communities in response to antigay and lesbian violence." Valerie Jenness & Kendal Broad, "Antiviolence Activism and the (In)Visibility of Gender in the Gay/Lesbian and Women's Movements," 8 Gender & Society 402, 408 (September 1994); see also, Valerie Jenness, "Social Movement Growth, Domain Expansion, and Framing Processes: The Gay/Lesbian Movement and Violence Against Gays and Lesbians as a Social Problem, 42 Social Problems 145 (February 1995).

117. Abramovsky, "Bias Crime," pp. 875, 913.

Chapter 5

1. See Richard Bernstein, Dictatorship of Virtue (New York: Vintage, 1994); Todd Gitlin, The Twilight of Common Dreams (New York: Metropolitan Books, 1995); Gordon MacInnes, Wrong For the Right Reasons (New York: New York University Press, 1995); Jim Sleeper, In Defense of Civic Culture (Washington, D.C.: Progressive Foundation, 1993); Michael Tomasky, Left For Dead (New York: Free Press, 1996); Arthur Schlesinger, Jr., The Disuniting of America (New York: W.W. Norton, 1992).

2. Sleeper, In Defense of Civil Culture, p. 1.

3. Norman Dorsen, ed., The Evolving Constitution (Middletown, CT: Wesleyan University Press, 1987); David J. Garrow, ed., We Shall Overcome (Brooklyn, NY: Carlson Publishing, 1989); Chester J. Antieau, Federal Civil Rights Acts: Civil Practice, 2d ed. (Rochester, NY: Lawyers Co-operative Publishing, 1980); Derrick A. Bell, Race, Racism and American Law, 2d ed. (Boston, MA: Little, Brown, 1980).

4. Shelby Steele, The Content of Our Character (New York: St. Martin's Press, 1990).

5. For discussions of the politics of victimization, see Sleeper, In Defense of Civic Culture; Joseph Epstein, "The Joys of Victimhood," New York Times Magazine, July 2, 1989, p. 20; Charles Sykes, A Nation of Victims (New York: St. Martin's Press, 1992); Jonathan Rauch, "Beyond Oppression," The New Republic, May 10, 1993, pp. 18–23.

6. Jim Sleeper explains the debate and angst among subcontinental Indian Americans over seeking to be defined as a disadvantaged group, despite their outstanding record of accomplishment in the United States. Ultimately, explains Sleeper, the lure of special benefits attendant upon designation as a disadvantaged group proved too strong. Sleeper, In Defense of Civic Culture. See also, Note, "Violence Against Asian Americans," 106 Harvard Law Review 1926, 1935–36 (1993).

7. Steele, The Content of Our Character, p. 14.

8. W. Chambliss & R. Seidman, Law, Order and Power, 2d ed. (Reading, MA: Addison Wesley, 1982); E. S. Fairchild & V. J. Webb, The Politics of Crime and Criminal Justice (Beverly Hills, CA: Sage, 1985); J.R. Gusfield, Symbolic Crusade (Urbana, IL: University of Illinois Press, 1963).

9. Valerie Jenness, "Social Movement Growth, Domain Expansion, and Framing Processes: The Gay/Lesbian Movement and Violence Against Gays and Lesbians as a Social Problem," 42 Social Problems 145 (February 1995); Valerie Jenness, "Hate Crimes in the United States: The Transformation of Injured Persons into Victims and the Extension of Victim Status to Multiple Constituencies," in Joel Best, ed., Images of Issues: Typifying Contemporary Social Problems (New York: Aldine De Gruyter, 1989).

10. Stuart Scheingold, The Politics of Rights (New Haven, CT: Yale University Press, 1974); Stuart Scheingold, The Politics of Law and Order: Street Crime & Public Policy (New York: Longman, 1984).

11. Gallup Poll, April 28, Homosexuality and Gay Rights, p. 83 (1993).

12. Joseph M. Fernandez, "Bringing Hate Crime into Focus: The Hate Crimes Statistics Act of 1990," 26 Harvard Civil Rights–Civil Liberties Law Review 261, 274 (1991), citing telephone interviews with Susan Armsby, lobbyist, People for the American Way (Oct. 30, 1990), and Michael Lieberman, counsel, ADL (Oct. 30, 1990). H.R. 775, 99th Cong., 1st sess., 131 Cong. Rec. 1311 (1985).

13. Ethnically Motivated Violence Against Arab-Americans: Hearings Before the Subcommittee on Criminal Justice of the House Committee on the Judiciary, 99th Cong., 2d sess. (1986).

14. Anti-Asian Violence: Hearings Before the Subcommittee on Civil and Constitutional Rights of the House Committee on the Judiciary, 100th Cong., 1st sess. (1987).

15. Crimes Against Religious Practices and Property: Hearings on H.R. 665 Before the Subcommittee on Criminal Justice of the House Committee on the Judiciary, 99th Cong., 1st sess. (1985).

16. Racially Motivated Violence: Hearings Before the Subcommittee on Criminal Justice of the House Committee on the Judiciary, 100th Cong., 2d sess. (1988).

17. 131 Cong. Rec. H5988–93 (daily ed. July 22, 1985).

18. Fernandez, "Bringing Hate Crime Into Focus," p. 274.

19. Ibid., p. 271.

20. Ibid.; Anti-Gay Violence: Hearings Before the Subcommittee on Criminal Justice of the House Committee on the Judiciary, 99th Cong., 2d sess. 15 (1986) (statement of Representative Conyers).

21. H.R. 3193, 100th Cong., 2d sess., 133 Cong. Rec. H7350 (daily ed. Aug. 7, 1987).

22. Hate Crime Statistics Act of 1988: Hearings Before the Subcommittee on the Constitution of the Senate Committee on the Judiciary, 100th Cong., 2d sess. (1988) [hereinafter, 1988 Senate Hearings].

23. 1988 Senate Hearings, p. 73 (statement of Joan Weiss, National Institute Against Prejudice and Violence).

24. Representative Barbara Kennelly (D-Conn.) was also a sponsor. In the Senate, the bill was sponsored by Senators Paul Simon, Howard Metzenbaum, and Alan Cranston.

25. H. Rep. 575, 100th Cong., 2d sess. 3 (April 20, 1988).

26. S. Rep. No. 21, 101st Cong., 1st sess., at 3 (1989).

27. 136 Cong. Rec. S1067, S1080 (daily ed. Feb. 8, 1990).

28. 135 Cong. Rec. H3179, H3183 (daily ed. June 27, 1989).

29. H. Rep. 575, 100th Cong., 2d sess. 12–13 ((April 20, 1988) dissenting views of Representatives Gekas (R-Pa.), McCollum (R-Fla.), Coble (R-N.C.), Dannemeyer (R-Cal.), and Smith (R-Tex.)).

30. 136 Cong. Rec. S1169 (daily ed. Feb. 8, 1990).

31. Pub. L. No. 100–275, 104 Stat. 140 (1990); Fernandez, "Bringing Hate Crime Into Focus," p. 278.

32. 136 Cong. Rec. S1092 (1990).

33. 136 Cong. Rec. H1460 (1990).

34. Andrew Rosenthal, "President Signs Law for Study of Hate Crimes," New York Times, April 24, 1990, p. B6.

35. "Bush Signs Act Requiring Records on Hate Crimes," Washington Post, April 24, 1990, p. A6.

36. Rosenthal, "President Signs Law for Study of Hate Crimes," p. B6.

37. Eric Rothschild, "Recognizing Another Face of Hate Crimes: Rape as a Gender-Bias Crime," 4 Maryland Journal of Contemporary Legal Issues 231 (1993).

38. Senate Hearings on S. 702, S. 797, and S. 2000 Before the Subcommittee on the Constitution of the Committee of the Judiciary, 100th Cong. 2d sess. 264 (June 21, 1988) (statement of Molly Yard, president, National Organization for Women).

39. Fernandez, Bringing Hate Crime Into Focus," p. 275.

40. ADL, Hate Crime Statutes: Including Women as Victims 12 (1990).

41. Marguerite Angelari, "Hate Crime Statutes: A Promising Tool for

Fighting Violence Against Women," 2 American University Journal of Gender & Law 63, 83–86 (1994).

42. Elizabeth Pendo, "Recognizing Violence Against Women: Gender and the Hate Crimes Statistics Act," 17 Harvard Women's Law Journal 157 (1994).

43. C. J. Sheffield, "Hate Violence," p. 396, in P. Rothenberg, ed., Race, Class, and Gender in the United States (New York, St. Martin's Press, 1992).

44. See Center For Democratic Renewal, When Hate Groups Come to Town 35–37 (1992) (summarizing argument against treating gender crimes as hate crimes). See also Pendo, "Recognizing Violence Against Women" (arguing for inclusion of gender as a hate crime trigger).

45. Pub. Law No. 103–322, 108 Stat. 1796 (Sept 13, 1994).

46. The chief sponsor in the House was Representative Barbara Boxer (D-Cal.). Once Boxer won a seat in the Senate, Representatives Pat Schroeder (D-Cal.), Louise Slaughter (D-N.Y.), and Charles Schumer (D-N.Y.) became the House sponsors.

47. Cong. Rec., June 19, 1990, at S8263. Cong. Rec., Jan 14, 1991, p. S597.

48. Pub. Law No. 102–322, 108 Stat. 1796, tit. IV (Sept. 13, 1994).

49. H.R. 1133, 103d Cong. 1st sess. (Feb. 24, 1993).

50. 42 U.S.C. § 13981 (e) (2).

51. 42 U.S.C. 13981 (c).

52. Numerous representatives from rape crisis centers and battered women's shelters testified in support of the VAWA. Women and Violence: Hearings on Legislation to Reduce the Growing Problem of Violent Crime Against Women Before the Senate Committee on the Judiciary, 101st Cong. 2d sess. 79 (1990); Crimes of Violence Motivated by Gender: Hearings Before the Subcommittee on Civil and Constitutional Rights of the House Committee on the Judiciary, 103d Cong., 1st sess. (1993). Opposition to the bill came from federal judges and others concerned about bringing large numbers of domestic violence lawsuits in the federal courts. The ACLU, while supporting the purpose of the bill, expressed concern that the intent/motive requirement was too vague.

53. Hearings: Crimes of Violence Motivated by Gender, p. 3 (statement of Sally Goldfarb, senior staff attorney, NOW Legal Defense and Education Fund).

54. Hearings: Crimes of Violence Motivated by Gender, pp. 114–15 (statement of Eleanor Smeal, president, Fund for the Feminist Majority).

55. Ibid., p. 113 (statement of Patricia Ireland, president, National Organization for Women).

56. Until recently, women abused by their spouses were precluded from bringing a civil suit by the intrafamily immunity doctrine, a common law rule codified by statute in some states, which prohibited tort action between family members. Today, all but ten states have repudiated that doctrine. W. H. Hallock, "The Violence Against Women Act: Civil Rights for Sexual Assault Victims," 68 Indiana Law Journal 577, 596 n.134 (Spring 1993).

57. Hearings: Crimes of Violence Motivated by Gender, p. 17 (statement of Elizabeth Symonds, legislative counsel, ACLU).

58. Ibid.

59. Doe v. Doe, 929 F. Supp. 608 (D. Conn. 1996); Brzonkala v. Virginia Polytechnic, 1996 U.S. Dist. LEXIS 10766 (W.D. Va. 1996). In both cases, the defendants challenged the civil rights provision claiming that Congress lacked the power to enact this law under either the Commerce Clause or the Fourteenth Amendment. A federal district court in Connecticut upheld the provision, whereas a federal district court in West Virginia struck down the law as unconstitutional. Both courts relied on United States v. Lopez (115 S.Ct. 1624 (1995)), in which the Supreme Court struck down, as beyond Congress's power under the Commerce Clause, a law making it a federal offense to possess a firearm within 1,000 feet of a school.

60. Statement of Representative Charles Schumer (D-N.Y).

61. Hate Crimes Sentencing Enhancement Act of 1992: Hearings on H.R. 4797 Before the Subcommittee on Crime and Criminal Justice of the House Committee on the Judiciary, 102d Cong., 2d sess. 157 (July 29, 1992) (statement of Robert K. Lifton, American Jewish Congress) [hereinafter, HCSEA House Hearings].

62. HCSEA House Hearings, p. 67 (statement of Elizabeth R. OuYang, staff attorney, Asian American Legal Defense and Education Fund).

63. Pub. Law No. 103–322, 108 Stat. 1796 (Sept. 13, 1994).

64. 60 Fed. Reg. 25,082 (May 10, 1995).

65. Pub. Law No. 103–322, 108 Stat. 1796 (Sept. 13, 1994).

66. 60 Fed. Reg. 25,074, 25,083 (1995).

Chapter 6

1. Jeffrie G. Murphy, "Bias Crimes: What Do Haters Deserve?" 11 Criminal Justice Ethics 23 (Summer/Fall 1992).

2. Lawrence Crocker, "Hate Crime Statutes: Just? Constitutional? Wise?" 1992/1993 Annual Survey of American Law 485, 493 (1992/1993).

3. Crocker, "Hate Crime Statutes," p. 492.

4. Ibid., p. 493.

5. 113 S. Ct. 2194 (1993).

6. Jack Levin & Jack McDevitt, Hate Crimes: The Rising Tide of Bigotry & Bloodshed (New York: Plenum Press, 1993), p. 11; Joan Weiss, "Ethnoviolence: Impact and Response in Victims and the Community," in Robert J. Kelly, ed., Bias Crime: American Law Enforcement and Legal Responses (Chicago: Office of International Criminal Justice, 1991), p.179.

7. Levin & McDevitt, Hate Crimes, p. 100 (emphasis in original).

8. Ibid.

9. Ibid.

10. Wisconsin v. Mitchell, 113 S. Ct. at 2201.

11. Bennett Weisburd & Brian Levin, "On the Basis of Sex: Recognizing

Gender-Based Bias Crimes," 5 Stanford Law & Policy Review 21, 25 (Spring 1994).

12. National Institute Against Prejudice and Violence, National Victimization Survey (1989).

13 Weiss, "Ethnoviolence: Impact and Response in Victims and the Community," p. 179.

14. Ibid., p. 182.

15. Ibid.

16. American Psychological Association Task Force on the Victims of Crime and Violence, Final Report (Nov. 30, 1984), p. 23.

17. APA Task Force, p. 24; M. Bard & D. Sangrey, The Crime Victim's Book (New York: Basic Books, 1979); A. W. Burgess & L. L. Holstrom, "Rape Trauma Syndrome," 131 American Journal of Psychiatry 981–85 (1974); A. W. Burgess & L. L. Holstrom, "Rape: Sexual Disruption & Recovery," 49 American Journal of Orthopsychiatry 658–69 (1979); D. Forman, "Psychotherapy With Rape Victims," 17(3) Psychotherapy: Theory, Research, Practice 304–11 (1980); W. G. Skogan & M. G. Maxfield, Coping With Crime: Individual & Neighborhood Reactions (Beverly Hills, CA: Sage, 1981); M. Symonds, "The 'Second Injury' to Victims," in L. Kivens, ed., Evaluation & Change: Services for Survivors (Minneapolis, MN: Minneapolis Medical Research Foundation, 1980).

18. APA Task Force, p. 25.

19. Ibid., p. 25–27.

20. Ibid., p. 29.

21. Arnold Barnes & Paul H. Ephross, "The Impact of Hate Violence on Victims: Emotional and Behavioral Responses to Attacks," 39 Social Work 247 (May 1994).

22. Barnes & Ephross, "The Impact of Hate Violence," p. 250.

23. 491 U.S. 397 (1989).

24. See Lu-in Wang, Hate Crime Laws (New York: Clark, Boardman, Callaghan, 1995), chapter 13, for an overview of state-venerated object laws.

25. The ADL's model "institutional vandalism" statute requires only "knowledge of the character of the property." ADL, Hate Crimes Statutes: A 1991 Status Report (1992), p. 2.

26. Justice Brennan, writing for the majority, stated in a footnote that "our analysis does not rely on the way in which the flag was acquired, and nothing in our opinion should be taken to suggest that one is free to steal the flag so long as one uses it to communicate an idea. We also emphasize that Johnson was prosecuted *only* for flag desecration—not for trespass, disorderly conduct, or arson." Johnson, 491 U.S. at 412, note 8.

27. Kent Greenawalt, "Reflections on Justifications for Defining Crimes by the Category of Victim," 1992/1993 Annual Survey of American Law 617, 627 (1992/1993).

28. William Marovitz, "Hate or Bias Crime Legislation," in Robert J. Kelly, ed. Bias Crime: American Law Enforcement and Legal Responses (Chicago: Office of International Criminal Justice, 1991), p. 48.

29. James Weinstein, "First Amendment Challenges to Hate Crime Legislation: Where's the Speech," 11 Criminal Justice Ethics 6, 10 (1992).

30. State v. Plowman, 838 P.2d 558 (1992).

31. Plowman at 564.

32. John Carman, "Haunting Images Cling to Polly Klaas," San Francisco Chronicle, Dec. 8, 1993, p. E1; Andy Newman, "Megan, Her Law and What it Spawned," New York Times, Feb. 25, 1996, §13 NJ, p. 1.

33. "More Words of Teacher Are Found on Tape," New York Times, March 28, 1996, p. B7.

34. Bureau of Justice Statistics, Sourcebook of Criminal Justice Statistics—1994, Tables 2.1 and 2.2.

35. The Gallup Poll, Public Opinion 1994, p. 28. The 1994 Gallup Poll asked respondents to rank the most important noneconomic problem facing the country.

36. Richard Perez-Pena, "Man Said to Admit a Week of Attacks," New York Times, June 14, 1996, p. A1.

37. Frederick Kunkle, "Suspect Held in N.Y.C. Attacks," The Bergen [County, N.J.] Record, June 14, 1996, p. A1.

38. APA Task Force, p. 36; Skogan & Maxfield, "Coping With Crime"; Kevin N. Wright, The Great American Crime Myth (New York: Praeger, 1985), p. 2–15, 70–83.

39. FBI, Uniform Crime Reports, Hate Crime Statistics: 1993 (1995).

40. John P. Cook, "Collection and Analysis of Hate Crime Activities," in Robert J. Kelly, ed., Bias Crime: American Law Enforcement and Legal Responses (Chicago: Office of International Criminal Justice, 1993), p. 149.

41. Taking into account the impact on third parties should be distinguished from victim impact statements submitted at a sentencing hearing. Although the majority of states currently permit the use of victim impact statements at the time of sentencing, the use of victim impact statements is limited to relatives of the victim, and not frightened neighbors or the community at large.

42. Thanks to Susan Gellman for this example.

43. Levin & McDevitt, Hate Crimes, p. 217.

44. Unpublished document, New York City Police Department, "Bias Incident Investigating Unit, 1990 Annual Report" (1991). James C. McKinley, Jr., "Tracking Crimes of Prejudice: A Hunt for the Elusive Truth," New York Times, June 29, 1990, p. A1.

45. Tom Metzger, head of the violent white supremacist group, White Aryan Resistance, advised callers to his telephone hotline that hate crime sentence enhancements could be avoided by remaining silent during a bias-motivated crime. Miriam Rozen, "Wielding a Strong Hate Crime Statute, Luis Aragon Brings Racists and Homophobes to Justice," The American Lawyer, June 1992, p. 58.

46. Weisburd & Levin, "On the Basis of Sex," p. 27.

Chapter 7

1. Peter Finn & Taylor McNeil, Bias Crimes and the Criminal Justice Response: A Summary Report Prepared for the National Criminal Justice Association (Boston: Abt Associates, 1988), p. 4.

2. Bureau of Justice Statistics, Local Police Departments 1993, p. 2, Table 2 (April 1996). Of 12,361 police departments, only 3.9 percent employ 100 or more officers, 17.3 percent employ 25 to 99 officers, and 27.2 percent employ 10 to 24 officers.

3. Ian Fisher, "Gay Groups Call Police Decoys Ineffective," New York Times, Jan. 1, 1992, p. A35.

4. One member of a neighborhood resident anti-crime patrol said, "I don't think it does any good. It's a waste of taxpayers' money." Fisher, "Gay Groups Call Police Decoys Ineffective."

5. Gary Marx & Chuck Wexler, "When Law and Order Works: Boston's Innovative Approach to the Problem of Racial Violence," 32 Crime & Delinquency 205, 210 (April 1986).

6. Marx & Wexler, "When Law and Order Works," pp. 211–12.

7. Ibid., p. 208.

8. Ibid., p. 212.

9. New York City Gay & Lesbian Anti-Violence Project, NYPD Bias Unit Downgraded, Stop the Violence, Winter/Spring 1995, p. 3.

10. New York City Police Department, Background Information on the Bias Incident Investigating Unit, pp. 4–5 (undated document).

11. Helen Benedict, Virgin or Vamp: How the Press Covers Sex Crimes (New York: Oxford University Press, 1992), pp. 201–03, 209.

12. Migdalia Maldonado, "Practical Problems with Enforcing Hate Crimes Legislation in New York," 1992/1993 Annual Survey of American Law, 555, 557–58 (1992/1993).

13. Bias Incident Investigating Unit, undated document, p. 4. Emphasis added.

14. Ibid.

15. New York City Police Department, Inspector William T. Wallace, Bias Incident Investigating Unit (Sept. 1991), p. 22.

16. New York City Police Department, Bias Incident Investigating Unit, Year End Report 1994, p. 15.

17. The Bias Unit keeps arrest statistics for all bias crimes, and does not separately break down crimes against the person and property.

18. Bias Incident Investigating Unit, Year End Report 1994, p. 13.

19. National Coalition of Anti-Violence Programs & New York City Gay & Lesbian Anti-Violence Project, Anti-Lesbian/Gay Violence in 1995 (1996), p. 51.

20. Anti-Lesbian/Gay Violence in 1995, p. 52.

21. Ibid., p. 52–53.

22. James C. McKinley, "Tracking Crimes of Prejudice: A Hunt for the Elusive Truth," The New York Times, June 29, 1990, p. A1.

23. Cathy Perkins, ed., Cointelpro (New York: Monrad Press, 1975); Pat Watters & Stephen Gillers, eds., Investigating the FBI (Garden City, NY: Doubleday, 1973).

24. Don Whitehead, Attack on Terror: The FBI Against the KKK in Mississippi (New York: Funk & Wagnall, 1970).

25. Paul G. Chevigny, "Politics and Law in the Control of Local Surveillance," ′69 Cornell Law Review 735 (1984).

26. Telephone interview with Camilla Nelson, Civil Rights Policy Director, State of Minnesota Office of the Attorney General (October 31, 1996).

27. California Division of Criminal Justice Information Services, California Department of Justice, Hate Crime in California 1995 (1996).

28. Telephone interview with Migdalia Maldonado, former assistant district attorney, Civil Rights Bureau, Kings County District Attorney's Office (August 20, 1996).

29. Hate Crime in California 1995, p. 6.

30. Ibid., p. 20.

31. Ibid., p. 21.

32. Telephone interview with Chuck Haines, assistant district attorney for the city and county of San Francisco (October 15, 1996).

33. Hate Crime in California 1995, p. 19, 26.

34. Virginia Nia Lee & Joseph M. Fernandez, "Legislative Responses to Hate-Motivated Violence: The Massachusetts Experience and Beyond," 25 Harvard Civil Rights, Civil Liberties Law Review 287, 290 (1987).

35. Lee & Fernandez, "Legislative Responses," p. 293–94.

36. Ibid., p. 294.

37. Ibid., p. 294, 305.

38. Jack Levin & Jack McDevitt, Hate Crimes: The Rising Tide of Bigotry and Bloodshed (New York: Plenum Press, 1993), p. 194–95.

39. Jack O'Malley, Cook County State's Attorney's Office, A Prosecutor's Guide to Hate Crime (1994).

40. Telephone interview with Ellen Meyers, Cook County State's Attorney's Office (November 7, 1996).

41. Miriam Rozen, "Wielding a Strong Hate Crime Statute, Luis Aragon Brings Racists and Homophobes to Justice," The American Lawyer, June 1992, p. 58.

42. Ibid.

43. Telephone interview with Chuck Haines.

44. Maldonado, "Practical Problems with Enforcing Hate Crimes Legislation," p. 556.

45. White Los Angeles police officers beat intoxicated black motorist, Rodney King, after a high-speed vehicle pursuit. The beating was captured on video by a passerby. The officers were acquitted of assault by an all-white jury in April 1992. Following the acquittal, there were riots in South Central Los Angeles for nearly a week. Report of the Independent Commission on the LAPD (Warren Christopher, Chair, 1992); Mark Baldassare, ed. The Los

Angeles Riots: Lesson for the Urban Future (San Francisco: Westview Press, 1994); Robert Gooding-Williams, ed., Reading Rodney King: Reading Urban Uprising (New York: Routledge, 1993).

Reginald Denny, a white truck driver, stopped at an intersection in South Central Los Angeles, where most of the rioting took place. He was pulled out of his truck by two black rioters who beat him, smashed his head with a brick, and gleefully danced around his unconscious body. Denny's attack was also captured on video. The defendants were acquitted of the more serious felony charges, but convicted of "mayhem," a misdemeanor. Mary Schmich, "Denny Case: Step Back or Justice?" Chicago Tribune, Oct. 20, 1993, p. N1.

46. See Maldonado, "Practical Problems with Enforcing Hate Crime Legislation."

47. Prosecutors and defense counsel are permitted to strike potential jurors from the panel through the use of peremptory challenges or "for cause." When a juror is struck "for cause," it means that the prosecutor or defense counsel has demonstrated to the judge's satisfaction, after questioning, that the juror is not impartial. Each side has a limited number of peremptory challenges (the number varies from state to state). No reason need be given for using a peremptory challenge.

48. Batson v. Kentucky, 476 U.S. 79 (1986) (holding that a prosecutor may not use peremptory challenges to exclude blacks from a jury that is to try a black defendant solely on account of their race); Georgia v. McCollum, 112 S.Ct. 2348 (1992) (holding that a defendant may not use peremptory challenges solely on the basis of race); J.E.B. v. Alabama, 114 S.Ct. 1419 (1994) (holding unconstitutional the dismissal of jurors based on gender).

49. 114 S.Ct. 1419 (1994).

50. United States v. Chalan, 812 F.2d 1302 (10th Cir. 1987).

51. United States v. Biaggi, 673 F. Supp. 96 (E.D.N.Y. 1986), aff'd, 853 F.2d 89 (2d Cir. 1988).

52. People v. Trevino, 704 P.2d 719, 217 Cal. 39 Cal. 3d 667, Rptr. 656 (1985).

53. Ristaino v. Ross, 424 U.S. 589 (1976).

54. Ann Fagan Ginger, Jury Selection in Civil and Criminal Trials, 2d ed. (Tiburon, CA: Lawpress Corp., 1984), 1990 Supp., p. 108–09.

55. James J. Gobert & Walter E. Jordan, Jury Selection: The Law, Art, and Science of Selecting a Jury, 2d ed. (New York: McGraw-Hill, 1990), p. 249.

56. Ginger, Jury Selection, p. 537.

57. Ibid., p. 540.

58. Ibid., p. 541.

59. Maldonado, "Practical Problems with Enforcing Hate Crimes Legislation," p. 559.

60. Ibid.

61. 19 Cal. Rptr. 2d 444 (1993).

62. Aishman, 19 Cal. Rptr. 2d at 453.

63. State v. Wyant, 597 N.E.2d 450 (1992), vacated and remanded, 113 S. Ct. 2954 (1993), reversed, 624 N.E.2d 722 (1994).

64. 932 F.2d 674 (1991).

65. 457 N.E.2d 50 (1983).

66. The Violent Crime Control and Law Enforcement Act of 1994, mandated a revision of the U.S. Sentencing Guidelines to provide an automatic enhancement for hate crimes of three offense levels above the base level for the underlying offense. However, the Sentencing Guidelines scheme does not remove the issue of bias motivation from the jury. Indeed, the jury must find "beyond a reasonable doubt that the defendant intentionally selected any victim or any property as the object of the offense because of the actual or perceived race, color, religion, national origin, ethnicity, gender, disability, or sexual orientation of any person." 18 U.S.C. Appendix § 3A1.1 (1996).

67. George James, "Court Orders Students in Bias Case to Take Sensitivity Course," New York Times, Aug. 31, 1995, p. B5.

68. Linda Saslow, "Juveniles Who Commit Bias Crimes Confront Their Hate and 'Hot Buttons,'" New York Times, June 12, 1994, p. LI14.

69. Ibid.

70. Ibid.

71. James B. Jacobs, "Stratification and Conflict Among Prison Inmates," 66 Journal of Criminal Law & Criminology 476 (1976); James B. Jacobs, New Perspectives on Prisons and Imprisonment (New York: Cornell University Press, 1983); Report of the Disturbance Cause Committee, Findings: Southern Ohio Correctional Facility Riot (June 10, 1993).

72. According to Kevin Berrill, director of the Anti-Violence Program of the National Gay & Lesbian Task Force, "[n]owhere is anti-gay violence more trivialized and more inescapable than in prisons and jails." Kevin Berrill, "Anti-Gay Violence: Causes, Consequences and Responses," in Nancy Taylor, ed, Bias Crime: The Law Enforcement Response (Chicago: Office of International Criminal Justice, 1991), p. 118.

Chapter 8

1. Henry Louis Gates, Jr., Anthony P. Griffin, et. al., Speaking of Race Speaking of Sex: Hate Speech, Civil Rights, and Civil Liberties (New York: New York University Press, 1994); Kent Greenawalt, "Criminal Coercion and Freedom of Speech," 78 Northwestern University Law Review 1081 (1984); David Goldberger, "Hate Crime Laws and Their Impact on the First Amendment," 1992/1993 Annual Survey of American Law 569 (1992/1993); Susan Gellman, "Sticks and Stones Can Put You in Jail, But Can Words Increase Your Sentence? Constitutional and Policy Dilemmas of Ethnic Intimidation Laws," 39 UCLA Law Review 333 (1991).

2. Brief of the American Civil Liberties Union as Amicus Curiae in Support of Petitioner, Todd Mitchell, in Wisconsin v. Mitchell, p.1, 4 (emphasis in original).

3. Brief of Center for Individual Rights as Amicus Curiae in Support of Respondent, Wisconsin, in Wisconsin v. Mitchell, p. 7–8 (emphasis in original).

4. "International Legal Colloquium on Racial and Religious Hatred and Group Libel," 22 Israel Yearbook on Human Rights 1–259 (1992); N. Lerner, The U.N. Convention on the Elimination of All Forms of Racial Discrimination (2d ed. 1980); United Kingdom Race Relations Act of 1965, ch. 73 § 6(1) (amended in 1976 and 1986); J. Griffiths, "Conflict in Society: Public Order v. Individual Liberty—Laws Against Incitement to Racial Hatred," paper delivered at Asia Pacific Lawyers Association Third General Assembly, Hawaii, Jan. 6–9, 1989. Canadian court decisions upholding hate speech restrictions include: Regina v. Keegstra, 19 C.C.C. (3d) 254 (Alta. Q.B. 1984), and Regina v. Zundel, 31 C.C.C. (3d) 97, 580 O.R. (2d) 129 (Ont. C.A. 1987).

5. Samuel Walker, Hate Speech: The History of an American Controversy (Lincoln: University of Nebraska Press, 1994).

6. Chaplinsky v. New Hampshire, 315 U.S. 568 (1942).

7. Chaplinsky at 571–72.

8. Gooding v. Wilson, 405 U.S. 518, 524 (1972).

9. Texas v. Johnson, 491 U.S. 397 (1989).

10. Gerald Gunther, Constitutional Law, 12th ed. (Mineola, NY: Foundation Press, 1991), p. 1073.

11. Gerald Gunther, Stanford University Campus Report, May 3, 1989, p. 18.

12. Walker, Hate Speech, p. 40.

13. Ibid., p. 64–65.

14. Lovell v. Griffin, 303 U.S. 444 (1938) (holding unconstitutional a permit requirement for distribution of literature by Jehovah's Witnesses); Martin v. Struthers, 319 U.S. 141 (1943) (upholding First Amendment right of Jehovah's Witnesses to solicit door-to-door); Cantwell v. Connecticut, 310 U.S. 296 (1940) (holding unconstitutional criminal conviction of a Jehovah's Witness based on offensive speech).

15. Walker, Hate Speech, p. 55.

16. 22 A.2d 877 (1941).

17. Klapprott at 877.

18. Floyd Abrams, "Hate Speech: An American View, Group Libel and Criminal Law: Walking on the 'Slippery Slope,'" 22 Israel Yearbook on Human Rights 85 (1992); Natan Lerner, "Incitement in the Racial Convention: Reach and Shortcomings of Article 4," 22 Israeli Yearbook on Human Rights 1 (1992); Kenneth Lasson, "Group Libel v. Free Speech, When Big Brother Should Butt In," 23 Duquesne Law Review 77 (1984).

19. 343 U.S. 250 (1952).

20. Beauharnais at 250.

21. Id.

22. Id.

23. Laurence Tribe, American Constitutional Law, 2d ed. (Mineola, NY:

Foundation Press, 1988), p. 926; Gerald Gunther, Constitutional Law, 11th ed. (Mineola, NY: Foundation Press, 1985), p. 1055.

24. 376 U.S. 254 (1964).

25. 578 F.2d 1197 (7th Cir. 1978).

26. Collin v. Smith at 1199.

27. Id. at 1206.

28. Texas v. Johnson, 491 U.S. 397, 414 (1989).

29. Walker, Hate Speech, p. 78.

30. Milton Heumann & Thomas W. Church, with David Redlawsk, Hate Speech on Campus: Cases, Case Studies, and Commentary (Boston: Northeastern University Press, 1997); Robert M. O'Neil, Free Speech in the College Community (Bloomington: University of Indiana Press, 1997).

31. Mari Matsuda, "Public Response to Racist Speech: Considering the Victim's Story," 87 Michigan Law Review 2320, 2340 (August 1989).

32. Charles R. Lawrence, III, "If He Hollers Let Him Go: Regulating Racist Speech on Campus," 1990 Duke Law Journal 431, 436 (1990).

33. Matsuda, "Public Response to Racist Speech," p. 2357.

34. Doe v. University of Michigan, 721 F. Supp. 852 (E.D. Mich. 1989); UWM Post v. Board of Regents of the University of Wisconsin, 774 F. Supp. 1163 (E.D. Wis. 1991); Dambrot v. Central Michigan University, 839 F. Supp. 477 (E.D. Mich. 1993).

35. 721 F. Supp. 852 (E.D. Mich. 1989). See also UWM Post v. Board of Regents of the University of Wisconsin, 774 F. Supp. 1163 (E.D. Wis. 1991) (declaring unconstitutional campus hate speech code).

36. Doe at 853.

37. Id. at 858.

38. Id.

39. Id. at 853.

40. Id. at 866.

41. Id.

42. 774 F. Supp. 1163 (E.D. Wis. 1991).

43. UWM Post at 1165.

44. Id. at 1167–68.

45. Id. at 1172.

46. Id. at 1173.

47. 771 F.2d 323 (7th Cir. 1985).

48. 106 S.Ct. 1172 (1986).

49. Code of Indianapolis and Marion County, Indiana, § 16-1(a) (2).

50. Hudnut at 328.

51. Tribe, American Constitutional Law, p. 925 (emphasis in original).

52. Martin H. Redish, "Freedom of Thought as Freedom of Expression: Hate Crime Sentencing Enhancement and First Amendment Theory," 11 Criminal Justice Ethics 29 (Summer/Fall 1992); Ralph S. Brown, "Susan Gellman Has It Right," 11 Criminal Justice Ethics 46 (Summer/Fall 1992); Larry Alexander, "The ADL Hate Crime Statute and the First Amendment," 11 Crimi-

nal Justice Ethics 49 (Summer/Fall 1992); Greenawalt, "Criminal Coercion and Freedom of Speech"; David Goldberger, "Hate Crime Laws and Their Impact on the First Amendment," 1992/1993 Annual Survey of American Law 569 (1992/1993); and Gellman, "Sticks and Stones Can Put You in Jail," p. 333.

53. For a view similar to ours, see Minnesota v. Maccholz, no. K096388 (Minn. district court, criminal division, 3d Dist., August 1996) (striking down a Minnesota harassment statute on vagueness grounds). The court said, "The state may surely make it illegal to ride a horse through a crowd [as did the defendant, while shouting anti-homosexual epithets], but it may not punish someone who does so because of his personal views on some issue."

54. Tribe, American Constitutional Law, p. 926 (emphasis in original). Professor Tribe testified in support of the Hate Crime Sentencing Enhancement Act of 1992. Hate Crime Sentencing Enhancement Act of 1992: Hearings on H.R. 4797 Before the House Subcommittee on Crime and Criminal Justice of the Committee on the Judiciary, 102d Cong., 2d sess. 7 (July 29, 1992) (statement of Laurence Tribe).

55. Abraham Abramovsky, "Bias Crime: A Call for Alternative Responses," 19 Fordham Urban Law Journal 875 (1992); Steven M. Freeman, "Hate Crime Laws: Punishment Which Fits the Crime," 1992/1993 Annual Survey of American Law 581, 585 (1992/1993); James Weinstein, "First Amendment Challenges to Hate Crime Legislation: Where's the Speech," 11 Criminal Justice Ethics 6 (Summer/Fall 1992).

56. Freeman, "Hate Crime Laws," p. 585.

57. 838 P.2d 558 (Or. 1992).

58. Plowman at 563.

59. Id.

60. 19 Cal. Rptr. 2d 444 (Cal. App. 4th Dist. 1993).

61. Aishman at 449.

62. 597 N.E.2d 450 (1992), vacated and remanded, 113 S.Ct. 2954 (1993).

63. Wyant at 450.

64. Id. at 457.

65. State v. Wyant, 624 N.E.2d 722 (1994) (reversing, 597 N.E.2d 450 (1992)).

66. 112 S.Ct. 2538 (1992).

67. The majority opinion was joined by Justices Scalia, Kennedy, Souter, Thomas, and Chief Justice Rehnquist. Justices Blackmun and Stevens filed concurring opinions, in which Justices O'Connor and White joined.

For an account of the facts as well as the events leading up to the Supreme Court's *R.A.V.* decision, *see* Edward J. Cleary, Beyond the Burning Cross: The First Amendment and the Landmark *R.A.V.* Case (New York: Random House, 1994).

68. R.A.V. at 2549.

69. Stevens, J., concurring p. 2570 (emphasis in original).

70. R.A.V. at 2571 (emphasis in original).

71. 113 S.Ct. 2194 (1993).

72. Brief for Respondent, p. 13.

73. State v. Mitchell, 485 N.W.2d 807 (1992).

74. Mitchell at 815.

75. Gellman, "Sticks and Stones," p. 333.

76. Mitchell at 813.

77. Mitchell at 810, quoting Susan Gellman, "Sticks and Stones," p. 363.

78. Wisconsin v. Mitchell, 113 S.Ct. 2200.

79. People v. Baker, 25 Cal. Rptr. 2d 372 (1993); In re M.S., 42 Cal. Rptr. 2d 355 (1995); People v. Ayers, 335 Md. 602 (1994); Dawson v. Delaware, 112 S.Ct. 1093 (1992); Barclay v. Florida, 463 U.S. 939 (1983).

80. Wisconsin v. Mitchell at 2199 (quoting LaFave & Scott, Substantive Criminal Law, Vol. 1, §3.6(b), p. 324 (1986).

81. 112 S.Ct. 1093 (1992).

82. Dawson at 1094.

83. 463 U.S. 939 (1983).

84. Barclay at 939.

85. Mitchell at 814.

86. Wisconsin v. Mitchell at 2200.

87. United States v. Schwimmer, 279 U.S. 644, 654–55 (1929) (Holmes, J., dissenting), *overruled*, Girouard v. United States, 328 U.S. 61 (1946).

Chapter 9

1. The phrase "content of our character" was coined by Martin Luther King in his famous "I Have a Dream Speech" delivered from the Lincoln Memorial in Washington, D.C. on August 28, 1963. King stated, "I have a dream that my four little children will one day live in a nation where they will not be judged by the color of their skin, but the content of their character." Recently, Shelby Steele used the phrase as the title of a book on racial identity from the 1950–60s civil rights movement to 1980s affirmative action. See Shelby Steele, The Content of Our Character: A New Vision of Race in America (New York: St. Martin's Press, 1990).

2. Emile Durkheim, Division of Labor in Society (New York: Free Press, 1964); see also David Garland, Punishment and Society: A Study in Social Theory (Chicago: University of Chicago Press, 1990).

3. See Arthur S. Schlesinger, Jr., The Disuniting of America (New York: Norton, 1992); Richard Bernstein, Dictatorship of Virtue (New York: Vintage Books, 1994); Donald L. Horowitz, Ethnic Groups in Conflict (Berkeley, CA: University of California Press, 1985).

4. Michael Tomasky, Left For Dead: The Life, Death and Possible Resurrection of Progressive Politics in America (New York: Free Press, 1996), p. 81.

5. Jim Sleeper, In Defense of Civic Culture (Washington, D.C.: Progressive Foundation, 1993), p. 2. See also Jim Sleeper, Liberal Racism, New York: Penguin Books, 1977, published after our book was already in press.

6. Bernstein, Dictatorship of Virtue, p. 9.

7. Editorial, "The Meaning of 'Hate,'" National Review, April 30, 1990, p. 17.

8. Klanwatch Intelligence Report, August 1995, p. 11.

9. Charles J. Sykes, A Nation of Victims (New York: St. Martin's Press, 1992) p. 15.

10. Kara Swisher, "Police, Gay Activists See Rise in Assaults on Homosexuals," Washington Post, September 17, 1989, p. A1.

11. Ann Pellegrini, "Rape is a Bias Crime," New York Times, May 27, 1990, section 4, p. 13.

12. Pedro Ponce, "Some Question Use of Hate Crime Laws by Victimized Whites," San Diego Union Tribune, May 5, 1994, p. A36.

13. Ibid.

14. Ibid.

15. Marc L. Fleischauer, "Teeth for a Paper Tiger: A Proposal to Add Enforceability to Florida's Hate Crimes Act," 17 Florida State University Law Review 697, 706 (1990); Note, "Combatting Racial Violence: A Legislative Proposal," 101 Harvard Law Review 1270 (1988); Mari J. Matsuda, "Public Response to Racist Speech: Considering the Victim's Story," 87 Michigan Law Review 2320 (1989).

16. Larry Tye, "Hate Crimes on Rise in US," The Boston Globe, July 29, 1990, p. 1.

17. Bernstein, Dictatorship of Virtue, p. 186–87.

18. Ibid., p. 187.

19. Ibid. By contrast, the 1991 statistics for "ordinary" crimes translated into one rape per 2,440 residents and one robbery per 1,000 residents.

20. Ibid.

21. Letter from Diane Knippers, President, The Institute on Religion and Democracy, to The Reverend Dr. Joan Brown Campbell, General Secretary, National Council of Churches of Christ in the USA, September 19, 1996.

22. Two recent books by black authors predict a race war. Carl T. Rowan, The Coming Race War in America: A Wake-up Call (New York: Little, Brown, 1996); Richard Delgado, The Coming Race War? and Other Apocalyptic Tales of America After Affirmative Action and Welfare (New York: New York University Press, 1996).

23. National Church Arson Task Force, First Year Report for the President, June 1997, p. 13 [hereinafter NCATF Report].

24. Jan Crawford Greenburg, "Ashes Yield No Proof of Conspiracy," Chicago Tribune, September 19, 1996, p. N1.

25. Ibid.

26. "Man Gets 5 Years for Burning Black Church," New York Times, October 9, 1996, p. A11.

27. Richard A. Serrano, "Blacks' Arrests Belie Church Fire Suspicions," Los Angeles Times, September 21, 1996, p. A1.

28. "Teenager Confesses to Burning Church," New York Times, July 21, 1996, p. A12.

29. Fox Butterfield, "Old Fears and New Hopes: Tale of Burned Black Church Goes Far Beyond Arson," New York Times, July 21, 1996, p. A12.

30. Greenburg, "Ashes Yield No Proof of Conspiracy," p. N1.

31. Ibid.

32. Letter from Diane Knippers.

33. Letter from Diane Knippers.

34. Institute on Religion and Democracy, IRD Responds to National Council of Churches' Claims about Arsons at Black Churches, September 19, 1996, p. 3.

35. Letter from Diane Knippers, IRD president.

36. NCATF Report, p. 12.

37. "Stein Criticizes Dinkins for Latest Crown Heights Statement," UPI, December 2, 1992.

38. Alan Finder, "Dinkins Confronts Jewish Critics in Crown Heights," New York Times, December 17, 1992, p. A1.

39. Ibid. For a comprehensive treatment of the Crown Heights riots see, Richard H. Girgenti, A Report to the Governor on the Disturbances in Crown Heights: An Assessment of the City's Preparedness and Response to Civil Disorder (New York: State Division of Criminal Justice Services, 1993).

40. "Stein Criticizes Dinkins for Latest Crown Heights Statement," UPI, December 2, 1992.

41. Dennis Hevesi, "Fatal Beating is Changed from Bias-Related Crime," New York Times, January 2, 1992, p. B3.

42. Wendell Jamieson, "A 'Macho' Fight Ends in Tragedy," Newsday, January 2, 1992, p. 7.

43. Michelle Fuller, "Bias Death, Biased Reporting," Newsday, January 10, 1992, p. 53.

44. Ibid.

45. Ian Katz, "Chill Farce at Court of Absurd," The Guardian, Feb. 2, 1995, p. 10.

46. Laurie Wilson, "Scholars Say NY Attack Hard to Assess," Dallas Morning News, December 9, 1993, p. A14.

47. Ibid.

48. Michael Hedges, "Study Shows Racial Crimes by Blacks on Rise," The Washington Times, December 15, 1993, p. A4.

49. Wilson, "Scholars Say NY Attack Hard to Assess," p. A14.

50. Jim Sleeper, "Racial Roots of the LIRR Massacre," Daily News, December 23, 1993, p. 49.

51. Richard F. Welch, "Unchallenged, Black Racism Grows," Newsday, February 10, 1994, p. 113.

52. Marc Fleisher, "Down the Passage Which We Should Not Take: The Folly of Hate Crime Legislation," 2 Journal of Law & Policy 1, 43 (1994). See also, John T. McQuiston, "Grand Jury Indicts Suspect on 93 Counts in Attack that Killed 6 on Long Island Rail Road," New York Times, January 19, 1994, p. B5.

53. N.Y. Penal Law § 240.30.

54. Fleisher, "Down the Passage Which We Should Not Take," p. 44.

55. Thomas F. McDermott, "He Stared Blankly at Me, Then Fired," New York Times, December 17, 1993, p. A39.

56. In New York, the definition of a hate crime does not include crimes motivated by gender bias.

57. Helen Benedict, Virgin or Vamp: How the Press Covers Sex Crimes (New York: Oxford University Press, 1992), p. 216.

58. Benedict, Virgin or Vamp, p. 216.

59. Ibid., p. 194

60. Ibid., p. 289, note 43.

61. Ibid., p. 214.

62. Ibid., p. 235.

63. Ibid.

64. Ibid. p. 238, 243. In the first trial, Antron McCray, Yusef Salaam, both fifteen at the time of the attack, and Raymond Santana, fourteen years old at the time of the attack, were convicted of rape and assault, but acquitted of attempted murder. Following the second trial, Kharey Wise and Kevin Richardson, sixteen and fourteen years old at the time of the attack, were sentenced to five-to-fifteen years and five-to-ten years, respectively. Wise was found guilty of sexual abuse and assault, but acquitted on charges of rape and attempted murder. Richardson was found guilty of all charges, including attempted murder. Steve Lopez, fifteen years old at the time of the attack, plead guilty to acting in concert and was sentenced to one and one-half to four and one-half years.

65. Mike Taibbi & Anna Sims-Phillips, Unholy Alliances: Working the Tawana Brawley Story (New York: Harcourt, Brace, Jovanovich, 1989); Robert D. McFadden, Ralph Blumenthal, M. A. Farber, E. R. Shipp, Charles Strum, & Craig Wolff, Outrage: The Story Behind the Tawana Brawley Hoax (New York: Bantam, 1990); Katheryn K. Russell, The Color of Crime: Racial Hoaxes, White Fear, Black Protectionism, Police Harassment, and Other Macro-Aggressions (New York: New York University Press, 1998).

66. Migdalia Maldonado, "Practical Problems with Enforcing Hate Crimes Legislation in New York," 1992/1993 Annual Survey of American Law 555, 557 (1992/1993).

67. Allison Mitchell, "Police Find Bias Crimes Are Often Wrapped in Ambiguity," New York Times, January 27, 1992, p. B2.

68. "A Case of Ethnic Attack is Called a Hoax," New York Times, November 4, 1995, p. A9.

69. Ibid.

70. Sykes, A Nation of Victims, p. 214.

71. Maria Newman, "Officials Pledge Drive to Counter Bias Attack," New York Times, January 8, 1992, p. B3.

72. Ray Sanchez, "Bias-Attack Doubts Hit," Newsday, February 7, 1992, p. 26; "Update: Leads Have Run Out in Youth Bias Attacks," New York Times, May 10, 1992, p. A42.

73. Lynda Richardson, "61 Acts of Bias: One Fuse Lights Many Different Explosions," New York Times, January 28, 1992, p. B1.

74. Richardson, "61 Acts of Bias," p. B1.

75. Ibid.

76. Ibid.

Chapter 10

1. David Rieff, Slaughterhouse: Bosnia and the Failure of the West (New York: Simon and Schuster, 1995), p. 108.

2. Richard Bernstein, Dictatorship of Virtue (New York: Vintage Books, 1995); Todd Gitlin, The Twilight of Common Dreams (New York: Metropolitan Books, 1995).

Bibliography

Abramovsky, Abraham. 1992. "Bias Crime: A Call For Alternative Responses." Fordham Urban Law Journal 19:875.

Abrams, Floyd. 1993. "Hate Speech: An American View, Group Libel and Criminal Law: Walking on the 'Slippery Slope.'" Israel Yearbook on Human Rights. 22:85.

Alexander, Larry. Summer/Fall 1992. "The ADL Hate Crime Statute and the First Amendment." Criminal Justice Ethics. 11:49.

Allport, Gordon. 1954. The Nature of Prejudice. Cambridge, MA: Addison-Wesley.

American Psychological Association Task Force on the Victims of Crime and Violence. Nov. 30, 1984. Final Report.

Angelari, Marguerite. 1994. "Hate Crime Statutes: A Promising Tool for Fighting Violence Against Women. American University Journal of Gender & the Law. 2:63.

Anti-Asian Violence: Hearings Before the Subcommittee on Civil and Constitutional Rights of the House Committee on the Judiciary, 100th Cong., 1st sess. (1987).

Anti-Defamation League. 1994. Audit of Anti-Semitic Incidents for 1993.

ADL. 1993. Audit of Anti-Semitic Incidents for 1992.

ADL. 1992. Hate Crimes Statutes: A 1991 Status Report.

ADL. 1990. Hate Crime Statutes: Including Women as Victims.

ADL. 1988. Hate Groups in America: A Record of Bigotry and Violence.

Antieau, Chester J. 1980, 2d ed. Federal Civil Rights Acts: Civil Practice. Rochester, NY: Lawyers Co-operative Publishing.

Anti-Gay Violence: Hearings Before the Subcommittee on Criminal Justice of the House Committee on the Judiciary, 99th Cong., 2d sess. (1986).

Baird, Robert M. & Rosenbaum, Stuart E., eds. 1992. Bigotry, Prejudice & Hatred: Definitions, Causes & Solutions. Buffalo, NY: Prometheus Books.

Baldassare, Mark, ed. 1994. The Los Angeles Riots: Lesson for the Urban Future. San Francisco: Westview Press.

Bard, M. & Sangrey, D. 1979. The Crime Victim's Book. New York: Basic Books.

Barnes, Arnold & Ephross, Paul H. 1994. "The Impact of Hate Violence on Victims: Emotional and Behavioral Responses to Attacks." Social Work. 39(3):247–51.

Barlet, Chip & Lyons, Matthew N. June 1995. "Militia Nation." The Progressive. 22.

Bell, Derrick A. 1980, 2d ed. Racism and American Law. Boston, MA: Little, Brown.

Benedict, Helen. 1992. Virgin or Vamp: How the Press Covers Sex Crimes. New York: Oxford University Press.

Bennett, David H. 1995. The Party of Fear: The American Far Right from Nativism to the Militia Movement. New York: Vintage Books.

Berk, Richard A., Boyd, Elizabeth A., & Hamner, Karl M. 1992. "Thinking More Clearly About Hate Motivated Crimes." in Herek, Gregory M. & Berrill, Kevin T., ed. Hate Crimes: Confronting Violence Against Lesbians and Gay Men. London: Sage Publications. 123–39.

Bernstein, Richard. 1995. Dictatorship of Virtue. New York: Vintage Books.

Berrill, Kevin T. 1992. "Anti-Gay Violence and Victimization in the United States: An Overview." in Herek, Gregory M. & Berrill, Kevin T., ed. Hate Crimes: Confronting Violence Against Lesbians and Gay Men. London: Sage Publications. 19–40

Berrill, Kevin T. 1993. "Anti-Gay Violence: Causes, Consequences, and Responses." in Kelly, Robert J., ed. Bias Crime: American Law Enforcement and Legal Responses. Chicago: Office of International Criminal Justice. 151–64.

Best, Joel. 1990. Threatened Children: Rhetoric and Concern About Child Victims. Chicago: University of Chicago Press.

Best, Joel. Summer 1988. "Missing Children, Misleading Statistics." The Public Interest. 84.

Brief Amicus Curiae of the American Civil Liberties Union in Support of Petitioner, Todd Mitchell, in Wisconsin v. Mitchell. 1993.

Brief of Center for Individual Rights as Amicus Curiae in Support of Respondent, Wisconsin, in Wisconsin v. Mitchell. 1993.

Brown, Dee. 1973. Bury My Heart at Wounded Knee. New York: Bantam.

Brown, Ralph S. Summer/Fall 1992. "Susan Gellman Has it Right." Criminal Justice Ethics. 11:46.

Bureau of Justice Statistics. 1995. Sourcebook of Criminal Justice Statistics—1994. Washington, D.C.: U.S. Department of Justice.

Bureau of Justice Statistics. April 1996. Local Police Departments. Washington, D.C.: U.S. Department of Justice.

Bureau of Justice Statistics. October 1993. Highlights from 20 Years of Surveying Crime Victims: The National Crime Victimization Survey, 1972–92. Washington, D.C.: U.S. Department of Justice.

Bureau of Justice Statistics. July 1990. Violent State Prisoners and Their Victims. Washington, D.C.: U.S. Department of Justice.

Bureau of Justice Statistics. August 1995. Violence Against Women: Estimates from the Redesigned Survey. Washington, D.C.: U.S. Department of Justice.

Burgess, A. W. & Holstrom, L. L. 1979. "Rape, Sexual Disruption, & Recovery." American Journal of Orthopsychiatry. 49:658–69.

Burgess, A. W. & Holstrom, L. L. 1974. "Rape Trauma Syndrome." American Journal of Psychiatry. 131:981.

Butler, Paul. 1995. "Racially Based Jury Nullification: Black Power in the Criminal Justice System." Yale Law Journal. 105:677.

California Division of Criminal Justice Information Services, California Department of Justice. 1996. Hate Crime in California 1995.

Carlson, Lewis H. & Colburn, George A. 1972. In Their Place: White America Defines Her Minorities, 1850–1950. New York: John Wiley & Sons.

Center for Democratic Renewal. 1992. When Hate Groups Come to Town.

Chaiken, Jan M. & Chaiken, Marcia R. 1983. "Crime Rates and the Active Criminal." in James Q. Wilson, ed., Crime and Public Policy. San Francisco: ICS Press.

Chalmers, David M. 1987. Hooded Americanism: The History of the Ku Klux Klan. Durham, N.C.: Duke University Press.

Chambliss, W. & Seidman, R. 1982. Law, Order & Power. Reading, MA: Addison Wesley.

Chevigny, Paul G. 1984. "Politics and Law in the Control of Local Surveillance." Cornell Law Review. 69:735.

Cleary, Edward J. 1994. Beyond the Burning Cross: The First Amendment and the Landmark R.A.V. Case. New York: Random House.

Coates, James. 1987. Armed and Dangerous: The Rise of the Survivalist Right. New York: Hill & Wang.

Cohen, Stanley. 1972. Folk Devils and Moral Panics. London: MacGibbon & Kee.

Cook, John P. 1993. "Collection and Analysis of Hate Crime Activities." in Kelly, Robert J. ed. Bias Crime: American Law Enforcement and Legal Responses. Chicago, IL: Office of International Criminal Justice.

Crimes Against Religious Practices and Property: Hearings on H.R. 665 Before the Subcommittee on Criminal Justice of the House Committee on the Judiciary, 99th Cong., 1st sess. (1985).

Crimes of Violence Motivated by Gender: Hearings Before the Subcommittee on Civil and Constitutional Rights of the House Committee on the Judiciary, 103d Cong., 1st sess. (1993).

Crocker, Lawrence. 1992/1993. "Hate Crime Statutes: Just? Constitutional? Wise?" Annual Survey of American Law. 1992/1993:485.

Curry, Richard O., ed. 1969. Radicalism, Racism and Party Realignment: The Border States During the Reconstruction. Baltimore, MD: Johns Hopkins Press.

D'Souza, Dinish. 1991. Illiberal Education: The Politics of Race and Sex on Campus. New York: Free Press.

Debo, Angie. 1983. A History of the Indians of the United States. Norman, OK: University of Oklahoma Press.

Delgado, Richard. 1996. The Coming Race War? and Other Apocalyptic Tales of America After Affirmative Action and Welfare. New York: New York University Press.

Democratic Leadership Council Symposium. Nov. 1993. "Getting Beyond Victimization." The New Democrat. 5:4.

Dilulio, John J., Jr. Spring 1996. "My Black Crime Problem, and Ours." City Journal. 14.

Dinnerstein, Leonard. 1994. Anti-Semitism in America. New York: Oxford University Press.

Dinnerstein, Leonard. 1987. Uneasy at Home: Anti-Semitism and the American Jewish Experience. New York: Columbia University Press.

Dorsen, Norman, ed. 1987. The Evolving Constitution. Middletown, CT: Wesleyan University Press.

Durkheim, Emile. 1964. Division of Labor in Society. New York: Free Press.

"Education." May 7, 1990. Time Magazine. 104.

Ehle, John. 1988. Trail of Tears: The Rise and Fall of the Cherokee Nation. New York: Doubleday.

Ehrlich, Howard J. 1990. Campus Ethnoviolence, Institute Report No. 4. Baltimore: National Institute Against Prejudice and Violence.

Ethnically Motivated Violence Against Arab-Americans: Hearings Before the Subcommittee on Criminal Justice of the House Committee on the Judiciary, 99th Cong., 2d sess. (July 16, 1986).

Fairchild, E. S. & Webb, V. J. 1985. The Politics of Crime & Criminal Justice. (Beverly Hills, CA: Sage.

Federal Bureau of Investigation Press Release, U.S. Dept. of Justice, January 1, 1993.

Federal Bureau of Investigation, Uniform Crime Reports. 1994. Hate Crime Statistics: 1992.

Federal Bureau of Investigation, Uniform Crime Reports. 1995. Hate Crime Statistics: 1993.

Fernandez, Joseph M. 1991. "Bringing Hate Crime Into Focus: The Hate Crime Statistics Act of 1990." Harvard Civil Rights, Civil Liberties Law Rev. 26:261.

Ferrell, Claudine L. 1986. Nightmare and Dream: Anti-Lynching in Congress, 1917–1922. New York: Garland Publishing.

Finn, Peter & McNeil, Taylor. 1988. Bias Crimes and the Criminal Justice Response: A Summary Report Prepared for the National Criminal Justice Association. Boston: Abt Associates.

Fleischauer, Marc L. 1990. "Teeth For a Paper Tiger: A Proposal to Add Enforceability to Florida's Hate Crimes Act." Florida State U. L. Rev. 17:697.

Fleisher, Marc. 1994. "Down the Passage Which We Should Not Take: The Folly of Hate Crime Legislation." Journal of Law & Policy. 2:1–53.

Foner, Eric. 1988. Reconstruction: America's Unfinished Revolution. New York: Harper & Row.

Forman, D. 1980. "Psychotherapy with Rape Victims." Psychotherapy, Theory, Research, Practice. 17(3):304.

Freeman, Steven M. 1992/1993. "Hate Crime Laws: Punishment Which Fits the Crime." Annual Survey of American Law. 1992/1993:581.

Gallup Poll. 1995. Public Opinion 1994.

Gallup Poll. 1994. Public Opinion 1993.

Garland, David. 1990. Punishment and Society: A Study in Social Theory. Chicago: University of Chicago Press.

Garrow, David J., ed. 1989. We Shall Overcome. Brooklyn, NY: Carlson Publishing.

Gates, Henry Louis, Jr., Griffin, Anthony P., Lively, Donald E., Post, Robert C., Rubenstein, William B., & Strossen, Nadine. 1994. Speaking of Race, Speaking of Sex. New York: New York University Press.

Gaumer, Craig Peyton. 1994. "Punishment for Prejudice: A Commentary on the Constitutionality and Utility of State Statutory Responses to the Problem of Hate Crimes." South Dakota L. Rev. 39:1.

Gellman, Susan. 1991. "Sticks and Stones Can Put You in Jail, But Can Words Increase Your Sentence? Constitutional and Policy Dilemmas of Ethnic Intimidation Laws." UCLA L. Rev. 39:333.

Gellman, Susan. 1992/1993. "Hate Crime Laws are Thought Crime Laws." Annual Survey of American Law. 1992/1993:509.

Gilbert, Neil. 1997. "Advocacy Research and Social Policy" in Michael Tonry, ed. Crime and Justice: A Review of Research, Vol. 22. Chicago: University of Chicago Press, 101–148.

Ginger, Ann Fagan. 1984, 2d ed. 1990 Supplement. Jury Selection in Civil and Criminal Trials. Tiburon, CA: Lawpress Corp.

Girgenti, Richard H. 1993. A Report to the Governor on the Disturbances in Crown Heights: An Assessment of the City's Preparedness and Response to Civil Disorder. New York State Division of Criminal Justice Services.

Gitlin, Todd. 1995. The Twilight of Common Dreams. New York: Metropolitan Books.

Gobert, James J. & Jordan, Walter E. 1990, 2d ed. Jury Selection: The Law, Art, and Science of Selecting a Jury. New York: McGraw-Hill.

Goldberger, David. 1992/1993. "Hate Crime Laws and Their Impact on the First Amendment." Annual Survey of American Law. 1992/1993:569.

Goldstein, Abraham. 1993. "Group Libel and Criminal Law: Walking on the 'Slippery Slope.'" Israel Yearbook on Human Rights. 22:95.

Gooding-Williams, Robert, ed. 1993. Reading Rodney King, Reading Urban Uprising. New York: Routledge.

Greenawalt, Kent. 1984. "Criminal Coercion and Freedom of Speech." Northwestern University Law Review. 78:1081.

Greenawalt, Kent. 1992/1993. "Reflections on Justifications for Defining Crimes by the Category of Victim." Annual Survey of American Law. 1992/1993:617.

Greene, Melissa Fay. 1996. The Temple Bombing. New York: Addison-Wesley.

Griffiths, J. January 1989. "Conflict in Society: Public Order v. Individual Liberty—Laws Against Incitement to Racial Hatred. Paper delivered at Asia Pacific Lawyers Association Third General Assembly, Hawaii.

Gunther, Gerald. 1991, 12th ed. Constitutional Law. Mineola, NY: Foundation Press.

Gunther, Gerald. 1985, 11th ed. Constitutional Law. Mineola, NY: Foundation Press.

Gunther, Gerald. May 3, 1989. Stanford University Campus Report.

Gurr, Ted Robert. 1989. Violence in America. Newbury Park, CA: Sage Publications.

Gusfield, J. R. 1963. Symbolic Crusade. Urbana, IL: University of Illinois Press.

Hallock, W.H. Spring 1993. "The Violence Against Women Act: Civil Rights for Sexual Assault Victims." Indiana Law Journal. 68:596.

Hate Crime Sentencing Enhancement Act of 1992: Hearings on H.R. 4797 Before the House Subcommittee on Crime and Criminal Justice of the House Committee on the Judiciary, 102d Cong., 2d sess. (July 29, 1992).

Hate Crimes Statistics Act of 1988: Hearings Before the Subcommittee on the Constitution of the Senate Committee on the Judiciary, 100th Cong., 2d sess. 261 (1988).

Hearings Before the House Subcommittee on Crime and Criminal Justice of the House Committee on the Judiciary, 102d Cong., 2d sess. (July 29, 1992).

Hearings Before the United States Commission on Civil Rights, Racial and Ethnic Tensions in American Communities: Poverty, Inequality, and Discrimination—A National Perspective (May 21–22, 1992).

Hearings on H.R. 4797 Before the House Subcommittee on Crime and Criminal Justice of the House Committee on the Judiciary, 102d Cong., 2d sess. (July 29, 1992).

Heumann, Milton, Church, Thomas, & Redlawsk, David. 1997. Hate Speech on Campus: Cases, Case Studies and Commentary. Boston: Northeastern University Press.

Holland, Gina. January 7, 1994. "Mississippi Ills Require Hate Crimes Bill Backers Maintain." The Commercial Appeal. B1.

Horowitz, Donald L. 1985. Ethnic Groups in Conflict. Berkeley, CA: University of California Press.

House Report 102–981, 102d Cong., 2d sess. (Oct. 2, 1992).

House Report 775. 99th Cong., 1st sess. 131 Congressional Record 1311. (1985).

House Report 575. 100th Cong., 2d sess. 3. (April 20, 1988).

House Report 1133, 103d Cong., 1st sess. (Feb. 24, 1993).

Howard, Walter T. 1995. Lynchings: Extralegal Violence in Florida During the 1930s. London: Associated University Press.

Hunter, Nan D. et al. 1992, 2d ed. The Rights of Lesbians and Gay Men. Carbondale, IL: Southern Illinois University Press.

Institute on Religion and Democracy. September 19, 1996. IRD Responds to National Council of Churches' Claims About Arsons at Black Churches.

"International Legal Colloquium on Racial and Religious Hatred and Group Libel." 1992. Israel Yearbook on Human Rights. 22:1–259.

Jacobs, James B. 1989. Drunk Driving: An American Dilemma. Chicago: University of Chicago Press.

Jacobs, James B. Summer/Fall 1992. "The War Against Hate Crimes: A New York City Perspective." Criminal Justice Ethics. 11:55.

Jacobs, James B. & Eisler, Barry. February 1993. "The Hate Crime Statistics Act of 1990." Criminal Law Bulletin 29:99.

Jacobs, James B. & Henry, Jessica S. Winter 1996. "The Social Construction of a Hate Crime Epidemic." Journal of Criminal Law & Criminology 86:366.

Jacobs, James B. 1992/1993. "Implementing Hate Crime Legislation: Symbolism and Crime Control." Annual Survey of American Law 1992/1993:541.

Jacobs, James B. Fall 1993. "Should Hate Be a Crime?" The Public Interest 113:3–14.

Jacobs, James B. 1993. "The Emergence & Implications of American Hate Crime Jurisprudence." Israel Yearbook on Human Rights. 22:113–139.

Jacobs, James B. 1992. "The New Wave of American Hate Crime Legislation." Report from the Institute of Philosophy & Public Policy. 12:9.

Jacobs, James B. 1983. New Perspectives on Prisons and Imprisonment. New York: Cornell University Press.

Jacobs, James B. 1976. "Stratification and Conflict Among Prison Inmates." Journal of Criminal Law & Criminology. 66:476.

Jenness, Valerie & Grattet, Ryken. 1996. "The Criminalization of Hate: A Comparison of Structural & Policy Influences on the Passage of 'Bias Crime' Legislation in the United States." Sociological Perspectives. 39:129.

Jenness, Valerie. 1995. "Social Movement Growth, Domain Expansion, and Framing Processes: The Gay/Lesbian Movement and Violence Against Gays and Lesbians as a Social Problem." Social Problems. 42:145.

Jenness, Valerie. 1989. "Hate Crimes in the United States: The Transformation of Injured Persons into Victims and the Extension of Victim Status to Multiple Constituencies," in Joel Best, ed., Images of Issues: Typifying Contemporary Social Problems. New York: Aldine De Gruyter. xv–xx.

Jenness, Valerie & Broad, Kendal. September 1994. "Anti-Violence Activism and the (In)Visibility of Gender in the Gay/Lesbian and Women's Movements." Gender & Society. 8:402.

Jukes, Adam. 1993. Why Men Hate Women. London: Free Association Books.

Klanwatch. February 1993. Intelligence Report No. 65. Montgomery, AL: Southern Poverty Law Center.

Klanwatch. August 1995. Intelligence Report No. 79. Montgomery, AL: Southern Poverty Law Center.

Kluckhohn, Clyde & Leighton, Dorothea. 1974. The Navaho. Cambridge, MA: Harvard University Press.

Knippers, Diane. Letter from Diane Knippers, President, Institute on Religion and Democracy, to The Reverend Dr. Joan Brown Campbell, General Secretary, National Council of Churches of Christ in the USA. September 19, 1996.

"Labels Mask 'Latino' Diversity." 1991. Ford Foundation Letter. 22:10.

Lasson, Kenneth. 1984. "Group Libel v. Free Speech, When Big Brother Should Butt In." Duq. Law Review. 23:77.

Lawrence, Charles R. III. 1990. "If He Hollers Let Him Go: Regulating Racist Speech on Campus." Duke L. J. 1990:431.

Lawrence, Charles R. III. 1987. "The Id, the Ego and Equal Protection: Reckoning with Unconscious Racism." Stanford L. Rev. 39:317.

Lawrence, Frederick M. 1994. "The Punishment of Hate: Toward a Normative Theory of Bias-Motivated Crimes." Michigan. L. Rev. 93:320.

Lawrence, Frederick M. 1993. "Civil Rights and Criminal Wrongs: The Mens Rea of Federal Civil Rights Crimes." Tulane Law Review. 67:2113.

Lee, Joann. April 30, 1994. "A Look at Asians as Portrayed in the News." Editor & Publisher Magazine. 56.

Lee, Virginia Nia & Fernandez, Joseph M. 1987. "Legislative Responses to Hate-Motivated Violence: The Massachusetts Experience and Beyond." Harvard Civil Rights, Civil Liberties Law Review. 25:287.

Leo, John. October 9, 1989. The Politics of Hate. U.S. News & World Report. 24.

Lerner, Natan. 1980, 2d ed. The U.N. Convention on the Elimination of All Forms of Racial Discrimination.

Letter from Mario M. Cuomo, Governor of the State of New York, to the New York State Legislature. August 16, 1991.

Levin, Brian. 1992/1993. "Bias Crimes: A Theoretical and Practical Overview." Stanford Law & Policy Rev. 4:165.

Levin, Jack & McDevitt, Jack. 1993. Hate Crimes: The Rising Tide of Bigotry and Bloodshed. New York; Plenum Press.

Levine, James P. 1992. "The Impact of Local Political Cultures on Jury Verdicts." Criminal Justice Journal. 14:163.

Litwack, Leon F. 1979. Been in the Storm So Long: The Aftermath of Slavery. New York: Knopf.

MacInnes, Gordon. 1995. Wrong For the Right Reasons. New York: New York University Press.

Maldonado, Migdalia. 1992/1993. "Practical Problems with Enforcing Hate Crimes Legislation in New York." Annual Survey of American Law. 1992/1993:555.

Marcus, Sheldon. 1973. Father Coughlin: The Tumultuous Life of the Priest of the Little Flower. Boston, MA: Little, Brown.

Marovitz, William A. 1993. "Hate or Bias Crime Legislation." in Kelly, Robert J., ed. Bias Crime: American Law Enforcement and Legal Responses. Chicago: Office of International Criminal Justice. 48–53.

Marx, Gary and Wexler, Chuck. 1986. "When Law and Order Works: Boston's Innovative Approach to the Problem of Racial Violence," Crime & Delinquency. 32:205.

Matsuda, Mari J. 1989. "Public Response to Racist Speech: Considering the Victim's Story." Michigan L. Rev. 87:2320.

McFadden, Robert D., Blumenthal, Ralph, Farber, M. A., Shipp, E. R., Strum, Charles, & Wolff, Craig. 1990. Outrage: The Story Behind the Tawana Brawley Hoax. New York: Bantam.

Morsch, James. 1991. "The Problem of Motive in Hate Crimes: The Argument Against Presumptions of Racial Motivation." Journal of Criminal Law & Criminology. 82:65.

Murphy, Jeffrie G. Summer/Fall 1992. "Bias Crimes: What Do Haters Deserve?" Criminal Justice Ethics. 11:23.

Murray, Charles & Herenstein, Richard. 1994. The Bell Curve. New York: Free Press.

National Church Arson Task Force, First Year Report for the President, June 1997.

National Coalition of Anti-Violence Programs and New York City Gay and Lesbian Anti-Violence Project. 1996. Anti-Lesbian/Gay Violence in 1995.

National Institute Against Prejudice & Violence. 1989. National Victimization Survey.

Nelson, Jack. 1996. Terror in the Night: The Klan's Campaign Against the Jews. Jackson, MS: University of Mississippi Press.

New York City Gay & Lesbian Anti-Violence Project. Winter/Spring 1995. NYPD Bias Unit Downgraded, Stop the Violence. New York: NYC Gay & Lesbian Anti-Violence Project.

New York City Police Department. 1996. Bias Incident Investigation Unit, Year End Report 1995.

New York City Police Department. 1995. Bias Incident Investigation Unit, Year End Report 1994.

New York City Police Department. 1991. Bias Incident Investigation Unit, 1990 Annual Report.

New York City Police Department. (undated). Background Information on the Bias Incident Investigation Unit.

New York City Police Department, Inspector William T. Wallace. September 1991. Bias Incident Investigation Unit.

Note. 1965. "Discretion to Prosecute Federal Civil Rights Crimes." Yale Law Journal. 74:1297.

Note. 1988. "Combatting Racial Violence: A Legislative Proposal." Harv. L. Rev. 101:1270.

Note. 1993. "Hate is Not Speech: A Constitutional Defense of Penalty En-
    hancement for Hate Crimes," Harv. L. Rev. 106:1314.
Note. 1993. "Violence Against Asian-Americans." Harv. L. Rev. 106:1926.
Olmstead-Rose, Lester. 1991. "Hate Violence: Symptom of Prejudice." Wil-
    liam Mitchell L. Rev. 17:439.
O'Malley, Jack. 1994. Cook County Attorney's Office: A Prosecutor's Guide
    to Hate Crime.
Padgett, Gregory L. 1984. "Racially-Motivated Violence and Intimidation:
    Inadequate State Enforcement and Federal Civil Rights Remedies."
    Journal of Criminal Law & Criminology. 75:103.
Pendo, Elizabeth A. 1994. "Recognizing Violence Against Women: Gender and
    the Hate Crime Statistics Act." Harvard Women's Law Journal 17:157.
Perkins, Cathy, ed. 1975. COINTELPRO. New York: Monrad Press.
Pinkney, Alphonso. 1994. Lest We Forget: White Hate Crimes. Chicago: Third
    World Press.
Racially Motivated Violence: Hearings Before the Subcommittee on Criminal
    Justice of the House Committee on the Judiciary, 100th Cong., 2d sess.
    (1988).
Rauch, Jonathan. May 10, 1993. "Beyond Oppression." The New Republic.
    18–23.
Redish, Martin H. Summer/Fall 1992. "Freedom of Thought As Freedom of
    Expression." Crim. Justice Ethics 11:29.
Report of the Disturbance Cause Committee. June 10, 1993. Findings: South-
    ern Ohio Correctional Facility Riot.
Report of the Independent Commission on the LAPD. 1992. Warren Chris-
    topher, Chair.
Rieff, David. 1995. Slaughterhouse: Bosnia and the Failure of the West. New
    York: Simon & Schuster.
Rothschild, Eric. 1993. "Recognizing Another Face of Hate Crimes: Rape as
    a Gender-Bias Crime." Maryland J. Contemp. Leg. Issues 4:231.
Rowan, Carl T. 1996. The Coming Race War in America: A Wake-up Call.
    New York: Little, Brown.
Rozen, Miriam. June 1992. "Wielding a Strong Hate Crime Statute, Luis
    Aragon Brings Racists and Homophobes to Justice." The American
    Lawyer. 58.
Russell, Katheryn K. 1998. The Color of Crime: Racial Hoaxes, White Fear,
    Black Protectionism, Police Harassment, and Other Macro-Aggressions.
    New York: New York University Press.
Sanderson, Paul M. 1991. "Investigation of Religious Bias-Motivated Crimes."
    in Taylor, Nancy, ed. Bias Crime: The Law Enforcement Response. Chi-
    cago, IL: Office of International Criminal Justice.
Sapp, Allen D., Holden, Richard N., & Wiggins, Michael E. 1992. "Value and
    Belief Systems of Right-Wing Extremists: Rationale and Motivation of
    Bias-Motivated Crimes." in Kelly, Robert J., ed. Bias Crime: American
    Law Enforcement and Legal Responses. Chicago: Office of International
    Criminal Justice. 105.

Sargent, Lyman Tower, ed. 1995. Extremism in America. New York: New York University Press.

Scheingold, Stuart. 1974. The Politics of Rights. New Haven, CT: Yale University Press.

Scheingold, Stuart. 1984. The Politics of Law and Order: Street Crime and Public Policy. New York: Longman.

Schlesinger, Arthur, Jr. 1992. The Disuniting of America. New York: W.W. Norton.

Schweitzer, Thomas A. 1995. "Hate Speech on Campus and the First Amendment: Can They Be Reconciled?" Conn. L. Rev. 27:493.

Senate Hearings on S. 702, S. 797, & S. 2000 Before the Subcommittee on the Constitution of the Committee on the Judiciary, 100th Cong., 2d sess. (June 21, 1988).

Senate Report No. 21. 1989. 101st Cong., 1st sess.

Senate Report No. 721. 1967. 90th Cong., 2d sess., reprinted in 1968 U.S.C.C.A.N. 1837.

Sigelman, Lee & Welch, Susan. 1991. Black Americans' Views of Racial Inequality. New York: Cambridge University Press.

Skerry, Peter. 1993. "The New Politics of Assimilation." City Journal. 3:6–7.

Skogan, W. G. & Maxfield, M. G. 1981. Coping with Crime: Individual and Neighborhood Reactions. Beverly Hills, CA: Sage.

Sleeper, Jim. 1990. The Closest of Strangers: Liberalism and the Politics of Race in New York. New York: W.W. Norton.

Sleeper, Jim. 1993. In Defense of Civic Culture. Washington, D.C.: The Progressive Foundation.

Steele, Shelby. 1990. The Content of Our Character. New York: St. Martin's Press.

Swinney, Everette. 1987. Suppressing the Ku Klux Klan: The Enforcement of the Reconstruction Amendments, 1870–1877. New York: Garland Publishing.

Sykes, Charles. 1992. A Nation of Victims. New York: St. Martin's Press.

Symonds, M. 1980. "The 'Second Injury' to Victims." in Kivens, L., ed. Evaluation and Change: Services for Survivors. Minneapolis, MN: Minneapolis Medical Research Foundation.

"Symposium: Penalty Enhancement for Hate Crimes." Summer/Fall 1992. Crim. Justice Ethics 11:3.

Taibbi, Mike & Sims-Phillips, Anna. 1989. Unholy Alliances: Working the Tawana Brawley Story. New York: Harcourt, Brace, Jovanovich.

Tomasky, Michael. 1996. Left For Dead: The Life, Death and Possible Resurrection of Progressive Politics in America. New York: Free Press.

Tribe, Laurence. 1988, 2d ed. American Constitutional Law. Mineola, NY: Foundation Press.

Tull, Charles J. 1965. Father Coughlin and the New Deal. Syracuse, NY: Syracuse University Press.

Uniform Crime Reporting. 1990. Hate Crime Data Collection Guidelines. Federal Bureau of Investigation, U.S. Dept. of Justice.

Uniform Crime Reporting. 1992. Hate Crime Statistics, 1990: A Resource Book. Federal Bureau of Investigation, U.S. Dept. of Justice.

Uniform Crime Reporting. 1991. Training Guide for Hate Crime Data Collection. Federal Bureau of Investigation, U.S. Dept. of Justice.

Uniform Crime Reports. 1991. Federal Bureau of Investigation, Crime in the United States: 1990.

Uniform Crime Reports. 1992. Federal Bureau of Investigation, Crime in the United States: 1991.

U.S. Departments of Commerce, Justice and State. May 3, 1994. Appropriations for 1995: Hearings on the Community Relations Service.

U.S. Department of Justice. 1994. Legal Activities, 1993–94.

Walker, Samuel. 1994. Hate Speech: The History of an American Controversy. Lincoln, Neb.: University of Nebraska Press.

Wang, Lu-in. 1995. Hate Crimes Laws. New York: Clark, Boardman, Callaghan.

Watters, Pat & Gillers, Stephen, eds. 1973. Investigating the FBI. Garden City, NY: Doubleday.

Weinstein, James. Summer/Fall 1992. "First Amendment Challenges to Hate Crime Legislation: Where's the Speech." Crim. Justice Ethics. 11:6.

Weiss, Joan. 1991. "Ethnoviolence: Impact and Response in Victims and the Community." in Robert J. Kelly, ed. Bias Crime: American Law Enforcement and Legal Responses. Chicago: Office of International Criminal Justice. 174–185.

Weisburd, Bennett & Levin, Brian. Spring 1994. "On the Basis of Sex: Recognizing Gender-Based Bias Crime." Stanford Law & Policy Review. 5:25.

Whitehead, Don. 1970. Attack on Terror: The FBI Against the KKK in Mississippi. New York: Funk & Wagnall.

Wills, Garry. August 10, 1995. "The Turner Diaries" (book review). New York Review of Books. 50.

Williams, Juan. 1987. Eyes on the Prize: America's Civil Rights Years. New York: Viking.

Winters, Paul A., ed. 1996. Hate Crimes. San Diego: Greenhaven Press.

Women and Violence: Hearings on Legislation to Reduce the Growing Problem of Violent Crime Against Women Before the Senate Committee on the Judiciary, 101st Cong., 2d sess. (1990).

Wright, Kevin N. 1985. The Great American Crime Myth. New York: Praeger.

1990 Census of Population and Housing for Census Tracts and Block Numbering Areas, New York, NY PMSA. 1990. "Table 5: General Characteristics of Asian or Pacific Islander Persons: 1990."

Table of Cases

199

Index